Reagan

The Next Four Years

Reagan

The Next Four Years

Congressional Quarterly Inc.
1414 22nd Street N.W.
Washington, D.C. 20037

Congressional Quarterly Inc.

Congressional Quarterly Inc., an editorial research service and publishing company, serves clients in the fields of news, education, business and government. It combines specific coverage of Congress, government and politics by Congressional Quarterly with the more general subject range of an affiliated service, Editorial Research Reports.

Congressional Quarterly publishes the *Congressional Quarterly Weekly Report* and a variety of books, including college political science textbooks under the CQ Press imprint and public affairs paperbacks on developing issues and events. CQ also publishes information directories and reference books on the federal government, national elections and politics, including the *Guide to Congress*, the *Guide to the Supreme Court*, the *Guide to U.S. Elections* and *Politics in America*. The *CQ Almanac*, a compendium of legislation for one session of Congress, is published each year. *Congress and the Nation*, a record of government for a presidential term, is published every four years.

CQ publishes *The Congressional Monitor*, a daily report on current and future activities of congressional committees, and several newsletters including *Congressional Insight*, a weekly analysis of congressional action, and *Campaign Practices Reports*, a semimonthly update on campaign laws.

The online delivery of CQ's Washington Alert Service provides clients with immediate access to Congressional Quarterly's institutional information and expertise.

Copyright © 1985 Congressional Quarterly Inc.

Printed in the United States of America

Library of Congress Cataloging in Publication Data

Main entry under title:

Reagan, the next four years.

Bibliography: p.
Includes index.
1. United States—Politics and government 1981-   . 2. Reagan, Ronald. I. Congressional Quarterly, inc.
E876.R413   1985   973.927'092'4
ISBN 0-87187-352-4

Editor: Nancy Lammers.

Major Contributors: Christopher R. Conte, Mary H. Cooper, John Felton, Carolyn Goldinger, Mary McNeil, John L. Moore, Steven Pressman, Donald Smith and Elder Witt.

Cover: Richard A. Pottern.

Photo Credits: Cover, David Marie/FOLIO Inc.; p. 3, Defense Department; p. 8, AP; p. 9, AP; p. 19, AP; p. 37, *Washington Post;* p. 41, AP; p. 48, White House; p. 59, General Motors; p. 70, *Minneapolis Star and Tribune;* p. 78, U.S. Department of Agriculture; p. 80, Ken Heinen; p. 83, *Washington Post;* p. 88, Louisville Times Co.; p. 95, Bill Fitzpatrick/White House; p. 139, Defense Department; p. 152, *Washington Post;* p. 154, *Washington Post.*

Indexer: Bernice Eisen.

Table of Contents

Preface

President Ronald Reagan took the oath for his second term in office in January 1985 with one of the most massive election victories of the 20th century behind him. But the question remained: Would this broad public support make any difference?

The president faced seemingly intractable problems in his final four years in office: a soaring deficit that was expected to exceed $200 billion each year under existing programs; an intense controversy over the size and necessity of the defense build-up that Reagan had supported so vigorously; the coldest relations with the Soviet Union since the days after World War II and the growing pressure worldwide for arms control agreements between the two superpowers.

To make his task even more complicated, Reagan faced a House of Representatives solidly controlled by the Democrats and a Senate barely controlled by his own party. Nevertheless, Congress handed President Reagan a victory on the first controversial vote of his second term by approving in March 1985 the funds to buy 21 MX missiles. The president had lobbied extremely hard to win on this hotly contested issue, and the favorable vote portended well for him.

Reagan: The Next Four Years explores the challenges facing Reagan as well as the events of his first four years in office. The introductory chapter takes a broad look at the changes, especially stylistic and economic, that Reagan introduced during his first term. Chapter 2 provides a detailed account of the 1984 election victory that returned Reagan to the White House. Reagan's relations with Congress during his first term and his future prospects for success are analyzed in Chapter 3. The next two chapters outline important developments in foreign policy, along with related arms control issues. The economic dilemma that faced Reagan when he took office in 1981 and his means of dealing with it are discussed in Chapter 6. This analysis is followed by a look at how domestic issues of perennial concern have fared under Reagan and how the additional budget cuts, required to reduce the deficit, could affect them in the future. Reagan's influence upon the judicial system, especially at the Supreme Court and federal appeals court levels, is outlined in Chapter 8. The final two chapters provide biographical sketches of the men and women Reagan has appointed to critical Cabinet-level and White House staff positions. Transcripts of important speeches delivered by Reagan and messages sent to Congress, including his second inaugural address and his economic report of Feb. 5, 1985, are provided in the appendix.

The analyses in this book have been gathered by CQ editors from expert reports in the *Congressional Quarterly Weekly Report,* from the forthcoming edition of CQ's *Congress and the Nation,* which covers Reagan's first term, and from special Editorial Research Report essays.

Nancy Lammers
April 1985

1

Reagan Departs from the Past

As impressive as Ronald Reagan's 1984 election victory was, two crucial questions remained unanswered. Were the results a mandate to continue the "Reagan Revolution," which admirers had taken to calling the president's distinct departure from the policies of previous administrations, both Democratic and Republican? Or was the election more an indication of the president's personal popularity, along with Walter F. Mondale's persistent inability during the campaign to excite voters and rally support for the Democratic cause?

Countering any claim to a mandate was the relatively unimpressive showing of Republican congressional candidates. Where GOP leaders once had held hopes of capturing as many as 25 to 30 House seats in the 99th Congress, they picked up only 14 — and lost two seats in the Senate. With such modest Republican House gains, Reagan clearly would not have the compliant working majorities in 1985 and 1986 that he enjoyed when he first came into office in 1981 and that allowed him to push his programs through Congress.

But whether the voters were handing Reagan a mandate or not, they clearly were satisfied with his performance, especially on economic policy. The economy had enjoyed a remarkable recovery during the last two years of Reagan's first term. The comeback had been unexpectedly strong, following the economy's sluggish performance the year Reagan entered the White House and during the deep recession that had followed.

In January 1981 the prime lending rate was fluctuating between 20 and 20.5 percent, while the Consumer Price Index measure of inflation was approaching 12 percent per year. Unemployment stood at 7.4 percent. By mid-term, interest rates and inflation had dropped, but at the heavy price of a 10.7 percent unemployment rate — the highest since the end of World War II.

The recession began to dissipate in 1983. Inflation held at only 3.8 percent during the 12-month period and unemployment dipped to 8.2 percent in December 1983. The prime interest rate, which had peaked at 21.5 percent in December 1980, had dropped back to 11 percent by the latter half of 1983. And the "real" gross national product (GNP) — the nation's total output of goods and services, adjusted for inflation — grew 2.6 percent during the first quarter of 1983, then 9.7 percent in the second quarter, 7.6 percent in the third and 4.9 percent in the fourth.

Continued high budget deficits throughout Reagan's first four years in office formed an ominous backdrop for this economic boom. But the theoretical effects of deficits seemed to matter little in the day-to-day lives of most Americans, the vast majority of whom, polls showed, considered themselves substantially better off after four years of Reagan in the White House. A key calculation in the minds of many Americans on the eve of the 1984 election was that they were sharing less of their income with the federal government, due to the personal income tax cut that had formed a centerpiece of Reagan's economic program.

Predecessor Jimmy Carter believed that tax reductions would only increase inflation, a principle reflected in the last budget he sent to Congress before leaving office on Jan. 20, 1981. But that document had no practical effect; soon after his swearing-in, Reagan sent to Congress his own budget plan, which called for the largest tax cut in American history. That same budget proposed massive, across-the-board spending cuts in all areas of domestic spending. The only budget category spared was defense. It was this budget, complete with its dramatic tax cut, that became the law of the land.

Another fact not lost upon voters was that America was at peace. Despite anxiety over U.S. involvement in Central America, the deaths of U.S. soldiers on a peacekeeping mission in Lebanon and a successful mini-war in Grenada, the nation was secure within its own borders, and none of its troops were exposed to hostile fire in a foreign country.

Perhaps one of the most dramatic differences between the just-concluded four years of the Reagan administration and the previous four under Carter — and to a large extent the whole period following the American withdrawal from Vietnam — was an evident renewal of national pride. During a summer 1979 speech ostensibly about the long-running energy crisis, President Carter had proclaimed that the country was suffering from a "crisis of confidence" and that the "erosion of our confidence in the future

is threatening to destroy the social and political fabric of America." Just five years later, patriotism and confidence in the nation's future were basic themes for both candidates in the 1984 presidential campaign.

How much credit Reagan could take for all this was arguable — especially in the case of the robust economic recovery. But that it did occur during his four years in office resulted, deservedly or not, in his taking the credit at the polls.

What was beyond dispute was that, after decades of dominance by New Deal liberalism and its offspring, the Great Society, Reagan brought to Washington a new philosophy. Among its most profound elements were the historic tax and spending cuts enacted in 1981. Although the economic effects were debatable, this program indisputably opened a new era of federal fiscal austerity.

On an equal scale of departure from previous administrations were Reagan's national security policies, the linchpins of which were his belief that the United States had fallen behind in the arms race with the Soviet Union, and his insistence on substantial "real," that is, after-inflation, increases in Pentagon spending. Underlying this was Reagan's undisguised mistrust of the Soviet Union, which he labeled an "evil empire."

Assessing the first four years of the Reagan administration shortly before the 1984 election, Thomas E. Mann, executive director of the American Political Science Association, declared: "The agenda really has changed. In spite of the fact that the Democrats are now resisting budget cuts, the calls for continued and massive increases in federal programs are gone. Reagan has altered the terms on which politicians talk about government."

The Reagan Style

How much of this change in agenda came about because some historic pendu-

As one party in honor of Reagan's second inauguration closed, the president and his wife, Nancy, joined some of Hollywood's brightest stars — among them Frank Sinatra and Elizabeth Taylor — to thank them for their entertainment.

lum was swinging in the other direction and Americans simply were ready for a change, and how much was because of Reagan's abilities as an ideological salesman, was debatable.

President Reagan was billed as the "great communicator" for his proven ability to project his ideas to audiences, both in person and via the electronic media. Much of this skill could be attributed to his professional training as an actor. Most observers agreed that his public relations success was undergirded by an infectious idealism about America. Some of the president's best public addresses, including his almost lyrical acceptance speech at the Republican National Convention in 1984, dealt with his optimistic vision of America.

"The guy has got four or five things he cares about deeply," said Rep. Dick Cheney, R-Wyo., a member of the House Republican leadership. "He comes back to those themes repeatedly and he's able to communicate them effectively to the country and that's reflected in how Congress responds."

The good-natured persona that Reagan projected in the media contributed to his popularity and hence to his ability to put ideas across. The president always seemed to have a quick quip and a broad grin to deflect criticism. He was even reported to have maintained his sense of humor while on his way to the operating room at George Washington University Hospital in March 1981, after having been wounded in the chest by a would-be assassin. Reagan told those who were caring for him that he hoped they were all Republicans.

Another noticeable difference in Reagan's Washington appeared on the social circuit. Where Carter had emphasized egalatarianism and homespun informality, Reagan came into the White House trailing clouds of Hollywood-style glitter. Carter's populist-tinged inauguration had cost $3.5 million to stage. Reagan's first inauguration was studded with personalities from the entertainment world and cost $16.3 million. His second was a more modest affair, but Reagan still managed to bring out the stars.

On a more substantive level of style, Carter was much more of a "hands-on" president than Reagan, who made a virtue of delegating authority. While Carter immersed himself in the details of government policy and administration, Reagan had made clear ever since his days as governor of California that he preferred to act in the role of a board chairman, overseeing the execution of his general philosophies by the officers of his "company."

Reagan's critics seized on this style, along with his sleeping and vacation habits, as evidence that the president lacked a personal interest in and grasp of important details of government. The president's detractors often pointed to Reagan's trips to his California ranch as evidence that he was too removed, physically and mentally, from the demands of his job.

Another factor raised by Reagan's critics during the 1984 campaign was age. On the day he took his first oath of office, Reagan was 69 years old, making him the oldest first-term president in history. However, age was not a major problem for Reagan during his first term. Unlike some other presidents who seemed to deteriorate visibly during their years in the White House, Reagan seemed to thrive. Americans were familiar with images of the president on horseback at his ranch, among other vigorous pursuits. Not long before the election he appeared on the cover of *Parade* magazine in an apparently strenuous workout session on an exercise machine.

In fact, none of these criticisms seemed to detract much at all from Reagan's popularity, a phenomenon that figured in a story told by newspaper columnist James J. Kilpatrick during the 1984 election campaign. Regarding Reagan's sleeping habits, one voter told Kilpatrick that he would rather have Reagan asleep in the White House than Mondale there awake.

Reagan's faculty for walking away from criticism apparently unaffected was matched by an almost uncanny ability to escape blame for a number of disasters that occurred during his first four years in office. Perhaps the most serious catastrophe of his first term was the collapse of his policy in Lebanon and the withdrawal of American troops in February 1984, preceded by the death of 241 U.S. Marines in a Beirut truck bombing the previous October.

Other setbacks stemmed from actions of the team Reagan brought with him into government, including the discrediting resignations of James G. Watt as interior secretary and Anne Gorsuch Burford as head of the Environmental Protection Agency. Both officials had drawn charges that they pursued agendas contrary to the basic purposes of their agencies.

Other troubles led to what critics labeled the "sleaze factor" in the Reagan administration. White House counselor Edwin Meese III's nomination to be attorney general was temporarily sidetracked after various allegations of unethical behavior surfaced during his confirmation hearings in March 1984. Seven months later, Labor Secretary Raymond J. Donovan became the first incumbent Cabinet officer to be indicted on criminal charges. Donovan asserted he was innocent of the charges of grand larceny, filing false instruments and falsifying business records, and he declared that the allegations were politically motivated. Nevertheless, he took a leave of absence from the Cabinet and then resigned in March 1985. But Reagan himself managed to insulate himself from all these controversies. Observing this, Rep. Patricia Schroeder, D-Colo., bestowed upon him the title of "Teflon president," since it seemed that blame did not stick to him.

Political Perspective

Reagan spent 20 years preparing for his 1984 triumph. He had begun his political career in California by campaigning for the presidential candidacy of Barry Goldwater with a powerful speech denouncing high taxes, government regulation and wasteful welfare programs. Those conservative precepts formed the central agenda that Reagan carried with him all the way to the White House.

In a broader historical sense, the election of Reagan in 1980 settled a generation-long struggle for the soul of the Republican Party. Republicans were sharply divided between moderate and conservative factions a generation earlier. The moderate side, largely based in the Eastern states, argued for an internationalist foreign policy. On domestic affairs, moderates were in favor of streamlining, without destroying, Franklin Roosevelt's New Deal. Conservatives, led by Robert A. Taft, took an essentially isolationist view of the world and scoffed at the moderates' accommodations to the New Deal as "me-tooism."

That schism within the GOP ended in San Francisco in 1964 with Goldwater's presidential nomination. The same pro-Goldwater majority booed Nelson A. Rockefeller's denunciation of right-wing extremism. Although Lyndon B. Johnson won the election in a landslide, observed Congressional Quarterly political editor Alan Ehrenhalt, Goldwater "won the argument over the Republican Party, and it has not really been reopened."

True to his philosophical moorings, Reagan during his first four years in office was one of the most doctrinaire presidents in modern times. But he also displayed a distinct streak of pragmatism at key turns. He declined, for example, to fight as vigorously for items on his conservative constituency's "social agenda," such as abortion and school prayer amendments to the Constitution, as he had for his economic program. In fact, to a large extent the developments of those four years can be seen in terms of Reagan balancing his strong ideological beliefs and pressures from conservative constituents with the practicalities of running the government, including dealing with Congress.

For the first two years, the president was able to get away with virtually ignoring his outnumbered political opponents in Congress. *Time* magazine's White House correspondent Laurence I. Barrett called the president's first year with Congress a "blitzkrieg" and a "fierce, rapid assault, not courtship."

Toward the end of 1982, House Speaker Thomas P. O'Neill Jr., D-Mass., grumbled, "The president doesn't know what compromise is. He thinks compromise is when we give him 80 percent of what he asks for and he gives us nothing. Cooperation is a two-way street. For two years, we have cooperated with the president and waited for him to cooperate with the congressional agenda. We are still waiting."

Reagan on occasion disappointed his conservative supporters who felt that the president did not press Congress forcefully enough to enact legislation dealing with a range of issues on which they took strong moral stands. During the 1980 campaign and after the election, Reagan took decisively conservative stands on abortion, busing and especially school prayer.

In 1982 he sent Congress a proposed constitutional amendment to allow organized voluntary prayer in public schools. The wording declared: "Nothing in this Constitution shall be construed to prohibit individual or group prayer in public schools or other public institutions. No person shall be required by the United States or any state to participate in prayer."

However, the lobbying muscle that Reagan applied so effectively in behalf of his economic and defense programs during his first term was lacking in the case of the "social agenda." Facing determined opposition in the Democratic-controlled House, Reagan's school prayer amendment died at the end of the 97th Congress without even emerging from the Senate Judiciary Committee.

Despite Reagan's efforts, conservatives suffered similar setbacks on the abortion issue. On June 15, 1983, the Supreme Court reaffirmed its landmark 1973 decision legalizing abortion. The Reagan administration had urged the court to leave "further refinements" of the law to the wisdom of state legislative bodies. Instead, the court told legislatures to stop trying to influence a woman's choice on whether to terminate a pregnancy. Her right to make that decision herself, along with a physician, was guaranteed by the Constitution as outlined in the 1973 *Roe v. Wade* decision, the court said.

Groups opposed to abortion vowed to redouble their efforts to win a constitutional amendment outlawing abortion. But less than two weeks after the decision, the Senate rejected an amendment designed to overturn *Roe v. Wade*. Despite lobbying by Reagan, the vote was 49-50, which was 18 votes short of the two-thirds majority needed for a constitutional amendment.

Legislative efforts to eliminate court-ordered busing suffered similar setbacks, with the Democratic-controlled House Judiciary Committee always ready to bury the bill should it have cleared the Senate.

Reagan's general handling of civil rights matters, including his restructuring of the Civil Rights Commission, angered many black leaders. On May 26, 1983, the president announced his intention to replace three commissioners who had often criticized the administration's civil rights policies. Reagan nominated three people with civil rights experience but who shared his opposition to hiring quotas and school busing to achieve racial integration. Civil rights groups complained that Reagan was undermining the traditional independence of the six-member, presidentially appointed panel, which had been created in 1957. After nearly five months of negotiations between the White House, members of the Senate Judiciary Committee and civil rights groups, Reagan abruptly fired the three commissioners he wanted to replace.

Congressional debates over items on the "social agenda," when they did take place, were often emotional and wearying. But during most of Reagan's first term in office, these issues took a back seat to the president's main concern: the economy.

2

Reagan's Landslide Victory

It would be hard to imagine a vote more decisive than the balloting Nov. 6, 1984, which gave Ronald Reagan his second presidential victory. Reagan's win was about as sweeping as they come; he drew 59 percent of the popular vote — just shy of the 61 percent standard established by President Lyndon B. Johnson in 1964. Reagan won all but one state, a feat performed previously only by Richard Nixon in 1972, and he won a record 525 electoral votes. That left 13 electoral votes for his Democratic opponent, former vice president Walter F. Mondale, who carried only the District of Columbia and his home state of Minnesota.

Reagan received at least 60 percent of the vote in nearly two-thirds of the states, including three of the largest electoral vote prizes — Florida, New Jersey and Texas. The 10 states in which Reagan drew his highest percentages were scattered all over the country. Six were in his native West, including his two best states, Utah (75 percent) and Idaho (73 percent). Other leading Reagan states in the region were Alaska, Arizona, Nevada and Wyoming. Two of the others, Kansas and Nebraska, were in the agricultural Midwest. New Hampshire and Oklahoma completed Reagan's top 10.

The results were hardly a surprise. The pollsters had been predicting a massive Reagan sweep since late summer 1984, with final election-eve surveys showing him far ahead. Unlike the 1980 race, which had a volatile finish that propelled Reagan to a decisive victory over President Jimmy Carter, most voters seemed to have their minds made up long before Election Day.

By early November, the only question was whether Reagan would become the first presidential candidate to sweep every state since the national popular vote tally was instituted in the early 1800s. He just missed. Although the president made a late campaign stop in Mondale's home state, Reagan lost Minnesota — but by less than 35,000 votes. *(Results, p. 14)*

Despite the size of the victory, its meaning remained unclear. The other landslide elections of recent times all created at least a temporary feeling of conclusiveness. Johnson began talking about "consensus government" almost immediately after his 1964 triumph. Nixon reacted to the 1972 result by planning a wholesale purge of top positions in the executive branch.

Reagan's re-election sweep had a different feeling about it. The president, talking to reporters the day after the balloting, made no use of the word "mandate"; he simply said the voters "made it clear they approved of what we've been doing." Had

President Ronald Reagan and Nancy Reagan wave to supporters celebrating his 49-state re-election victory.

he talked about a mandate, no one would have been sure what the mandate was for, since he had revealed none of his plans for a second term during his campaign.

Moreover, the results of the congressional elections indicated that Reagan would be hard pressed to translate his popularity into action. In the Senate, instead of gaining as most presidents do, Reagan lost two seats, reducing the Republican majority to 53-47. In the House of Representatives, the president's party gained 14 seats, far short of the historical average for landslides. The GOP gained one governor for a lineup of 16 Republicans and 34 Democrats.

Turnout

The Democrats' efforts to register millions of new voters, many of them black, were successful, but hopes of building a class-oriented anti-Reagan majority in 1984 evaporated with the improving economy. Efforts to expand and refashion the electorate were blunted dramatically, first by the Republicans, who mounted a well-financed registration effort of their own, and then by the common perception that developed in late summer that the race was not even close.

Instead of 100 million voters participating in the presidential election, as the

Democrats had hoped, about 93 million people voted. That vote total would be large enough to end the 20-year decline in the presidential-year voter turnout rate, which slumped to 52.6 percent of the voting-age population in 1980.

Census Bureau interviews, conducted two weeks after the election, revealed that higher voting rates among women, blacks and Hispanics accounted for the increased turnout. Sixty-one percent of women 18 or older voted, up two percentage points from 1980. The bureau put the turnout for men at 59 percent, the same as in 1980. Fifty-six percent of blacks voted, and among blacks aged 65 and above, 68 percent cast ballots.

Blacks aged 18 to 34 also voted in greater numbers — 47 percent in 1984, compared with 39 percent in 1980.

But the increased turnout was not large enough to do Mondale much good. While his national popular vote total was about 1 million votes higher than Carter's in 1980, Reagan's soared upward by nearly 10 million votes. Reagan became the first candidate to win more than 50 million votes in a presidential election.

Vote Analysis

Although the Democrats are known as a coalition party, it was Reagan who put

Democratic nominees Walter F. Mondale and Geraldine A. Ferraro ponder their defeat at a press conference.

together the grand coalition in 1984. He led in all sociological categories of voters except blacks, Hispanics, Jews, union members and people with low incomes. Of political groups, Reagan led among Republicans and independents; he led overwhelmingly among conservatives and fairly substantially among moderates. He trailed only among self-designated Democrats and self-designated liberals. The categories in which Reagan enjoyed support greater than his national average of 59 percent included the following: white Protestants (73 percent), born-again Christians (80 percent), Southerners (63 percent), self-designated Republicans (92 percent) and self-designated conservatives (81 percent).

As in 1980, he swept most of the suburbs, small towns and villages throughout the country, as well as the bulk of the high-growth population centers of the Sun Belt, a number of academic communities and many areas dominated by blue-collar voters. And to that large coalition, he added virtually all of the rural white South, where Carter had maintained a toehold four years earlier.

Reagan ran unusually well among young voters (aged 18 to 29). He won more than 55 percent of their ballots, according to an ABC News-*Washington Post* poll. Youth had been a weak link for the GOP in the past, supporting Democratic presidential candidates in recent elections more loyally than any other age group. But for whatever reason — economic self-interest, attraction to Reagan and his strong, "grandfatherly" qualities or distaste for the Democrats as the party of malaise and Carter — the youth vote broke overwhelmingly for Reagan.

There was no corresponding swing to the Democrats among older voters. Although polls showed Mondale running more strongly than Carter did in 1980 among voters over 30, the Democrats were hardly drawing a large enough share of their vote

to scare GOP strategists.

Democratic efforts to exploit the gender gap failed. Even with New York representative Geraldine A. Ferraro on the Democratic ticket, women preferred Reagan over Mondale. According to the exit poll conducted by the *New York Times*/CBS News, 56 percent of women voted for Reagan. (Sixty-two percent of men voted for Reagan.) And the extensive campaigning by Mondale and Ferraro on the West Coast produced no victories. The Democrats drew no more than 45 percent of the vote in Oregon, Washington and California.

Geographical Breakdown

Democratic nominee Mondale drew consistently strong support from only two significant voting areas, the declining cities of the industrial Frost Belt and the black-majority counties of the South. And even in the cities, there was evidence of a splintering Democratic alliance, with minorities voting in large numbers for the Democratic ticket but with white ethnic neighborhoods registering a larger-than-usual Republican vote.

In Chicago, for example, Reagan drew 35 percent of the ballots, 9 percentage points higher than his share in 1980. In New York's Queens, home base of the Democrats' vice presidential candidate, Reagan received 47 percent of the vote, 2 percentage points higher than his 1980 total. While solid support from minorities allowed Mondale to win a 500,000-vote plurality within New York City, that considerable margin did not make him competitive statewide.

The story was similar in other industrial Frost Belt states, with Mondale building a lead in the major cities that evaporated under a tide of Reagan votes in the suburbs and rural counties. The once-reliable base that Democrats had among blue-collar ethnics in older suburbs and smaller industrial centers provided Mondale little help. The votes generally divided in a way that reflected local economic conditions.

Rural America was a triumph for Reagan. This segment of the electorate usually votes Republican in presidential contests, but under favorable conditions Democrats have been able to make substantial inroads. Capitalizing on his rural roots, Carter carried more than 1,500 of the nation's nearly 3,000 counties in 1976. Four years later, he was still able to win nearly 900 counties. But Mondale could capture barely 300, a total much closer to George McGovern's meager harvest of about 130 counties in 1972 than to any of Carter's totals.

Mondale was even beaten soundly in rural portions of Minnesota. He carried barely 20 of the state's 87 counties, relying on substantial majorities in the populous Twin Cities area and the hardscrabble Iron Range to build his narrow margin of victory in the state.

Reagan's Southern Sweep

The big falloff in the rural Democratic vote, however, was in the South. Democrats were hoping to carry several Southern states in 1984 by constructing a biracial coalition of "have-nots." But the vote instead was extremely polarized, with whites voting decisively for Reagan and blacks for Mondale. Since whites hold the majority in every state, the result was a string of Reagan victories throughout the South.

Even though he was an unpopular incumbent four years earlier, Carter still had a strong base of support within his home region. He was able to carry more than half of the approximately 1,300 counties in the South, many of them with a majority-white population. In 1984 Mondale won fewer than 200 counties in the region, and many of them were majority black. In Alabama, for example, nine of the 13 counties that Mondale won had a black majority. So did 10 of the 12 he carried in South Carolina.

In the South, race tended to override economic considerations. While Alabama, for example, was one of four states with an unemployment rate above 10 percent, Mondale lost blue-collar counties such as Etowah (Gadsden) and Lauderdale (Florence), which Carter had won easily in 1980. And in the politically volatile rural counties that were fiercely loyal to Gov. George C. Wallace during his third-party presidential bid in 1968, Mondale's vote was often minuscule. In Geneva County, Ala., which gave Wallace 92 percent in 1968 and Carter 68 percent in 1976, Mondale received just 27 percent. In Coffee County, Alabama, a Wallace stronghold in 1968 and a county that Reagan carried by just 4 percentage points over Carter in 1980, Reagan beat Mondale by 39 percentage points.

By holding a significant share of the white vote in 1980, Carter won Georgia and finished within 3 percentage points of Reagan in seven Southern states. But with Reagan winning overwhelming white support in 1984, the votes from an enlarged and almost unanimously Democratic black community made little difference. Reagan carried every Southern state by at least 18 percentage points.

Reagan's emphasis on conservative religious issues helped him lock up the Southern white vote, but Democrats hoped that it would produce a backlash elsewhere. If it did, it was in the West, where the Democratic ticket showed its biggest gains from 1980. There, Mondale apparently won the bulk of the sizable vote that went for independent John B. Anderson in 1980.

West Loyal to Reagan

The Democratic presidential vote rose dramatically in a number of the more liberal Western population centers. Mondale ran 9 percentage points ahead of Carter's 1980 total in both Denver and Multnomah County (Portland), Ore., and 8 percentage points higher in King County (Seattle),

Wash. But Mondale's most striking Western gains were in the San Francisco Bay area. The Democratic presidential vote was up 16 percentage points in San Francisco and 11 percentage points in Alameda County (Oakland and Berkeley). And Mondale picked up two counties, Marin and Santa Cruz, that had voted for Reagan in 1980.

Still, in most of the high-growth, vote-rich territory of the West and Southwest, Reagan was awesome. He won 75 percent of the 820,000 votes cast in suburban Orange County, Calif.; 72 percent of the 570,000 votes cast in Maricopa County (Phoenix), Ariz.; 67 percent of the 610,000 votes cast in Dallas County, Texas; and 62 percent of the 870,000 votes cast in Harris County (Houston), Texas. Reagan not only won big in these population centers but increased his vote by at least 4 percentage points over his 1980 total in each of them.

Northern Vote Divided

While Reagan made significant inroads among white Southerners, he also was able to reclaim the support of many moderate Republicans, who showed signs of drifting away from the GOP in 1980. Yankee Republicans, in particular, seemed to have returned to the fold. Many of them supported Anderson's independent candidacy four years earlier, and Anderson was encouraging them to vote for Mondale. But few appeared to follow his lead. Reagan increased his vote percentage by at least 10 points from 1980 in five of the six New England states, all of which had given Anderson at least 10 percent of the vote.

The 10 states in which Mondale drew his highest percentages in 1984 were clustered in the Northeast Corridor (the District of Columbia, Maryland, Pennsylvania, New York, Massachusetts and Rhode Island) and the upper Midwest (Minnesota, Iowa and Wisconsin). West Virginia rounds out the list.

Mondale ran up some of his highest percentages in New England college towns, drawing 77 percent of the vote in Cambridge, Mass., home of Harvard University and the Massachusetts Institute of Technology, and 71 percent across the state in Amherst, home for both Amherst College and the University of Massachusetts. But in Centre County, Pa., which is dominated by Pennsylvania State University, Reagan received 63 percent of the vote.

But Reagan was able to make dramatic inroads in some of the ethnic mill towns of New England, a region with unemployment rates well below the national level. Reagan carried Lowell, Mass.; Woonsocket, R.I.; and Barre, Vt. — all towns carried by Carter in 1980 — and held Mondale to 51 percent of the vote in Lewiston, Maine, an aging factory town that George McGovern had carried in 1972 with 62 percent of the vote.

Midwestern Vote and the Economy

Unemployment was a decisive factor for many Midwestern voters. In areas of the industrial Frost Belt suffering double-digit unemployment rates, the Democratic presidential vote tended to go up. Mondale won easily in beleaguered St. Louis County (Duluth), Minn., where the Democratic vote jumped 9 percentage points from 1980 and in Mahoning County (Youngstown), Ohio, where it rose 8 percentage points. In these areas, the latest unemployment rates were more than 12 percent.

But in "smokestack" areas where economic conditions were better than they had been four years earlier, blue-collar voters continued their movement away from the national Democratic ticket. In much of Ohio's industrial sector, for instance, unemployment rates were significantly lower than in Youngstown, and Reagan ran well. He captured Lucas (Toledo), Lorain, Montgomery (Dayton), Stark (Canton) and Summit (Akron) counties, all of which were necessary for a Democratic victory in the state. Montgomery and Summit counties had voted for Carter in 1980.

But economic conditions did not explain everything, even in the Midwest. As the only major industrial state saddled with a double-digit unemployment rate, Michigan should have been fertile ground for Mondale. But he could carry only four of the state's 83 counties. Even his margin in Wayne County (Detroit) was sharply reduced from Carter's winning total in 1980, and he was shut out in the "Automobile Corridor" that extends north from Detroit to Bay City. Reagan swept blue-collar Macomb County, where Mondale's mentor, Democrat Hubert H. Humphrey, had won easily in 1968.

Even normally Democratic Washtenaw County, which includes the University of Michigan, abandoned Mondale. That switch seemed to typify the division within the academic world that was taking place throughout the country. Places with prestigious liberal arts colleges tended to give Mondale an overwhelming vote, while counties with large state universities were much more receptive to Reagan.

Mondale Performance

For the Democrats, the 1984 election was another in their growing string of presidential election drubbings. At no time in this century had a major party gone through a series of electoral debacles as one-sided as the Democrats experienced beginning with 1972. In two of these contests they carried only one state. In three, they carried no more than six.

In recent years it had taken unusual circumstances for the Democratic presidential ticket to be competitive. Carter capitalized on public disfavor with the Republicans generated by the Watergate scandal to win in 1976. Yet even then his victory margin was just 2 percentage points. In the other three elections after 1968, the Democrats had lost by margins of 23, 10 and 18 percentage points, respectively.

The election of 1984 was not a particularly auspicious one for the Democrats to attempt to break the GOP's White House dominance. Reagan was one of the most popular of recent presidents, and the perceived economic upswing served to underscore his themes of peace and prosperity. Adding to the Republican advantage was Mondale's relative unpopularity even within his own party. In the Democratic primaries, more than three voters out of every five cast ballots for a candidate other than Mondale.

Yet 1984 probably offered a more legitimate test of the Democrats' national appeal than any presidential campaign in the last two decades. There was no major independent or third-party candidate on the ballot to divert votes as in 1968 and 1980. There was no party "outsider" atop the ticket, like McGovern in 1972 and Carter in 1976. And with both Mondale and Reagan assured of more than $40 million in federal funds to conduct their fall campaigns, there was no shortage of money.

Democrats were hopeful that Reagan, the "great communicator" of the early 1980s, would be the "great polarizer" of 1984, helping to galvanize millions of voters who were hurt by his cutbacks in spending for social programs or objected to his redirection of the federal government. The outline of a massive anti-Reagan vote was evident in the mid-term elections of 1982, when a surge in the number of black, blue-collar and unemployed voters helped propel Democrats to some major gains.

The best news for the Democrats may have been that in most states Mondale was able to draw about 35 to 40 percent of the vote. There was no region where the party's presidential vote consistently collapsed below 30 percent, as it did for McGovern in the South in 1972 and for Carter in much of the West in 1980.

Official 1984 Presidential Election Results

	Ronald Reagan (R)		Walter F. Mondale (D)		Electoral Votes	
	Votes	%	Votes	%	Reagan	Mondale
Ala.	872,849	61	551,899	38	9	
Alaska	138,377	67	62,007	30	3	
Ariz.	681,416	66	333,854	33	7	
Ark.	534,774	60	338,646	38	6	
Calif.	5,467,009	58	3,922,519	41	47	
Colo.	821,817	63	454,975	35	8	
Conn.	890,877	61	569,597	39	8	
Del.	152,190	60	101,656	40	3	
D.C.	29,009	14	180,408	85		3
Fla.	2,730,350	65	1,448,816	35	21	
Ga.	1,068,722	60	706,628	40	12	
Hawaii	185,050	55	147,154	44	4	
Idaho	297,523	72	108,510	26	4	
Ill.	2,707,103	56	2,086,499	43	24	
Ind.	1,377,230	62	841,481	38	12	
Iowa	703,088	53	605,620	46	8	
Kan.	677,296	66	333,149	33	7	
Ky.	821,702	60	539,539	40	9	
La.	1,037,299	61	651,586	38	10	
Maine	336,500	61	214,515	39	4	
Md.	879,918	53	787,935	47	10	
Mass.	1,310,936	51	1,239,606	48	13	
Mich.	2,251,571	59	1,529,638	40	20	
Minn.	1,032,603	50	1,036,364	50		10
Miss.	582,377	62	352,192	37	7	
Mo.	1,274,188	60	848,583	40	11	
Mont.	232,450	60	146,742	38	4	
Neb.	460,054	71	187,866	29	5	
Nev.	188,770	66	91,655	32	4	
N.H.	267,050	69	120,347	31	4	
N.J.	1,933,630	60	1,261,323	39	16	
N.M.	307,101	60	201,769	39	5	
N.Y.	3,664,763	54	3,119,609	46	36	
N.C.	1,346,481	62	824,287	38	13	
N.D.	200,336	65	104,429	34	3	
Ohio	2,678,560	59	1,825,440	40	23	
Okla.	861,530	69	385,080	31	8	
Ore.	685,700	56	536,479	44	7	
Pa.	2,584,323	53	2,228,131	46	25	
R.I.	212,080	52	197,106	48	4	
S.C.	615,539	64	344,459	36	8	
S.D.	200,267	63	116,113	37	3	
Tenn.	990,212	58	711,714	42	11	
Texas	3,433,428	64	1,949,276	36	29	
Utah	469,105	75	155,369	25	5	
Vt.	135,865	58	95,730	41	3	
Va.	1,337,078	62	796,250	37	12	
Wash.	1,051,670	56	807,352	43	10	
W.Va.	405,483	55	328,125	45	6	
Wis.	1,198,584	54	995,740	45	11	
Wyo.	133,241	71	53,370	28	3	
Total	54,455,074	59	37,577,137	41	525	13

Source: Secretaries of state for the 50 states and the District of Columbia; compiled by Congressional Quarterly.

Yet while Mondale was able to tap a respectable vote, he was strong hardly anywhere. Carter came within 5 percentage points of carrying a dozen states in 1980; Mondale finished within 5 percentage points of winning just three more states — Maryland, Massachusetts and Rhode Island.

Mondale was unable to reach out beyond the traditional Democratic base. According to the ABC News-*Washington Post* poll, he won nine out of every 10 black votes, while winning with smaller majorities the support of Jews, union households, the unemployed and least educated.

Although GOP voters were nearly unanimous in their support for Reagan, nearly one Democrat out of every four deserted Mondale to back the incumbent. Among them were a large share of blue-collar, ethnic voters, indicating an erosion of the party's base.

Of the few highlights for the Democrats was their strong showing in the large Frost Belt urban centers. Not only did Mondale draw massive majorities in New York City (61 percent of the vote), Chicago (65 percent), Philadelphia (65 percent), Baltimore (71 percent) and Washington, D.C. (87 percent), but also there were significantly more votes cast in most of the large cities than in 1980.

But in no case was the urban vote large enough to swing the state to Mondale. The result was a party still struggling to find a reliable base. While Republican candidates were able to count on rolling up huge majorities in most states in the Western half of the country, Democratic strength often varied with their candidates.

Carter tended to be strongest in the South; McGovern ran well in states with large numbers of young voters and high-tech industries, such as Massachusetts, Wisconsin, California and Oregon; Humphrey had been particularly strong in the Northeastern industrial states.

Democratic Outlook

With his landslide victory President Reagan ripped apart what was left of the once-dominant Democratic coalition, demonstrating that the GOP, at least in presidential politics, was the real "umbrella" party. If Democrats were to regain the White House in 1988, it was likely to be with a coalition different from the one that elected Franklin D. Roosevelt, John F. Kennedy, Lyndon B. Johnson and Jimmy Carter.

From Roosevelt through Carter, the Democrats were able to win by combining disparate groups of voters under their umbrella, ranging from the most liberal of urban ethnics in the North to the most conservative rural whites in the South. But the 1984 presidential results showed that only a skeleton of that coalition remained.

After looking at the results, the best thing the Democrats could do was hope that history repeated itself in 1988. The last three presidents who won landslide re-election victories saw their own party lose the next presidential election. Four years after Republican Dwight D. Eisenhower won a second term in 1956, Kennedy, a Democrat, was elected. Four years after Johnson scored his landslide win in 1964, Nixon was swept into the White House. And four years after Nixon's big win over McGovern in 1972, Carter was on his way to Washington.

Presidents can take credit for any successes during their first term and blame the problems on their predecessors. But in their second terms, the blame is all theirs and their party's next standard-bearer hears the criticism.

The American people obviously wanted Reagan to be president for four more years, rejecting the appeals of Mondale and the national Democratic Party. Beyond that limited area of agreement, however, it remained to be seen what the victors could accomplish in terms of political action.

3

Can Reagan Win with Congress?

Questions of President Ronald Reagan's willingness to lead Congress, more unified Democratic opposition to his policies, and a growing split between moderate and conservative Republicans all cast doubt on the legislative success Reagan could expect in his second term. Furthermore, Reagan was likely to confront problems that usually hamper second-term presidents. Congress often grows weary of the incumbent, whose party traditionally loses strength in the House and Senate at the six-year mark.

Also basic to Reagan's success in a second term was the tone of his agenda. A common thread running through conversations with members of Congress from both parties was that he had to take the lead on trimming the deficit and, to do so, had to move from the broad budget- and tax-cutting and defense-increasing themes that marked his first term to a more specific outline for bringing government expenditures in line with receipts. Even some Republicans asserted that he could not avoid the unpopular step of raising taxes.

Some members of both parties predicted that Reagan would pursue his "place in history," perhaps by seeking better relations with the Soviet Union and avoiding the more contentious, domestic issues of abortion and school prayer. But, if he de-

cided to do so, relations with Democrats might improve whereas internal ideological splits among congressional Republicans were expected to pose a new problem.

Conservatives, who helped craft a 1984 GOP election platform that embodied the tenets of the "Reagan Revolution," were expected to urge the president to remain true to those principles. They stood in opposition to moderates, who would press Reagan to attack federal deficits and to adopt a more cooperative approach in his relations with Congress.

Factors in Second-term Success

Whatever Reagan's legislative plans were for his second term, he was not likely to be able to implement them without substantial help from the 99th Congress, which was expected to prove far less cooperative than the one that greeted him in 1981. Barring any election recount reversals, there were 14 more Republicans in the House in 1985 than in the previous year. But there were 10 fewer GOP votes than there were in 1981, when the Reagan economic program passed, and that difference may be an important one. The president's package of

Congressional Leadership, 99th Congress

House

Thomas P. O'Neill Jr., D-Mass., speaker of the House

Jim Wright, D-Texas, majority leader

Thomas S. Foley, D-Wash., majority whip

Robert H. Michel, R-Ill., minority leader

Trent Lott, R-Miss., minority whip

Richard A. Gephardt, D-Mo., chairman, House Democratic Caucus

Jack F. Kemp, R-N.Y., chairman, House Republican Conference

Senate

Strom Thurmond, R-S.C., president pro tempore

Robert Dole, R-Kan., majority leader

Alan K. Simpson, R-Wyo., majority whip

Robert C. Byrd, D-W.Va., Democratic leader

Alan Cranston, D-Calif., Democratic whip

Daniel K. Inouye, D-Hawaii, secretary, Senate Democratic Conference

John H. Chafee, R-R.I., chairman, Senate Republican Conference

$35 billion in spending cuts passed the House by six votes in 1981.

In the end, though, numbers would possibly be less important than psychology on the Democratic side. Reagan could not have won on the crucial economic votes in 1981 without massive help from conservative Democrats, and not all those defections were the result of ideological agreement. By addressing the nation on television and generating constituent pressure for his program, the president was able to persuade several dozen Democratic House members that it could be politically dangerous to oppose him.

Whatever he wanted to accomplish in 1985 and beyond, Reagan would need to reestablish that climate of fear among conservative Democrats on the House floor. At best, that would not be an easy task for a president in his final term and lacking the emotional following that he had as a charismatic newcomer. When that same president was arguing for some form of deficit-cutting austerity budget — rather than for tax cuts as he did in 1981 — it was doubly hard to imagine his winning many clear-cut victories in a Democratic House.

The Senate changes little, but the changes that resulted from the 1984 elections were expected to make Reagan's life harder, not easier. There were 53 Republicans and 47 Democrats in the chamber in 1985, a net Democratic gain of two. In ideological terms, the Democrats may have gained a shade more than that: Walter D. Huddleston, the Democrat unseated in Kentucky, was assailed as a liberal in the 1984 campaign, but his was a relatively conservative vote available to the administration on some issues. All five of the newly elected Senate Democrats were likely to oppose Reagan in nearly all major policy areas.

The Republican Senate contingent was expected to be dominated by Reagan loyalists, but, as in the 98th Congress, about two-fifths of the GOP seats would be held by a moderate bloc interested in protecting social spending and blocking New Right social initiatives on issues such as abortion and school prayer. In the past, this crucial GOP bloc was reluctant to act as a group or to make common cause with the Democrats across the aisle. If that situation changed, the Senate could come to be controlled at least temporarily by a "moderate coalition" comparable to the conservative one that controlled the House in 1981.

Divided Government

Divided government is seldom a pleasant enterprise for those involved, and it rarely produces much in the way of important legislation. The record of 1981 represented the exception, not the rule. President Richard Nixon's frustration after four years of dealing with stubborn Democratic legislators led him into some questionable approaches to domestic policy — such as impounding appropriated money that was legally obligated to be spent. President Gerald R. Ford never resorted to anything like that, but the massive Democratic majorities

that existed for all but a few months of his presidency prevented him from establishing any real legislative program at all.

During the past generation, the only extended period of divided government that seemed to work even tolerably well occurred during the second Eisenhower administration. As a man without strong partisan instincts — and without many controversial goals in domestic policy — President Dwight D. Eisenhower had little difficulty working with House Speaker Sam Rayburn and Senate Majority Leader Lyndon B. Johnson, both of whom were, like him, Texans. In the closing years of Eisenhower's presidency, it was the liberal Democrats in Congress who felt frustrated; the bipartisan consensus tended to exclude them. *(Box, second-term presidencies, p. 20)*

President Reagan lobbies members of Congress in the East Room of the White House. Sitting from left to right are Reps. Les Aspin, D-Wis., and Melvin Price, D-Ill., and Sens. Claiborne Pell, D-R.I., Paul Laxalt, R-Nev., and Strom Thurmond, R-S.C.

Second-term Success . . .

"Congress and I are like an old man and woman who've lived together for a hundred years," Lyndon Johnson once mused as he neared the end of his tenure in the White House. "We know each other's faults and what little good there is in us. We're tired of each other."

Sooner or later virtually all of Ronald Reagan's predecessors have had to face the truth that the longer a president remains in office, the more difficult his relations with Congress will become. The last president to serve two complete terms was Dwight D. Eisenhower, who occasionally was compared with Reagan because of the wide-scale personal popularity enjoyed by both men. In the early months of Reagan's first term, *Newsweek* magazine credited his success with Congress to "clothing his presidency — and smothering his opposition — in a blanket of personal goodwill unmatched since Dwight Eisenhower."

But Reagan was not likely to take much comfort in continued comparisons between himself and Ike.

"President Eisenhower has cause for disappointment with Congress," announced Congressional Quarterly in August 1957, the first year of his second term. The reason: Congress that year approved only 37 percent of Eisenhower's 206 legislative requests, his lowest score since he entered office. In 1953, his first year in office, Eisenhower won congressional passage of 73 percent of his requests.

By 1960, Eisenhower's last year in the White House, his congressional approval score had plummeted to 31 percent, the lowest of his eight years in office. "Mr. Eisenhower is a lame-duck president with no power, after he leaves office in January, to punish legislators who voted against his program," Congressional Quarterly wrote in September 1960. Bryce Harlow, Eisenhower's chief lobbyist, said Eisenhower spelled out his legislative program in great detail early in his first term and spent the rest of his presidency prodding Congress to enact pieces of it into law, with decreasing success.

In addition to his time in office, other factors worked to diminish Eisenhower's lobbying influence. A heart attack in 1955 slowed the president down. More important, a recession helped the Democrats to widen their congressional majorities in the 1958 midterm elections, adding 49 seats in the House and 17 in the Senate.

It was tempting to see the second Reagan term as comparable to those Eisenhower years, but Congress had changed too much in the intervening quarter-century for the analogy to be carried very far. No contemporary House or Senate leader possessed enough power to restrain congressional partisanship the way Johnson and Rayburn did, and Speaker Thomas P. O'Neill Jr., D-Mass., who publicly called Reagan's presidency "a shame" during 1984, would never develop the sort of relationship with this president that Rayburn had with Eisenhower. Among junior mem-

...Has Eluded Presidents

That further branded Eisenhower as a lame duck during his last two years in office.

Harlow also said there are important differences between Reagan's approach to Congress and the way Eisenhower dealt with legislators. Eisenhower often would meet "over bourbon and branch water" with House Speaker Sam Rayburn and then-Senate Majority Leader Lyndon Johnson in amiable White House sessions that would deal with legislative progress. "President Reagan is instinctively more partisan than Eisenhower in terms of his relations with Congress," said Harlow. "He kicks them good from time to time. Eisenhower never did that."

To be sure, presidents have won major legislative victories after being re-elected. In June 1938 Congress passed the Fair Labor Standards Act even though enthusiasm for Franklin D. Roosevelt's New Deal programs was waning. Eisenhower pushed through the 1957 Civil Rights Act, the first major civil rights measure of the 20th century. And Johnson won approval of the 1968 Open Housing Act, the third major civil rights bill of his administration, after he announced he would not run for a second four-year term. Johnson, however, conceded that national sympathy generated by the assassination of the Rev. Dr. Martin Luther King Jr. may have provided extra impetus to pass the housing bill.

Still, a landslide re-election victory offers no guarantee that the returning incumbent can have his way with Congress. Stephen Hess, a senior fellow at the Brookings Institution in Washington, noted that Roosevelt was rebuffed in his ill-fated plan to "pack" the Supreme Court only a year after his crushing win over Alf Landon in 1936.

Hess also observed that Johnson's Vietnam buildup canceled the effects of his 1964 landslide over Barry Goldwater. After two years of persuading, a reluctant Congress in 1968 passed an income tax surcharge that Johnson wanted badly, but he was also forced to swallow more budget cuts than he wanted. Vietnam ultimately was the issue that drove Johnson from office.

There have been exceptions: Woodrow Wilson's second term and Roosevelt's third were marked by cooperative Congresses while the country waged two world wars. "Generally, however, at least since Jefferson, the second term is downhill," said Hess.

bers, partisan bickering in the House grew more intense in 1984 than it had been in any recent Congress.

Meanwhile, the election results confirmed another division that was impossible to ignore. The nation was operating under one political alignment for presidential campaigns and another for congressional campaigns.

Few in either party were shocked that one of the most sweeping presidential landslides of the century had brought only meager Republican gains in the House and a net loss in the Senate. There had been, after all,

Reagan's Relationship with Congress . . .

President Reagan had his ups and downs with Congress during his first administration. The following is a brief summary of his legislative successes and failures between 1981 and 1984:

1981

- Congress passed Reagan's three-year program of tax cuts.
- Congress cut federal spending for fiscal 1982 by $35 billion, close to Reagan's $40 billion request.
- In the first major test of Reagan's authority in foreign policy, the Senate voted to uphold a White House decision to provide sophisticated AWACS planes to Saudi Arabia. The House earlier voted a resolution disapproving the move.
- Reagan prevailed in an early test of fiscal policies when Congress canceled a scheduled increase in dairy price supports.
- Reagan was forced to withdraw a proposal to cut Social Security benefits in the wake of strong congressional opposition.
- Congress ignored a White House proposal to abolish the federally financed Legal Services Corporation, the agency that provides legal aid to the poor.

1982

- Congress rejected nuclear weapons freeze resolutions, which were strongly opposed by the administration.
- The House passed "domestic content" legislation to require minimum levels of U.S. parts and labor in foreign-made cars. The Senate did not consider the measure, which Reagan opposed.
- Reagan vowed in his State of the Union message not to raise taxes but eventually agreed to a $98.3 billion, three-year package of tax hikes.
- Congress voted to override Reagan's veto of a $14.2 billion supplemental appropriations bill.
- The Senate passed a proposed constitutional amendment requiring a balanced budget, favored by the administration. But the House refused to go along.
- The House voted a contempt citation for Anne M. Burford, Reagan's first head of the Environmental Protection Agency.
- In two tests of government spending levels, the House passed a $5.4 billion jobs program and the Senate approved $5.1 billion in housing aid. Reagan vetoed a $3 billion version of the housing bill, and it failed to become law. He threatened to veto the jobs bill, and it, too, never became law.

...Was Both Up and Down in First Term

1983

• Reagan beat back congressional efforts to place limits on the third-year installment of his 1981 tax cuts.

• The Senate voted to confirm Reagan's nomination of Kenneth L. Adelman to head the Arms Control and Disarmament Agency. Arms control advocates claimed Adelman was not qualified for the position.

• Congress approved a resolution permitting the administration to keep Marines in Lebanon for 18 months. But Congress soured on the deal after an Oct. 23 terrorist attack killed 241 Americans at their Beirut airport camp. Reagan withdrew the Marines in February 1984.

• The Senate twice voted to begin manufacturing chemical weapons for the first time since 1969, action favored by Reagan. In both cases, Vice President George Bush broke a tie in favor of the weapons. But chemical weapons were deleted in a defense appropriations bill at the insistence of the House.

• The Senate rejected by 18 votes a constitutional amendment to overturn a 1973 Supreme Court decision legalizing abortion.

• The House twice voted to end secret U.S. aid, sought by the White House, to support guerrillas battling the leftist Sandinista government in Nicaragua.

1984

• Congress continued to support production of the MX missile, though by an increasingly smaller margin in the House.

• Reagan won most of the money he sought in military and economic assistance to the U.S.-backed government in El Salvador.

• Congress passed a major anti-crime bill strongly pushed by Reagan.

• The administration failed to win enactment of legislation deregulating the banking industry after the House fashioned a bill aimed toward more, rather than less, regulation.

• For the second straight year, Congress refused to enact Reagan's proposal for "enterprise zones" to boost businesses in inner cities.

• The Reagan administration's efforts to aid anti-Sandinista guerrillas in Nicaragua through "covert" aid from the CIA were thwarted temporarily by strong House-led opposition. The compromise ban on aid to the "contras" called for another vote in spring 1985.

• With deficits a major campaign issue, the House passed a bill that would require the president to submit a balanced budget. But the Senate did not consider the measure, which was opposed by the administration.

an experience very much like this in 1972, when Nixon's crushing victory over Democrat George McGovern yielded virtually the same congressional result: a Republican gain of 12 in the House and a GOP loss of two in the Senate.

But from a Republican point of view, there existed powerful reasons why 1984 should not have turned out like 1972. At that time, there was no national party apparatus to help finance or plan congressional challenges; the National Republican Congressional Committee, which finances GOP House campaigns, was a somnolent institution interested only in passing money to incumbents. By 1984 that committee was a multimillion-dollar enterprise that not only financed House candidates but recruited them, coached them in campaign technique and, in some cases, produced their advertising.

Moreover, President Nixon did everything he could to avoid his party's congressional candidates. A personal triumph was exactly what he wanted. In contrast, President Reagan stressed party goals from start to finish. That he did not make special visits to boost House candidates until the last week of the campaign should not be over-emphasized; it had never been proven that those visits accomplished much anyway.

The Republican congressional campaigns were as well-coordinated a national enterprise as they possibly could have been. In key districts around the nation, voters watched television commercials in which a Republican son talked his father out of voting Democratic for the House. Those ads, designed and produced in Washington, left many Democrats worrying about a last-minute landslide as Election Day approached.

That the congressional landslide did not occur entitled any thoughtful Republican to ask: If not now, when? If a GOP presidential landslide and a well-executed national campaign effort could not shake the large Democratic House majority, what could?

There was growing speculation that much of the electorate divided its vote intentionally, supporting Republicans for president and Democrats for Congress, to avoid concentrating too much influence in one party. It was far from certain, however, that many voters had the constitutional separation of powers in mind when they went to the polls.

What was certain was that Democrats, whatever their weaknesses in presidential politics, produced some remarkable talent at the congressional level. They demonstrated a consistent ability to win even the most unfavorable districts in good years for their party and then used incumbency to hold those seats in bad years.

Reagan as Lame Duck

Beyond the crucial question of how many House and Senate votes Reagan could count on in the 99th Congress, the outcome of the congressional elections in November also had a psychological effect on how Reagan would be perceived, according to various political analysts.

Speculating before the election, Austin Ranney, a political scientist at the American Enterprise Institute in Washington, said "If it's another 1972 or 1956 where the president wins big but Republicans don't pick up much in Congress, nobody takes that as any big mandate for his policies. Under those circumstances, Reagan is a lame duck the day he is inaugurated." Ranney maintained that Reagan's effectiveness with Congress would diminish dramatically the moment he was tagged with the lame-duck label by the media and others. "Reagan no longer can denounce Congress and the Democrats because he will no longer be a political threat to them," said Ranney.

Reagan's own political past offered

mixed clues as to whether he would remain rigidly loyal to his conservative principles and political allies or if a second term would be marked by more flexibility and conciliation in his relations with Congress. His success in the national political arena stemmed from his image as the consummate Washington outsider who eschewed a business-as-usual approach to government and rode that theme all the way into the Oval Office. Once there, Reagan drew on the perceived strength of his 1980 victory and his personal popularity for his early first-term successes on Capitol Hill.

After Reagan's first year, however, relations with Congress grew more strained, and congressional support of his legislative program steadily declined. In 1981, Congress backed Reagan 82 percent of the time, according to Congressional Quarterly's system of rating presidential support on Capitol Hill. After House Republicans lost strength in the 1982 elections, his support slipped to 67 percent in 1983 and 66 percent in 1984. *(Presidential support study details, p. 26)*

More important, Reagan no longer was able to count on Congress' agreeing with his position on issues of the greatest concern to the administration. As the votes slipped away, Reagan and his lieutenants found themselves having to work out compromises with Congress on the size of the defense budget, production of the MX missile and aid to anti-Sandinista forces in Nicaragua. Reagan also found himself in 1982 signing the largest tax increase in the history of the country, a $98 billion measure that came in stark contrast to the tax cut bulldozed into law by the White House in 1981. *(Reagan's legislative successes and failures, box, p. 22)*

Reagan's eight-year tenure as California governor offered clues to what his second-term relations with Congress might be like. Reagan's "sense of purpose was keener and his goals more focused in his second term," wrote *Washington Post* reporter Lou

Cannon in a 1982 biography entitled *Reagan.*

Some said that Reagan came of age as a politician in his second gubernatorial term, dropping doctrinaire ideology in favor of a more pragmatic and conciliatory approach toward state legislators. Enactment of a landmark welfare reform measure, Reagan's cherished legislative centerpiece, involved intense negotiations rarely seen during Reagan's first four years in Sacramento.

"He was a compromising and approachable governor and in retrospect was responsive to a lot of requests from Democrats," said Rep. Mervyn M. Dymally, D-Calif., a member of the California Legislature during both Reagan terms. Dymally said Reagan's relations with state legislators were not so ideologically polarized as they sometimes appeared to be in Washington. "He's not the same person anymore. Here, his appointment book is based on ideology, camera situations and plain old gimmickry," charged Dymally.

Retiring Rep. Barber B. Conable Jr. disagreed, arguing that "the second Reagan administration will be even more government-oriented and less ideologically oriented than it has been in the first four years." The task for Reagan and his aides will be harnessing the personal popularity he continued to enjoy among the public into effective lobbying clout in Congress.

Democrats who opposed Reagan's policies said that his ability to charm voters might not rub off so easily on lawmakers, particularly in a second term. "I think the president is popular with the public because they do not know the president as we know him in Congress," said Rep. Bill Alexander, D-Ark. "But we know him now. We know Ronald Reagan. We know he is a wolf in sheep's clothing."

Others maintained that Reagan had the capacity to get Congress to follow his lead. "My impression would be that Ronald

Reagan in the next term is going to have to worry about his place in history and that he is going to know something that he may not have known before.... You do the tough things you have to do in the first year of a four-year term," said Conable.

"I think he can lead the right wing of the party. I think he can lead the left wing of the party. I think he can lead Americans generally," said Sen. Mark Andrews, a Republican from North Dakota. "But he has to get out and do it. He can't sit back and hide."

Congress' Backing for Reagan Declines

While Reagan's support from Congress was likely to decline in his second term, his first-term success provided a comfortable margin for the descent. Congressional backing for his positions had dropped steadily since 1981, his first year in office, but it waned only slightly in 1984, almost stopping the decline. Congressional Quarterly's annual presidential support study showed that Congress agreed with the president on 66 percent of the roll-call votes on which his stance was well known. That is about 1 percentage point less than in 1983, and a fraction of the 5 percentage point erosion between 1982 and 1983 and the 10 percentage point drop between 1981 and 1982. *(box, p. 27)*

The study showed the dip even though support for Reagan's positions increased in the House and stayed the same in the Senate. This resulted because far more of the votes on which Reagan had a clear stand took place in the Democratic-controlled House, where he was less likely to win, than in the Republican Senate.

Overall, Reagan's support in Congress slipped nearly 17 percentage points from the level of his first year in office, a year in

which Congress reacted to the mandate of his landslide victory by enacting much of his program. Reagan's slippage from his 1981 success rate of 82 percent was the third largest decline of the last seven presidents. President Eisenhower suffered a 19 point drop in his first term, and President Johnson had an 18 point loss over his term that began in 1965.

In 1984, on recorded Senate votes on which he took a stand, Reagan won 86 percent of the time, the same success rate he enjoyed in 1983. In the House, Reagan's support increased slightly more than 4 percentage points from 1983, to just over 52 percent.

While the volume of partisan, election-year rhetoric increased in the Democratic-controlled House in 1984, the presidential support scores took a curious turn. Democrats' scores went up, while those of Republicans went down.

Study's Findings

For its analysis, CQ considered 190 recorded votes in 1984 on which Reagan had a known position. Of those, 77 votes were in the Senate; 113 were in the House. Had there been a more equal division of votes between the chambers, Reagan's overall score of 66 percent likely would have been higher, benefiting from his broader Senate support. The 1983 study was almost an even split — 85 Senate votes and 82 House votes.

Although the study illustrated the political differences between Reagan and Congress, it did not measure how much of his program actually was enacted. And as an indicator of a member's loyalty to the president, the study should be used with care, caution and caveats.

First, the study counted only issues that reached a roll-call vote on the House or Senate floor. It did not consider items on the White House agenda that were scuttled or defeated before they reached the floor, privately compromised or passed on a voice vote.

Second, the analysis counted only votes where Reagan's public support or opposition was clear.

Third, all votes received equal weight. No distinction was made between major and minor votes, narrow and overwhelming outcomes, administration initiatives and congressional proposals. For example, a close, largely party-line Senate vote to reject conditions on military aid to El Salvador, which was a major foreign policy victory for Reagan, counted the same in CQ's analysis of Senate support as the unanimous vote on a popular bill aimed at collecting money from parents who fail to make child-support payments.

Finally, issues that took many roll calls to resolve may have influenced the study more than matters settled by a single vote. The classic recent example was in 1978, when President Jimmy Carter's Senate support score was dramatically enhanced by 55 winning roll-call votes — mostly procedural — on ratification of the Panama Canal treaties.

In 1984 some controversial issues required several roll calls, giving them added importance in assessing Reagan's support rating. To illustrate, 17 roll-call votes were taken when the Senate debated a supplemental appropriations bill that included Reagan's request for aid to El Salvador and to Nicaraguan rebels, and 11 of those votes were considered in the CQ study.

In contrast, the Senate had one roll call on its first budget resolution to set spending and revenue targets for fiscal 1985. The vote, a clear party split, was a key indicator of support for the president's economic policy.

Although some issues were important to the president, he did not take an evident position on various aspects of legislation. In such cases, CQ's study did not reflect Rea-

gan's stance, or whether Congress supported it.

(A reporter or researcher interested in how an individual member of Congress voted on aspects of the president's program is advised to look at the specifics of the member's legislative actions, including his or her record on CQ's selected key votes.)

Still, the presidential support score provided a rough gauge of the relationship between the president and Congress. Over time, the score reflected numerically the rises and dips in those relations, and the individual ratings showed how particular members fit the trends.

Success Rate

Following are the annual percentages of presidential victories since 1953 on congressional votes where the presidents took a clear-cut position:

Eisenhower		Nixon	
1953	89.0%	1969	74.0%
1954	82.8	1970	77.0
1955	75.0	1971	75.0
1956	70.0	1972	66.0
1957	68.0	1973	50.6
1958	76.0	1974	59.6
1959	52.0		
1960	65.0	**Ford**	
		1974	58.2%
		1975	61.0
Kennedy		1976	53.8
1961	81.0%	**Carter**	
1962	85.4	1977	75.4%
1963	87.1	1978	78.3
		1979	76.8
Johnson		1980	75.1
1964	88.0%	**Reagan**	
1965	93.0	1981	82.4%
1966	79.0	1982	72.4
1967	79.0	1983	67.1
1968	75.0	1984	65.8

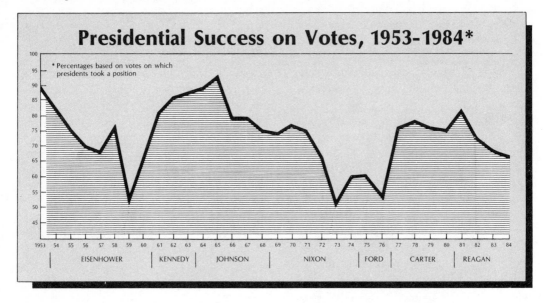

Presidential Success on Votes, 1953-1984*

* Percentages based on votes on which presidents took a position

EISENHOWER | KENNEDY | JOHNSON | NIXON | FORD | CARTER | REAGAN

The study was begun in 1953, Eisenhower's first year in office, and long was considered a yardstick of presidential success on Capitol Hill. A careful reading of the study's ground rules shows its drawbacks as a measure of executive clout, but not all readers have used the figures with discrimination. During the 1980 presidential campaign, President Carter's supporters cited his 77 percent support score for 1979 as evidence that Congress had passed four-fifths of the president's program. A Carter aide later acknowledged that CQ's statistics had been "mistranslated or misused."

Party, Regional Differences

As would be expected, Republicans agreed with Reagan more often than did Democrats. In the Senate, the Republican majority supported his positions on 76 percent of the votes, for a 3 point increase. But the president lost 10 points among House Republicans, falling from a 70 percent to a 60 percent support score. Among Senate Democrats, Reagan's support barely changed, slipping a single point, from 42 percent to 41 percent. House Democrats backed the president on 34 percent of the

roll calls, up six points from 1983.

A breakdown by party and region (East, West, South, Midwest) showed that, in the Senate, Reagan had greatest support in 1984 among Southern Republicans (84 percent, up 10 points) and the least backing from Western Democrats (32 percent, down 6 points). In the House, agreeing with Reagan most often were Western Republicans (65 percent, down 10 points), and least often were Democrats from the same area (28 percent, up 8 points).

In both chambers, Democrats from every region gave Reagan low support scores; only Southern senators backed him more than half the time (52 percent, a 10 point rise). But House Democrats from all four regions voted more often with the president in 1984 than 1983, while his support declined among House Republicans.

Senate

The president's biggest supporters in the Senate, both Republicans with tie scores of 92 percent, were Richard G. Lugar, Ind., also the top scorer of 1983 and 1981, and Majority Leader Howard H. Baker Jr., Tenn., the top scorer of 1982.

Ground Rules for CQ Presidential Support Study

Presidential Issues

CQ tries to determine what the president personally, as distinct from other administration officials, does and does not want in the way of legislative action by analyzing his messages to Congress, press conference remarks and other public statements and documents. Members must be aware of the position when the vote is taken.

Borderline Cases

By the time an issue reaches a vote, it may differ from the original form in which the president expressed himself. In such cases, CQ analyzes the measure to determine whether, on balance, the features favored by the president outweigh those he opposed or vice versa. Only then is the vote classified.

Some Votes Excluded

Occasionally, important measures are so extensively amended on the floor that it is impossible to characterize final passage as a victory or defeat for the president.

Procedural Votes

Votes on motions to recommit, to reconsider or to table often are key tests that govern the legislative outcome. Such votes are necessarily included in the presidential support tabulations.

Appropriations

Generally, votes on passage of appropriations bills are not included in the tabulations, since it is rarely possible to determine the president's position on the revisions Congress almost invariably makes in the sums allowed. However, votes on amendments to cut or increase specific amounts requested in the president's budget are included.

Failure to Vote

In tabulating the support or opposition scores of members on the selected presidential-issue votes, CQ counts only "yea" and "nay" votes on the ground that only these affect the outcome. Most failures to vote reflect absences because of illness or official business. Failures to vote lower both support and opposition scores equally.

Weighting

All presidential-issue votes have equal statistical weight in the analysis.

Changed Positions

Presidential support is determined by the position of the president at the time of a vote, even though that position may be different from an earlier position, or may have been reversed after the vote was taken.

Next were two influential Republicans who were absent from the 1983 list of Reagan's top supporters: Robert Dole, Kan., with 90 percent, and Pete V. Domenici, N.M., with 88 percent. Both men parted with Reagan on key economic questions in 1983. Thad Cochran, R-Miss., joined the field of Reagan's top Senate supporters for the first time. His score of 87 percent was 16 points higher than 1983.

Among Senate Republicans, only Lowell P. Weicker Jr., Conn., voted contrary to the president's position more than half the time — 55 percent. Others who disagreed most often with Reagan included Weicker's moderate-to-liberal cohorts, except for conservative Gordon J. Humphrey, N.H.

Reagan's top eight Democratic supporters in the Senate included two Southerners who more often opposed him in 1983. Howell Heflin, Ala., led Democrats in support for the president with a score of 75 percent — 33 percentage points higher than 1983. David L. Boren, Okla., tied for third at 62 percent — 21 points higher than 1983.

Eleven Democrats agreed with Reagan more than half the time, including Minority Leader Robert C. Byrd, W.Va., who scored 53 percent. Democrats voting against the Reagan position most often were Howard M. Metzenbaum, Ohio, and John Melcher, Mont., both of whom opposed the president 69 percent of the time, and Donald W. Riegle Jr., Mich., whose opposition score was 68 percent. Metzenbaum and Riegle made the list of top Reagan foes in every year of the president's term.

Two names from the 1983 list of chief opponents were notably missing in 1984. David Pryor, Ark., who opposed Reagan more than any other Senate Democrat in 1983, had an opposition score of 47 percent — down 24 points from 1983. And Walter D. Huddleston, Ky., who disagreed with Reagan on 59 percent of 1983 roll calls, opposed the president 40 percent of the time in 1984.

House

In the House, Steve Bartlett, R-Texas, backed Reagan's position more frequently than any other member — 81 percent of the time. Other strong supporters included some of the House's most conservative members, and Minority Leader Robert H. Michel, Ill., who had a 75 percent score.

Liberal-to-moderate "Gypsy Moth" Republicans from the North and East once again composed the GOP group most often voting against Reagan's stance. They were led, as in 1983, by Claudine Schneider, R.I., who opposed the White House position 57 percent of the time. Schneider was on the list of House Republicans frequently at odds with Reagan in every year of his term.

So was Jim Leach, Iowa, whose 1984 opposition score was 53 percent. Prior to the 1984 Republican National Convention, Leach was the organizer, and Schneider an early supporter, of a moderate group trying to fight the party's rightward drift.

Among House Democrats, the group most supportive of the president was led, as twice before, by Dan Daniel, Va., with 64 percent. G. V. "Sonny" Montgomery, Miss., and Charles W. Stenholm, Texas, were next with support scores of 59 percent and 58 percent, respectively. With Daniel, they are the only House Democrats who have appeared every year on CQ's list of Reagan's top backers.

Other top Democratic supporters were mostly "Boll Weevils" and two other conservatives — Ike Skelton, Mo., at 54 percent and Samuel S. Stratton, N.Y., at 53 percent. Not surprisingly, Reagan's most consistent opponents in the House included its most liberal Democrats. Charles A. Hayes, Ill., topped their ranks, with an opposition score of 80 percent.

Average Scores

Following are composites of party scores for 1984 and 1983:

Average Scores

	1984		1983	
	Dem.	**Rep.**	**Dem.**	**Rep.**
SUPPORT				
Senate	41%	76%	42%	73%
House	34	60	28	70
OPPOSITION				
Senate	49%	18%	51%	22%
House	58	33	66	25

Regional Averages

SUPPORT

Regional presidential support scores for 1984; scores for 1983 are in parentheses:

	East		**West**		**South**		**Midwest**	
DEM.								
Senate	35%	(42)	32%	(38)	52%	(42)	40%	(45)
House	31	(22)	28	(20)	43	(42)	30	(21)
REP.								
Senate	63	(68)	79	(73)	84	(74)	76	(77)
House	54	(60)	65	(75)	62	(74)	60	(71)

OPPOSITION

Regional presidential opposition scores for 1984; scores for 1983 are in parentheses:

	East		**West**		**South**		**Midwest**	
DEM.								
Senate	57%	(54)	52%	(49)	37%	(49)	53%	(51)
House	61	(73)	64	(73)	48	(52)	63	(75)
REP.								
Senate	30	(27)	14	(20)	10	(23)	19	(20)
House	40	(35)	28	(19)	30	(22)	33	(25)

(CQ defines regions of the United States as follows: *East:* Conn., Del., Maine, Md., Mass., N.H., N.J., N.Y., Pa., R.I., Vt., W.Va. *West:* Alaska, Ariz., Calif., Colo., Hawaii, Idaho, Mont., Nev., N.M., Ore., Utah, Wash., Wyo. *South:* Ala., Ark., Fla., Ga., Ky., La., Miss., N.C., Okla., S.C., Tenn., Texas, Va. *Midwest:* Ill., Ind., Iowa, Kan., Mich., Minn., Mo., Neb., N.D., Ohio, S.D., Wis.)

High Scorers — Support

Highest individual scorers in presidential support — those who voted most often for Reagan's position in 1984:

SENATE

Democrats		Republicans	
Heflin, Ala.	75%	Lugar, Ind.	92%
Nunn, Ga.	69	Baker, Tenn.	92
Long, La.	62	Dole, Kan.	90
Boren, Okla.	62	Domenici, N.M.	88
Stennis, Miss.	61	Abdnor, S.D.	88
Zorinsky, Neb.	61	Denton, Ala.	87
Johnston, La.	61	Thurmond, S.C.	87
Exon, Neb.	58	Cochran, Miss.	87

HOUSE

Democrats		Republicans	
Daniel, Va.	64%	Bartlett, Texas	81%
Montgomery, Miss.	59	Nielson, Utah	80
Stenholm, Texas	58	Lungren, Calif.	78
Hutto, Fla.	57	Badham, Calif.	77
Thomas, Ga.	54	Dannemeyer, Calif.	77
Sam B. Hall Jr.,		Mack, Fla.	76
Texas	54	Livingston, La.	75
Sisisky, Va.	54	Michel, Ill.	75
Skelton, Mo.	54	Conable, N.Y.	74
Whitley, N.C.	53	Hansen, Utah	74
Stratton, N.Y.	53	Shumway, Calif.	74
Bevill, Ala.	53	Robinson, Va.	74
		Bliley, Va.	74

High Scorers — Opposition

Highest individual scorers in presidential opposition — those who voted most often against Reagan's position in 1984:

SENATE

Democrats		Republicans	
Metzenbaum, Ohio	69%	Weicker, Conn.	55%
Melcher, Mont.	69	Hatfield, Ore.	45
Riegle, Mich.	68	Mathias, Md.	42
Pell, R.I.	66	Pressler, S.D.	39
Biden, Del.	65	Specter, Pa.	35
Sarbanes, Md.	64	Humphrey, N.H.	32
Leahy, Vt.	62	Boschwitz, Minn.	31

HOUSE

Democrats		Republicans	
Hayes, Ill.	80%	Schneider, R.I.	57%
Owens, N.Y.	78	Conte, Mass.	56
Dellums, Calif.	78	Green, N.Y.	56
Wheat, Mo.	77	Gilman, N.Y.	55
Wolpe, Mich.	76	Leach, Iowa	53
Edwards, Calif.	75	Snowe, Maine	51
Wyden, Ore.	75	McKernan, Maine	50
Mineta, Calif.	74	Ridge, Pa.	50
Weiss, N.Y.	74	Evans, Iowa	49
Kildee, Mich.	74	Rinaldo, N.J.	49
Lowry, Wash.	74	Petri, Wis.	46

4

Foreign Policy

Ronald Reagan entered office in January 1981 a novice in foreign affairs but with a fixed view of the role of the United States in the world. Time in office forced him to adapt those ideas to the realities a president faces every day.

As stated in countless speeches and interviews, Reagan's essential ideas were in 1980, and remained in 1985, that the Soviet Union was the chief source of trouble in the world and that the United States had to strengthen itself diplomatically and militarily to counter the Soviet threat.

Reagan tended to put all foreign policy issues into an East-West context. Thus, Lebanon, Grenada and Central America all were transformed into high-profile tests of will between the United States and the Soviet Union. For Reagan, the Soviet Union pulled the strings and its puppets danced: Syria in Lebanon, Cuba in Grenada and Nicaragua in Central America.

But Reagan discovered that trouble often comes from places other than the Soviet Union, that Soviet puppets sometimes danced to their own tunes, and that U.S. allies and friends often had differences with Washington. Talking tough and flexing military muscle did not always make troubles disappear.

The president undoubtedly created an image at home and abroad of a United States ready and willing to use military power to assert itself — a contrast with a widely held perception under Jimmy Carter of a United States reluctant to defend itself. Carter entered only one military engagement: the unsuccessful attempt to rescue the hostages in Iran. During his first term alone, Reagan sent U.S. combat troops to Lebanon and Grenada, used surrogates to conduct war in Nicaragua, and boosted many times over U.S. arms sales and military aid overseas.

Reagan seemed to be running against the Carter record. In one of his most important foreign policy speeches of 1984, on April 6, he defended the use of military force and said: "Peace through strength is not a slogan; it's a fact of life — and we will not return to the days of hand wringing, defeatism, decline and despair."

In accepting the Republican renomination for president in Dallas Aug. 23, he reiterated that theme: "In the four years before we took office, country after country fell under the Soviet yoke. Since Jan. 20, 1981, not one inch of soil has fallen to the communists." Vice President George Bush, in his speech the same night, praised Reagan's toughness. The U.S. invasion of Grenada in October 1983, he said, was "a proud moment." Added Bush: "Because our president stood firm in defense of freedom,

America has regained respect throughout the world."

But there was another edge to the military sword. Reagan's get-tough attitude had led some allies to fear that he was more interested in confrontation than in negotiation or diplomacy. U.S. foreign policy under Reagan was "more predictable" than under Carter, said a senior diplomat from a European country, but it also had caused "many more sleepless nights" for the rest of the world.

With the possible exception of any positive legacy from the Grenada invasion, at the end of his first term Reagan did not have an enduring foreign policy success — measured in treaties or other initiatives. That empty ledger of diplomatic victories contrasted sharply with Carter's record, which included the Panama Canal treaties, the normalization of relations with China, the Camp David accords between Egypt and Israel, generally improved ties with most Third World nations, and the never-ratified SALT II arms control treaty.

The only major successful diplomatic negotiation for which the Reagan administration could take credit was the Israeli-Lebanese troop pullout agreement signed on May 17, 1983. But that success was reversed a year later when U.S. influence in Lebanon had dipped to an all-time low and Lebanon abrogated the agreement at Syrian insistence. In early 1985 the Arab world was watching anxiously to see if Reagan would take advantage of his overwhelming re-election victory, and the historic opportunity it gave him, to press for peace.

Reagan asserted that he strengthened the North Atlantic Treaty Organization (NATO) and improved U.S. ties with the European allies. The most specific action to boost NATO militarily was the installation of medium-range Pershing and cruise missiles in Western Europe. But Reagan was carrying out a plan developed during the Carter administration, and his accompany-

ing anti-Soviet rhetoric helped foment massive anti-nuclear protests in Europe. *(Chapter 5,* Arms Control Developments, *p. 43)*

Toward racially segregated South Africa the president had adopted a policy of "constructive engagement," aimed at encouraging reform there by working with the government, rather than by bluntly attacking it. On Dec. 7, 1984, Reagan met with South Africa's most famous black leader, Anglican Bishop Desmond Tutu, winner of the 1984 Nobel Peace prize. After their meeting, Tutu and Reagan disagreed about the impact of American policy toward South Africa. Tutu said U.S. policy "had in fact worsened the situation of blacks there," but Reagan said the United States had made "sizable progress" and would continue its policy. A sudden wave of U.S. protest against apartheid that began in November 1984 was expected to provide renewed impetus in Congress to impose economic sanctions against the government there.

In time, it could be that Reagan's most measurable accomplishment would be the emergence of more responsible government in El Salvador. Steady support and encouragement from the United States enabled the Salvadoran government to carry out its freest elections in a half-century, over the opposition of leftist guerrillas. As of early 1985 it was too soon to tell, however, whether the government could reconcile with its opposition and add substance to the form of democracy.

Reagan made surprisingly few departures from the basic elements of post-World War II foreign policy. He embraced foreign aid and maintained the U.S. presence in the United Nations, the World Bank and other international bodies. He held negotiations, reluctantly, with Cuba, Nicaragua and the Soviet Union.

Reagan's difficulties in obtaining congressional support for his policies in El Salvador and elsewhere stemmed in part from his treatment of Capitol Hill as a hostile foreign country. Members, including some leading Republicans, berated the president and his administration for working against, rather than with, Congress.

The president's attitude toward congressional involvement in foreign affairs was laid out in his April 6 speech calling on critics to mute their voices. "If we are to have a sustainable foreign policy, the Congress must support the practical details of policy, not just the general goals," he said. Secretary of State George P. Shultz, who once was Reagan's best lobbyist on Capitol Hill, played on the same theme with a call for repeal of the War Powers Resolution, which gives Congress a role in deciding where and when U.S. combat troops are deployed.

In addition to his troubles with Congress, Reagan suffered the usual affliction of infighting in the foreign policy bureaucracy. Alexander M. Haig Jr., Reagan's first secretary of state, battled constantly with the White House staff and was forced to resign in mid-1982; Shultz and Defense Secretary Caspar W. Weinberger reportedly disagreed on just about everything; and the president's policy toward Central America was eternally buffeted by spats between so-called "hard-liners" and "moderates."

Reagan, who often seemed aloof from the discord, had a spotty record of personal familiarity with foreign policy problems. According to members of Congress who met with him, Reagan continued to have trouble with the nuances of complicated issues and with questions that were not put before him every day. But over time he had belatedly grasped some details of nuclear arms issues and had developed a good working knowledge of Central America, a region of special concern to him.

Central America

No news story during Reagan's presidency occupied the American press so con-

tinuously or troubled the American people more than the bloody fighting in Central America. Increased American involvement there, together with the invasion of Grenada, raised the specter of "another Vietnam." An official response was slowly shaped that would define a region of special U.S. interest, the "Caribbean Basin," and new policies to deal with it. These would combine a much-increased military presence and a new regionwide program of American economic assistance to be called the Caribbean Basin Initiative (CBI). Many believed both the military and economic thrusts were inevitable. In this region, wrote Robert W. Tucker in *Foreign Affairs*, "our pride is engaged as it cannot possibly be engaged in Africa or Southeast Asia."

Soviet, Cuban Influence

When Reagan took office in 1981, Nicaragua's Sandinista government was well into its second year and appeared to be slipping steadily into a Marxist format, while Cuban-sympathizing governments had taken power by coups in Grenada in the Caribbean and Suriname on the South American mainland. El Salvador was reeling under the so-called final offensive by leftist guerrillas and was losing the public relations battle in the United States. The killing of three nuns and a Catholic lay worker in 1979 had underscored the brutality of the country's right-wing goons and death squads, while unproven charges of guerrilla atrocities were written off as propaganda. To the north, Guatemala was in the throes of a guerrilla war of its own, and for the first time in history leftist agitation appeared to be penetrating that country's normally apolitical Indian population.

Rightly or wrongly, President Reagan and Secretary of State Haig saw a planned regional pattern of Soviet-Cuban subversion and takeover that directly threatened the United States "in its own back yard." *The Economist*, the London-based magazine, wrote: "The fires in Nicaragua, El Salvador and Guatemala did not ignite in swift succession by accident. . . . They seem to be flowing together in a single isthmus-wide conflagration."

Almost immediately, the new administration moved to isolate Nicaragua and step up support for the Salvadoran junta then running the country. A Gallup Poll in March 1981 indicated that American opinion for these measures was sharply divided, but with an overwhelming majority opposed to any use of American troops. Congressional critics, and there were many in the president's own party, argued that Haig's Cold War rhetoric, in particular, was frightening the American people as well as America's allies, while the roots of the Caribbean's problems could be laid more to poverty than subversion.

Caribbean Basin Initiative

Indeed, within a year the president embraced a more balanced approach. On Feb. 24, 1982, he went before the Organization of American States (OAS) in Washington to propose the Caribbean Basin Initiative to upgrade the region's crippled economies. His proposal set off a debate over whether the initiative's true goal was economic development or a cover for pouring more money into tottering Central American governments.

Reagan's speech was in fact two in one: the velvet glove of aid and trade benefits, but still the mailed fist of anti-communism. "Guerrillas, armed and supported by and through Cuba, are attempting to impose a Marxist-Leninist dictatorship on the people of El Salvador as part of a larger imperialistic plan," he said. Nonetheless, most of the address was oriented to economic assistance, and it was received with a sigh of relief in Latin America and Congress.

Yet in 1982 Reagan also initiated covert aid administered by the CIA to several thousand guerrillas — he called them "free-

dom fighters" or "contras" — who were battling the leftist government of Nicaragua. President Reagan had tried with moderate success to renew this aid every year thereafter, touching off congressional controversy with each attempt.

Reagan Backs 'Contras'

By the time of President Reagan's second inaugural, the political situation in Central America appeared to be stabilizing. Christian Democrat José Napoleón Duarte had been elected president in El Salvador, and the rightist elements grouped around Major Roberto D'Aubuisson were in retreat. A constituent assembly had been elected in Guatemala with centrists in control, holding out the prospect for return to civilian rule in 1985. Fears of a war between Nicaragua and Honduras, with the clear potential for full-scale U.S. intervention, were much diminished. The leftist government in Grenada was toppled by a U.S. military invasion in November 1983 and replaced by a new government of the center that was elected overwhelmingly in December 1984. Colonel Desi Bouterse, Suriname's strongman, had been alarmed by events in Grenada and sent home most of his Cuban advisers.

President Reagan in February 1985 acknowledged publicly for the first time that he was seeking to oust the leftist government of Nicaragua, and he appealed to Congress to assist in that goal. Reagan and his aides for three years had given several purposes for the U.S. policy of aiding anti-government guerrillas in Nicaragua, but the ousting of that regime never had been among Washington's official aims. In his Feb. 16 radio broadcast, Reagan compared the contras to Americans who fought the British during the American Revolution. The United States should aid the contras now, he said, just as the French aided the Americans then.

Administration critics said that the

United States should take its case against Nicaragua to the OAS. But at a February House Foreign Affairs Committee meeting Secretary of State Shultz insisted that the United States was "looking at all alternatives." He declined to discuss the OAS and the Rio Treaty, under which most countries in the Western Hemisphere had pledged to come to each other's aid to thwart aggression. Instead, Shultz said, "We have a moral duty to support people who are trying to bring about the freedom of their country."

The Middle East

American prestige and power in the Middle East suffered a sharp decline during Reagan's first term after major diplomatic and military efforts by the Reagan administration to bring peace to war-torn Lebanon ended in failure.

Other events also challenged U.S. influence and contributed to turmoil and violence in the region. Continued hostility toward Israel by the Arab states wiped out the optimism engendered by the 1979 Egyptian-Israeli Peace Treaty. The 1981 assassination of Egyptian President Anwar Sadat removed from the scene America's most loyal and understanding ally in the Arab world and threw into question the future of the peace treaty. The fate of the Palestinians residing in Israeli-occupied territories remained a basic cause of instability in the region.

The Iran-Iraq war that began in 1979 had escalated by 1984 to threaten shipping in the Persian Gulf, the key transportation link for much of the Western world's oil supplies.

With events spinning out of control in the Middle East, the political consensus on the policies America should pursue in the region disintegrated. As the Reagan administration moved from diplomacy and mediation to increased military involvement

Nicaraguan rebels are fighting for liberty and democracy, and the United States should aid them, just as the French aided American revolutionaries, Reagan said.

through the use of American troops in Lebanon and the sale of arms to moderate Arab states, Reagan and Congress clashed repeatedly over the direction in which the United States was moving.

U.S. Involvement in Lebanon

The debate focused on Lebanon, a country that had suffered nearly 10 years of civil war and occupation by Syrian and Palestinian troops. Lebanon both dominated the Middle East agenda and symbolized the problems faced by the Reagan administration as it sought to shore up moderate governments in the region as a buffer against Soviet influence.

The administration initially undertook a mediating role among the rival religious factions in Lebanon to help bring stability to the Christian-led government, while it also tried to persuade the Syrians and Palestinians to withdraw their forces from the country. But by 1983 that diplomatic role had been altered considerably by increased American military activity, including the stationing of 1,800 Marines in Lebanon as part of a four-nation peacekeeping force.

As the Marines were drawn into the hostilities in Lebanon, coming under fire and shelling, some members of Congress began questioning the U.S. military presence in the country. A controversy also developed between Reagan and Congress over the 1973 War Powers Resolution, which limited the president's power to keep American armed forces in hostile situations without congressional approval.

Congress reluctantly approved a resolution in September 1983 authorizing the Marines to remain in Lebanon for another 18 months. But 11 days after the president signed the resolution a truck carrying more than 10,000 pounds of explosives rammed into Marine headquarters at Beirut airport, killing 241 U.S. servicemen. It was the biggest daily casualty of U.S. military forces since the Vietnam War.

The attack led to strong public sentiment for withdrawal of the Marines and provoked sharp debate in Congress over the American role in Lebanon. The debate intensified after U.S. naval and air forces clashed with Syrian forces in eastern Lebanon in December 1983, heightening fears of a war with Soviet-backed Syria that would have risked a superpower confrontation.

President Reagan at first insisted that any withdrawal of the Marines would lead to the collapse of the Lebanese government, a takeover of Lebanon by Syria and a security threat to Israel. But faced with the likelihood of a congressional resolution calling for the removal of the Marines, the president in February 1984 withdrew the Marines to offshore ships. Within a few weeks Reagan ended all U.S. participation in the peacekeeping force, blaming Congress for any loss of U.S. credibility in Lebanon and the Middle East.

With the departure of the Marines and the near-collapse of the government of Lebanon, Syria emerged once again as the dominant force there. In return for its assistance in negotiating a coalition government, Syria pressured Amin Gemayel, Lebanon's president, into scrapping the U.S.-mediated agreement his country had signed with Israel the previous year.

Lebanon faded from the headlines in the United States until another terrorist attack in September 1984 — this time on the newly opened U.S. Embassy annex in East Beirut — pushed the country back into public attention. The attack was the third in 17 months and came only seven weeks before the U.S. elections. Reagan was forced on the defensive by congressional critics and Democratic presidential challenger Walter F. Mondale over the adequacy of security arrangements for Americans in Lebanon. Reagan infuriated Democrats by appearing at first to be shifting blame to the Carter administration for the "near-destruction" of intelligence operations, thus jeopardizing the country's ability to predict and forestall terrorist attacks. The president later backed off these charges and said he assumed all responsibility for the security failures, as he had done after the Marine headquarters attack.

Arab-Israeli Conflict

While the Reagan administration was preoccupied with Lebanon, little progress was being made on Arab-Israeli relations. Hopes for a lasting accommodation between Israel and its Arab neighbors after the peace treaty had been negotiatied with Egypt already had begun to evaporate when Egyptian President Sadat was gunned down by extremists on Oct. 6, 1981. U.S. policy in the Middle East had to be formulated and implemented thereafter without the help of a major ally.

Although Sadat's successor, former vice president Hosni Mubarak, pledged to adhere to the pact and continue Sadat's moderate foreign policy line, by 1984 Egypt had begun to move back into the Arab fold.

Israel met one of its obligations under the peace treaty when it withdrew all its forces from the Sinai Peninsula on April 25, 1982, a move much sought by Egypt. But other actions the Israelis pursued under Prime Minister Menachem Begin caused tensions to develop between the United States and its closest ally in the Middle East.

Repeatedly ignoring Washington's pleas for restraint, Israel bombed a nuclear reactor in Iraq in June 1981 and the headquarters of the Palestine Liberation Organization (PLO) in Beirut one month later. The Iraqi raid strained American support for Israel, although many in Congress and elsewhere defended the pre-emptive strike as, in Begin's phrase, "an act of supreme, legitimate self-defense."

The Iraqi and PLO raids seemed to demonstrate nothing so much as Israeli frustration at administration efforts to court the Arabs through a policy of "strategic consensus" among moderate Arab states to counter Soviet influence.

In December 1981 Begin pressured the Israeli parliament, or Knesset, to extend Israeli law to the Golan Heights, despite American efforts to persuade Israel not to extend its settlements. In June 1982 Israel invaded Lebanon to free its southern region of PLO guerrillas. The invasion brought the first U.S. troops to Lebanon in the 1980s to be part of a peacekeeping force with Italian and French troops to monitor the withdrawal of the Israelis and the eviction of the PLO.

Criticized for overemphasizing the Soviet threat in the Middle East to the detriment of progress on Arab-Israeli conflicts, President Reagan tried to seize the diplomatic offensive in September 1982 with his own Mideast peace plan. The plan involved Palestinian self-government for the West Bank in association with Jordan, but it was immediately rejected by the Israelis and faltered when Jordan was unable to secure approval from the PLO to negotiate on behalf of the Palestinians.

President Reagan moved to improve relations with Israel after Begin resigned for health reasons in September 1983. By the end of 1984, a new Israeli coalition government was seeking U.S. assistance in solving Israel's economic crisis and the involvement of the United States as a mediator with the Syrians over the removal of both Israeli and Syrian troops from Lebanon.

Proposed Arms Sales

Despite improved cooperation with Israel, the administration continued to promote arms deals with Jordan and Saudi Arabia, which Israel and its supporters viewed with alarm. Reagan's first major arms initiative in 1981 was a proposed sale of five Airborne Warning and Control System (AWACS) radar planes to Saudi Arabia. The proposal caused heated debate in Congress, but Reagan won a major foreign policy victory when the sale was narrowly approved in October 1981. Further administration arms sales proposals ran into stronger resistance from Congress in 1983 and 1984. Reagan had to pull back a proposed arms package for Jordan and ship missiles to Saudi Arabia under a special emergency power.

Reagan, like his predecessor, attempted to draw Jordan into the Arab-Israeli peace process. The president offered Jordan's King Hussein financial aid and equipment and training for a Jordanian "rapid deployment force" that could respond to military crisis in the region. The package also was to include sale of 1,613 "Stinger" portable anti-aircraft missiles.

When Hussein visited Washington in early 1984, he reportedly received assurances from Reagan that the president would press Congress for approval of the weapons and aid requests. Hussein angered members of Congress, however, by his unwillingness to enter into peace negotiations with Israel and by remarks he made in newspaper and television interviews in which he called the United States the major stumbling block to peace in the Middle East.

In the face of mounting opposition in Congress, Reagan in March 1984 withdrew the proposed sale of the Stingers to Jordan and a companion sale to Saudi Arabia. The Saudi sale was going to be resubmitted at some future date, according to administration officials. Within two months Reagan decided not to press Congress on the Jordanian "rapid deployment force," and he shipped 400 Stingers to Saudi Arabia under an "emergency" authority. This enabled the president to avoid a 30-to-50-day review by Congress. The missiles were supposed to boost Saudi Arabia's ability to protect its oil fields as well as shipping in the Persian Gulf.

Israel and many of its allies in Congress objected to the sale of any Stingers to Arab countries, saying the missiles could fall into the hands of terrorists. Saudi Arabia became the first country outside NATO or Japan to get Stingers.

The decisions on arms for Jordan and Saudi Arabia came as Iran and Iraq were extending their five-year-old war to shipping in the Persian Gulf. Iraq in late April 1984 had begun attacking Saudi shipping in the gulf. Iran responded in mid-May with attacks on ships belonging to Kuwait, Saudi Arabia and other countries. It was widely assumed that Iraq began the attacks in an effort to force the United States or other Western countries to enter the war and prevent an Iranian victory.

The administration took a cautious view of involvement, with Reagan telling a May 22 news conference that the United States was consulting with its allies and with countries in the region. "We have not volunteered to intervene," he said, "nor have we been asked to intervene."

1985 Peace Negotiations

By the beginning of Reagan's second term, however, some developments had given rise to the hope that moderation might yet prevail in the Middle East. Egypt moved in early 1985 toward re-establishing its claim to leadership of the Arab world, and it did so in a particularly bold and useful way — by suggesting a path to a possible Middle East peace settlement.

Egyptian President Mubarak urged Reagan on Feb. 24, 1985, to invite to the United States representatives of Israel, Jordan and Palestinian Arab groups for exploratory talks. If subsequent negotiations were agreed to at that time, Mubarak said, Egypt would be willing to act as host for the meeting.

These proposals dominated the meeting between Mubarak and President Reagan, which began March 12 in Washington. The idea already had been warmly received by administration officials, who noted that U.S. policy long had stressed the importance of direct Arab-Israeli negotiations to solve the Palestinian problem.

Saudi Arabian King Fahd, who visited Washington Feb. 11-12, also had urged Reagan to reassert a U.S. role in the peace process. In particular, Fahd asked Reagan to support the "just cause" of the Palestinians — an action he said would "earn the United States the respect and appreciation not only of the Arab and Muslim worlds but also of freedom-loving peoples everywhere." U.S. officials also quoted Fahd as saying privately that Reagan, because of his overwhelming re-election victory, had a "historic opportunity" to press for peace.

Lasting peace was an ambitious goal, but signs were hopeful. Chief among them was the successful meeting in Amman Feb. 11 between Jordan's King Hussein and Pal-

President Reagan greets King Fahd at the White House. U.S. officials quoted the Saudi Arabian as saying Reagan has a "historic opportunity" to press for peace.

estine Liberation Organization (PLO) Chairman Yasir Arafat. Formerly bitter enemies, the two men agreed on a "framework for common action" in reaching a settlement with Israel on the future of Palestinians living in the Israeli-occupied Gaza Strip and West Bank.

The Hussein-Arafat accord doubtless inspired Mubarak to float his proposal on peace talks. After being briefed in Jerusalem by Egyptian envoys, Israeli Prime Minister Shimon Peres said he endorsed the Mubarak plan. However, one sticking point could be Israel's longstanding refusal to negotiate directly with known members of the PLO.

Egypt was looking to the United States to enter the peace process. As Egyptian ambassador El Sayed Abdel Raouf el Reedy put it, "The re-election of President Reagan for a second term gives the American administration the chance to initiate a more active role in the search for peace in the Middle East."

Against the backdrop of increasing attention to the Middle East peace front, Congress and the administration were girding for another battle over arms sales to what it described as moderate Arab countries. Fahd's visit was used to warn Congress to expect proposals in 1985 for Middle East arms sales, especially to Saudi Arabia.

5

Arms Control Developments

In contrast to the skepticism with which he regarded weapons negotiations during his first term, President Ronald Reagan welcomed an agreement reached in January 1985 between the United States and the Soviet Union to resume nuclear arms control talks. After discussions Jan. 7-8 in Geneva, Secretary of State George P. Shultz and Soviet Foreign Minister Andrei A. Gromyko announced that the two superpowers would negotiate over three kinds of weapons, including a category never before given special consideration — space weapons. In a statement issued Jan. 22, 1985, the day after his inauguration, Reagan asserted that he had "no more important goal" in his second term than to "achieve a good agreement — an agreement which meets the interests of both countries, which increases the security of our allies and which enhances international stability."

At the same time, Reagan was seeking significant increases in defense spending for fiscal 1986, reinforcing his position that the United States should enter into negotiations with the Soviet Union only from a position of strength. Two days after it agreed to the arms control talks, the Reagan administration cited them as a reason Congress should support the president's nuclear arms build-up. Secretary of State Shultz maintained in a briefing to congressional members that

the U.S. negotiating position would be undermined if Congress scrapped the controversial MX missile or cut back on other defense efforts "necessary to the security of the nation."

In addition, the administration had stepped up its campaign calling into question Soviet compliance with the terms of past arms control agreements. In a February 1985 report to Congress, the administration cited 13 areas of "concern" but focused its attention on one "clear violation" of the 1972 Anti-Ballistic Missile Treaty: a phased-array, early warning radar system under construction near the Siberian city of Krasnoyarsk. Calling the provision controlling deployment of phased-array radar "the linchpin of the ABM Treaty," a senior administration official termed Soviet non-compliance "a dagger pointed at the whole arms control process in the future."

With public opinion apparently solidly behind the newly elected president and such misgivings about Soviet trustworthiness, why was Reagan embarking on new arms control negotiations? Kenneth Adelman, director of the U.S. Arms Control and Disarmament Agency, gave three reasons: "New arms control agreements, if soundly formulated, can serve U.S. security interests; entering into new negotiations does not in any way condone past Soviet behavior; and arms control gives us leverage and another way to get the Soviets to abide by existing agreements."

But the political climate no doubt also contributed to Reagan's new sentiments. The resumption of negotiations — broken off by Moscow in late 1983 — complemented the increasingly conciliatory tone that had characterized the official stance toward Moscow in the last two years of Reagan's first administration. In 1981-82 the president's nuclear arms programs encountered unprecedented domestic opposition, reflecting widespread alarm over the confrontational approach to the Russians that had characterized Reagan's first two years. By the time he squared off against Democratic presidential rival Walter F. Mondale in 1984, the shift to more conciliatory rhetoric evidently had neutralized the "war-peace" issue as a Reagan liability. Others speculated that Reagan wished to make his mark on history by attaining an arms control agreement before his inevitable retirement from the presidency at the end of his second term.

But while agreement to resume talks conformed to the political imperative of a more conciliatory tone, the administration argued that it also vindicated a fundamental premise of Reagan policy: that Moscow would negotiate away its existing advantage in nuclear weaponry only if it faced a U.S. arms buildup.

Reagan's Defense Buildup

Even as the administration was elaborating its negotiating position for the arms control talks, it was trying to build support in the United States and Europe for its defense modernization program, including Reagan's Strategic Defense Initiative (SDI). Dubbed "Star Wars" by its critics, SDI envisioned a new type of non-nuclear, space-based defense against nuclear attack that its supporters said would remove the enemy's incentive to use nuclear weapons. Reagan's defense buildup, the administration argued, was necessary to persuade the Soviet Union to bargain in good faith. The administration requested that Congress approve a $2 trillion military budget over the following five years, beginning with $313.7 billion for fiscal 1986, which was to begin Oct. 1, 1985. Part of the money was to be used to reinforce the arsenal of strategic nuclear weapons: the budget included $3.2 billion for 48 land-based MX missiles, $5.6 billion for 48 B1 bombers and $5 billion for a Trident submarine and Trident missiles.

Administration spokesmen, led by Defense Secretary Caspar W. Weinberger, maintained that Reagan's four-year-old program to "rearm America" was what led the Soviet Union back to the bargaining table and that efforts to reduce the Pentagon's budget would only undermine the American position at the talks. Because of widespread bipartisan concern over the $200 billion federal budget deficit, however, the administration's defense budget request undoubtedly would be pared. Reflecting this sentiment, Sen. Sam Nunn, D-Ga., told Weinberger during hearings on the budget proposal before the Armed Services Committee: "It's not a question of whether it will be cut, it's a question of how much it will be reduced."

Another concern to the administration was the controversial MX missile. Dubbed the "peacekeeper" by Reagan because of its purported contribution to nuclear deterrence, the MX was a new, more accurate intercontinental ballistic missile (ICBM) armed with 10 nuclear warheads. The administration was trying to increase support for the MX in Congress, which had delayed production of the weapon, before it came to another vote in early spring. "I must tell you, frankly," Weinberger told the Senate Foreign Relations Committee Jan. 31, "that cancellation of key programs, such as MX, will prolong negotiations, not facilitate them, and will reduce our ability to achieve arms reductions."

Further complicating the administration's effort to boost defense spending on Capitol Hill were the changes in leadership on several key congressional committees. In particular, Rep. Les Aspin, D-Wis., elected chairman of the House Armed Services Committee at the beginning of the 99th Congress, suggested that he might drop his support for the MX, a weapon he said may be unnecessary if Reagan's strategic defense initiative proved feasible.

By early 1985 SDI itself had overtaken the MX as the most controversial element of the administration's defense modernization program. In its preliminary research phase alone, SDI was expected to cost $26 billion, while some estimates of its final figure had reached $1 trillion. But budget concerns were only a small element of the growing criticism over SDI. While supporting the existing research effort, former secretary of state Cyrus R. Vance said he was "strongly opposed" to pursuing strategic defense beyond the research stage. "Once we cross the line from basic research to deployment," he told the Senate Foreign Relations Committee Feb. 4, "we have very radically changed the basic strategic doctrine." He voiced the concern of many arms control advocates in Congress that the deployment of a strategic defense system in space would set off a new arms race. They expressed the fear that the Soviet Union would try to penetrate the defense with new offensive weapons and the United States then would be compelled to build even more elaborate defenses.

Until recently the debate over SDI had been largely confined to the scientific community, where technical considerations were called into play either to boost or to debunk the program. Some of its supporters were physicists working in arms research facilities. Others, however, opposed SDI as technically unfeasible. Some said that even

if it were possible to extend a nuclear umbrella over the United States, SDI would pose grave dangers. According to a study conducted by the Union of Concerned Scientists: "If the president's vision is pursued, outer space could become a battlefield. An effective defense against a missile attack must employ weapons operating in space. This now peaceful sanctuary, so long a symbol of cooperation, would be violated. And the arduous process of arms control, which has scored so few genuine successes in the nuclear era, would also be imperiled — perhaps terminated — by the deployment of weapons in space."

Anti-nuclear Sentiment

It was feared that the debate over SDI might reawaken anti-nuclear sentiment in other countries, a worrisome prospect to Reagan supporters. The opposition Liberal Party in Canada in early February challenged the Conservative government of Prime Minister Brian Mulroney over its ongoing negotiations with the U.S. government to modernize an early warning system in northern Canada. The Liberals said that the modernization would draw Canada into participation in SDI. Defense Minister Robert Coates denied that the new $1 billion North Warning System would be a part of SDI.

Far more troubling to the administration was the prospect of an anti-SDI campaign among NATO's European members. As of late February the initiative had elicited no official opposition from the allied governments. President Reagan got some high-powered support for his controversial space-based defense program on Feb. 20, when British Prime Minister Margaret Thatcher addressed a joint session of Congress. Speaking of the need of Western countries to deter a potential nuclear attack, Thatcher said, "It is essential that our research and development capacities do not fall behind the work being done by the

Soviet Union. That is why I firmly support President Reagan's decision to pursue research into defense against ballistic nuclear missiles — the strategic defense initiative."

But SDI alarmed many European observers who feared that the creation of an anti-ballistic defense over North America would encourage the United States to withdraw into a "Fortress America," abandoning Western Europe to its own defenses. With the United States safely protected behind its space-based shield, they maintained, Europe would become an attractive battlefield for a nuclear exchange. The governments of allied nations — West Germany, Britain, Italy, Belgium and the Netherlands — that supported a 1979 NATO decision to deploy 572 new intermediate-range nuclear weapons on their soil may have had special cause for alarm. The deployment began on schedule in December 1983, but it fueled a widespread anti-nuclear movement that undermined the ruling governments' political strength. The conservative government of West German Chancellor Helmut Kohl was particularly vulnerable. Already weakened by economic stagnation, the government faced elections in 1987 and could expect strong opposition from the country's peace movement.

Only days after it was announced that U.S.-Soviet arms talks would resume, Belgian Prime Minister Wilfried Martens dismayed the Reagan administration by refusing to permit the cruise missile deployment scheduled in March. He said his government would decide by the end of that month when to begin deployment, but observers predicted that Martens, who was under pressure from anti-nuclear forces, would delay such a decision until after national elections were held in December. The Netherlands was exhibiting similar sensitivity to domestic anti-nuclear sentiment. The government there had delayed deployment of 48 cruise missiles until November.

U.S. allies in the southern Pacific also

dealt the administration an unexpected blow. First, New Zealand's Prime Minister David Lange, following up on a campaign promise to prohibit nuclear weapons in the country, announced his government would deny port access to a U.S. warship scheduled to arrive for joint naval exercises within the ANZUS alliance (Australia, New Zealand and the United States). The United States, which for security reasons does not reveal whether Navy vessels at sea are carrying nuclear weapons, responded by canceling the exercises altogether. Days later, Australian Prime Minister Robert Hawke told the administration that U.S. aircraft could not use Australian bases to monitor a test of the MX missile scheduled for this summer.

Soviet Pressure for Arms Control

While pursuing arms modernization, the Reagan administration had maintained consistently that it was willing to resume arms control negotiations at any time the Soviet Union wished. It was, after all, the Soviet side that abandoned both the strategic arms reductions talks (START) and the intermediate-range nuclear force talks (INF) in 1983, spokesmen maintained. First, Moscow broke off the INF negotiations in November 1984 to protest the initial NATO deployment of new Pershing and cruise missiles. The following month it refused to agree to a date for the next round of START talks. Soviet leader Konstantin U. Chernenko insisted as recently as October 1984 that Moscow would not resume INF talks until the NATO weapons were removed from Europe. In agreeing to resume talks, Moscow reversed its position. It also appeared to have dropped its prior insistence on a moratorium on testing anti-satellite weapons as a condition for negotiations on space weaponry.

After the agreement to negotiate, the Soviet Union began to focus its attention on SDI, repeatedly asserting that no progress could be made on INF and strategic weapons unless some agreement could be worked out to prevent the "militarization of space." Some Western observers deduced from such statements that Moscow was desperately trying to head off a new and highly expensive round of the arms race that it could ill afford. The Soviet economy had for the previous several years suffered from repeated crop failures as well as depressed world prices for its oil exports.

Shultz expressed this view during testimony before the Senate Foreign Relations Committee in January 1985. In contrast to the growing military and economic might of the West, he said, "the Soviets face ... profound structural economic difficulties, a continuing succession problem and restless allies; its diplomacy and its clients are on the defensive in many parts of the world." But this picture was not shared by all administration officials. Defense Secretary Weinberger told the same hearing that the Soviet Union boasted a numerically stronger nuclear arsenal and was "dramatically improving" its quality, while "expanding the geographical reach" of its conventional forces.

Resumption of Talks

The talks between the two superpowers, which began March 12, 1985, in Geneva, Switzerland, were for the first time to encompass three separate categories of arms: strategic nuclear weapons, intermediate-range nuclear weapons located in Europe and space weapons.

But no sooner was the agreement to resume negotiations announced than the prospects for their successful outcome were clouded by conflicting interpretations of the ambiguously worded announcement itself. The document to which both delegations agreed Jan. 8, 1985, specified that all three areas be "considered and resolved in their interrelationship." Subsequent statements

by Foreign Minister Gromyko made clear the Soviet position that no agreement could be reached in any one area unless agreement also was reached in the other two. "If no progress were made in space," he said Jan. 13 in a television interview with Soviet journalists, "then none could be made in the question of strategic weapons." American spokesmen denied such iron-clad "linkage" was intended. "Interrelationships, yes," explained White House spokesman Larry Speakes, "but as far as linkage where one doesn't proceed without the other, no, that's not our position."

Another potential conflict that became immediately apparent centered around SDI. Advocates contended that the research program did not violate the terms of the 1972 ABM Treaty, which forbids the deployment of weapons in space, and said it should not be used as a "bargaining chip" in Geneva. Only if the program passed from the research stage to the development and deployment of weapons, they maintained, should SDI be a subject of negotiation. President Reagan reiterated this position in an interview with the *New York Times*. Asked if he would halt SDI research in return for Soviet concessions on offensive weapons, he replied: "No, I would want to proceed with what we're doing. . . ."

The Soviet Union was adamantly opposed to SDI and clearly intended to place the program at the top of its agenda during the first round of the talks. Far from being a benign defensive system, the Soviets maintained, SDI would guarantee the success of an American first strike against them. As such, it could be interpreted only as a destabilizing offensive weapons system to be banned before it ever got off the ground.

The negotiating teams also provided clues to each side's opening positions. On the U.S. side, the delegation was to be headed by a newcomer to nuclear arms talks, Max M. Kampelman. On record as a hard-liner toward the Soviet Union and a

President Reagan and Vice President Bush with the U.S. negotiating team; from left, chief Max M. Kampelman, John Tower and Maynard W. Glitman.

supporter of SDI, he was chosen to lead the American team dealing with space weapons. John Tower, a former senator (R-Texas, 1961-85) and chairman of the Senate Armed Services Committee who supported Reagan's military buildup, was to be the chief negotiator on strategic, or long-range, weapons. The only delegation head with negotiating experience in the area to which he was assigned was Maynard W. Glitman, a career diplomat who served as deputy head of the delegation in previous INF talks. He was to lead the delegation on INF talks in Geneva.

Veteran arms negotiator Paul H. Nitze would play an important behind-the-scenes role. By far the most experienced arms control expert connected with the new talks, Nitze was to be a "special adviser" to the proceedings. Hard-liners were encouraged by the selection of Kampelman and Tower. At the same time, however, supporters of arms control were encouraged by the surprise replacement of Edward L. Rowny, chief negotiator in the stalemated strategic

arms reductions talks, and his relegation to a less visible advisory position. Rowny, a retired general with strong conservative backing, had criticized past arms control efforts.

The Soviet delegation would bring greater experience in arms control negotiations. Chosen as delegation head and chief negotiator on strategic arms was Viktor Karpov, who also led his party to the START talks. The space weapons team would be led by Yuli Kvitsinsky, former INF negotiator and co-author, with Nitze, of the ill-fated "walk-in-the-woods" proposal before those talks collapsed. *(Details, p. 53)* Aleksei Obukhov, another experienced arms control negotiator, would replace Kvitsinsky as chief negotiator for the INF talks.

History of Arms Control

The Geneva negotiations were but the most recent chapter in the turbulent history of arms control. Ever since the nuclear genie was let out of the bottle in 1945, negotiators have tried in vain to halt the development of nuclear weapons.

The first country to explode nuclear devices, the United States was also the only country to have used them, destroying the Japanese cities of Hiroshima and Nagasaki in August 1945. Only by bringing Japan quickly to its knees, it was reasoned, could the Pacific war be ended without the additional loss of thousands of U.S. servicemen. Ten months later, on June 14, 1946, the United States presented a plan to the newly created United Nations to ban the production of nuclear weapons and to place all peaceful applications of nuclear technology under international control.

The Baruch plan, which was named for one of its authors, financier Bernard Baruch, called for the creation of an agency to oversee nuclear development and inspect member nations' facilities. The United States, which alone possessed the technology to produce nuclear weapons at that time, pledged to destroy its bombs as soon as the agency was established. The Soviet Union, however, insisted that the American arsenal be dismantled before it would agree to the agency's creation, and the Baruch plan became the first of many arms control proposals to fall victim to disagreements between the postwar superpowers.

Deterrence, MAD and SALT

The next two decades witnessed a steady worsening of U.S.-Soviet relations. It was during this so-called Cold War period of frosty diplomatic exchanges that the Soviet Union developed a nuclear capability of its own and rapidly built an arsenal of atomic weaponry to counter that of the United States. Both sides began modernizing their weapons, and the arms race was on. The first breakthrough in technology came as a result of reducing warhead size and weight. The bombs dropped over Japan

were so heavy that they had to be transported by large bombers. By making them smaller and lighter, arms designers on both sides were able to load them instead onto rockets, which were a faster, and thus less vulnerable, means of delivering the bomb to its target. In time, both the United States and the Soviet Union developed intercontinental ballistic missiles, large rockets that could be shot up into the atmosphere to release their payload — the nuclear bomb — which would then follow a path determined by the physical law of "ballistic trajectory" toward its ultimate target halfway around the Earth.

The unprecedented danger and expense entailed in the spiraling weapons race prompted both sides to propose several arms control initiatives during the 1950s and 1960s. This period saw considerable progress in areas not directly concerned with the armaments themselves. The bilateral Hot Line Agreement (1963) set up a direct link between the White House and the Kremlin to facilitate emergency communications and reduce the risk of war. Four multilateral agreements of the same period also were aimed at reducing the risk of nuclear conflict. The Antarctic Treaty (1959) banned "any measures of a military nature" on that continent; the Limited Nuclear Test Ban Treaty (1963) banned weapons tests under water, in the atmosphere and in outer space, including "the moon and other celestial bodies"; the Peaceful Uses of Outer Space Treaty (1966) went a step further and banned all nuclear weapons from space; and signatories to the Nuclear Non-Proliferation Treaty (1968) agreed not to transfer nuclear weapons to nations that do not possess them. These agreed in turn not to embark on nuclear weapons programs of their own.

Agreement to negotiate the far more difficult issue of existing weapons was longer in coming. After its humiliation in the Cuban missile crisis of 1962 — under

U.S. pressure Russia withdrew its missiles from the island — the Soviet Union rapidly increased its nuclear arsenal. By the time agreement was finally reached to begin arms negotiations in 1968, each side already possessed nuclear arsenals capable of destroying the other. Deterrence was based on the mutual realization that a nuclear first strike could not destroy all the enemy's warheads and would merely provoke a retaliatory response. The concept, known as mutual assured destruction — or MAD — was to dominate the strategic thinking of both sides. President Lyndon B. Johnson's defense secretary, Robert S. McNamara, gave top priority to the limitation of anti-ballistic missiles. He believed ABMs would be ineffective against an all-out attack and were destabilizing, in that each side was rushing ahead to develop newer offensive weapons to counter ABMs.

Delayed first by the Soviet invasion of Czechoslovakia in August 1968 and then by the election of a new president, Richard Nixon, the Strategic Arms Limitation Talks — SALT — finally began in Vienna April 16, 1970. After two years of hard bargaining, President Nixon went to Moscow and joined Soviet Communist Party Secretary Leonid I. Brezhnev on May 26, 1972, in signing the two accords that made up the first strategic arms limitation agreement — SALT I. The first accord, the ABM Treaty, reflected the shared belief that ABM systems are destabilizing and ineffective. The treaty, which is of unlimited duration but subject to review every five years, allowed each side only two ABM deployment sites — later amended to one — and strictly limited the technological development of ABM weaponry, including radar and interceptor missiles.

SALT I's second component, an interim agreement on offensive strategic arms, was less sweeping in its effect. It froze the numbers of ICBMs and submarine-launched ballistic missiles (SLBMs) on each side for five years. The Soviet Union was left with more missile launchers and land-based ICBMs than the United States, while the United States retained its technological superiority and numerical advantage in long-range strategic bombers.

It was this discrepancy in the nuclear balance, which allowed both sides to perceive themselves at a disadvantage, that was to spell eventual failure for the SALT process. The agreement also left unaddressed an important technological advance already under development. This was the multiple, independently targetable reentry vehicle, or MIRV. A single missile could now be armed with several warheads, each aimed at different targets. MIRVs made simple missile counts obsolete at a single stroke and vastly complicated the already sticky problem of counting nuclear warheads. Although the Senate ratified SALT I by an 88-to-2 margin in September 1972, U.S. misgivings over the interim agreement were expressed in an amendment sponsored by Sen. Henry M. Jackson, D-Wash., that directed the president in future negotiations to accept arms levels equal or superior to those of the Soviet Union.

Both sides continued to modernize their nuclear weapons while observing the numerical limits imposed by SALT I. On Nov. 24, 1974, Brezhnev and President Gerald R. Ford agreed to the framework for its successor, SALT II. The Vladivostok accord, named for the Soviet Pacific port city where the two leaders met, set an overall ceiling on the number of delivery vehicles, including strategic bombers, permitted each side. Of the 2,400 total, 1,320 missile launchers could be fitted with MIRVs. Both sides were allowed leeway to allocate their forces as they saw fit. The Soviet Union would continue to concentrate its nuclear warheads on ICBMs, while the United States distributed its arsenal among the strategic "triad" of land-based missiles, submarines and strategic bombers.

An Arms Control Glossary

Anti-Ballistic Missile (ABM): A defensive system to intercept and destroy strategic ballistic missiles or their elements during flight, consisting of interceptor missiles, launchers and radars.

Cruise Missile: A small (18-ft.), jet-powered guided missile that can fly at very low altitudes to minimize radar detection.

Intercontinental Ballistic Missile (ICBM): A land-based, rocket-propelled missile with an intercontinental range (defined in SALT as more than 5,500 kilometers). Usually launched from an underground silo, it is vulnerable to attack but is also the most destructive strategic weapon.

Intermediate Range Nuclear Forces (INF): Land-based missiles and aircraft with ranges of up 5,500 kilometers that are capable of striking targets beyond the general region of the battlefield but not capable of intercontinental range.

Multiple Independently Targetable Re-entry Vehicle (MIRV): The portion of a strategic missile that carries a number of nuclear warheads, each of which can be directed to a separate target.

Mutual Assured Destruction (MAD): The ability of opposing sides to inflict an "unacceptable" degree of damage upon an aggressor after absorbing any first strike, or first offensive move of a nuclear war.

MX (Missile Experimental): A new, 10-warhead U.S. ICBM developed to replace the increasingly vulnerable Minuteman ICBM force and to counter the SS-18 and SS-19, Soviet ICBMs.

Short-Range Nuclear Forces: Land-based missiles, rockets and artillery capable of striking only targets in the general region of the battlefield.

Strategic Defense Initiative (SDI): This plan, known to its critics as "Star Wars," envisions a non-nuclear, space-based defense against nuclear attack. SDI would constitute a "layered defense" using different technologies to destroy attacking missiles during each phase of the ballistic trajectory.

Strategic Nuclear Forces: Ballistic missiles and bomber aircraft that have intercontinental range. U.S. strategic nuclear forces directly threaten Soviet territory and vice versa.

Submarine-Launched Ballistic Missile: Ballistic missiles carried in and launched from a submarine. These are harder to detect than land-based or air-launched missiles.

Once again, however, weapons designers in the military-industrial complex of both nations worked faster than the arms control negotiators. The Vladivostok agreement did not cover the American cruise missile or the Soviet Backfire bomber, presented as a medium-range bomber but considered capable of intercontinental missions as well. The impasse over these weapons was sidestepped under a compromise negotiating framework of September 1977, in which both sides agreed to observe the SALT I Interim Agreement until they could produce its successor.

The three-part SALT II accord that Brezhnev and President Jimmy Carter signed in Vienna on June 18, 1979, featured a Treaty on the Limitation of Strategic Offensive Arms. It set a limit of 2,400 on the total number of nuclear delivery vehicles and the following individual limits: 1,320 MIRV launchers (missiles and bombers carrying cruise missiles); 1,200 MIRVed ballistic missiles; 820 MIRVed land-based ICBMs; and 308 "heavy" ICBMs. No additional fixed launchers were permitted. It also banned any increase in the maximum number of warheads on existing types of ICBMs and limited the number of warheads allowed for each new type of ICBM to 10. Each SLBM was allowed to carry 14 warheads while an average of 28 long-range cruise missiles was permitted for each bomber. SALT II also banned the flight-testing and deployment of several missiles and the construction of new fixed ICBM launchers.

SALT II immediately came under fire from critics who said it enabled the Soviets to maintain nuclear superiority over the United States. For the next two years, as U.S.-Soviet relations deteriorated, the agreement was subjected to mounting criticism. In protest over the Soviet invasion of Afghanistan in December 1979, Carter himself stopped the ratification process by asking the Senate in January 1980 to "delay consideration" of SALT II. It was never ratified.

Reagan's Grudging Efforts

Elected in the fall of 1980, Ronald Reagan came to office vowing to "rearm America." The SALT process was denounced as a failure and arms control figured hardly at all during the first 18 months of his administration. The Soviet Union, he and his officials repeatedly suggested, had deftly used the negotiations to slow U.S. weapons modernization while boldly forging ahead themselves to a position of military superiority over the United States.

While the strategic arms negotiations were placed on hold and the Pentagon was given the green light for increased military spending, the administration had to deal with the issue of intermediate-range nuclear forces in Europe. NATO in 1979 had announced its decision to pursue a "dual track" path to counter the Soviet Union's growing arsenal of intermediate-range missiles, the SS-4, SS-5 and the new SS-20, pointed toward Western Europe. NATO announced it would seek to draw the Soviet Union into negotiations and to begin deploying American-made Pershing II and cruise missiles on allied territory if agreement had not been reached by December 1983.

Secretary of State Alexander M. Haig and Gromyko pledged in September 1981 "to spare no effort" to conclude an agreement before the NATO deadline. Talks opened in Geneva on Nov. 30 of that year. Only days earlier, Reagan had offered his own solution to the INF dilemma with his "zero-zero option": NATO would cancel deployment of the American missiles if the Soviet Union agreed to dismantle all its SS-4, SS-5 and SS-20 missiles.

But the Soviet position on INF proved irreconcilable with the U.S. contention that the SS-20s constituted a new and destabilizing class of weapons. Moscow rejected U.S. insistence on global limits of the SS-20, which, with a range of 5,000 kilometers, could threaten not only Western Europe but also American allies in Asia, including Japan. The Soviet Union insisted that British and French nuclear missiles be counted as part of NATO's arsenal; the United States refused, saying that these forces were purely national in scope and did not contribute to allied defense.

The two chief negotiators at Geneva attempted to resolve the impasse on their own during a private conversation in July 1982 later known as the "walk in the woods." U.S. chief negotiator Nitze — founder of the Committee on the Present Danger and leader of the fight against SALT II — and his Soviet counterpart Yuli Kvitsinsky drove to a secluded mountaintop in the Jura range near the French border, ordered the driver to meet them at the bottom and started to walk down. According to one account: "Once they got down to business, Nitze and Kvitsinsky were sitting on a log. It was starting to rain. Nitze had brought along a typed outline of an agreement, from which he began to read aloud. Kvitsinsky listened for a while, then suggested some modifications. Incorporating these changes would make it a joint paper. Nitze asked Kvitsinsky if he realized that. 'Yes,' replied the Soviet. 'Let's go through with the rest of it.' "

By the time they had reached their car, Nitze and Kvitsinsky reportedly had defined a compromise agreement that prohibited the Soviet Union from developing a long-range ground-launched cruise missile and froze SS-20s deployed in the Asian U.S.S.R. at existing levels. In exchange, the United States would cancel deployment of the Pershing. Their efforts were to prove fruitless. Both governments disavowed the proposal and the stalemate persisted. On Nov. 23, 1983, Kvitsinsky announced the Soviet decision to "discontinue" the talks in protest against NATO's resolve to deploy the Pershing and cruise missiles on schedule the following month.

Meanwhile, after 16 months in office, Reagan outlined his first strategic arms control proposal. In an effort to distinguish it from the "failed" SALT process, Reagan named his proposal START, for Strategic Arms Reduction Talks. START's basic aim, as described by chief negotiator Rowny, was "to break the mold of past negotiations which concentrated on limiting strategic offensive arms at high levels" and "to improve strategic stability through substantial reductions in the more destabilizing strategic offensive arms." The initial proposal, which Reagan presented May 9, 1982, called for both sides to reduce the number of land- and sea-based missile warheads by about one-third to 5,000 and to reduce the number of deployed ballistic missiles to no more than 850, a cut of one-half for the United States, somewhat more for the Soviet Union.

Reagan subsequently modified his START proposal to accommodate the recommendations of the Commission on Strategic Forces — known as the Scowcroft commission after its head, former National Security Council member Brent Scowcroft. While reaffirming the goal of reducing each side's ballistic-missile warheads to 5,000, the president in June 1983 relaxed the overall limit of 850 deployed ballistic missiles. These changes were included in a draft treaty that the United States offered July 7.

Under pressure from congressional arms control advocates, Reagan in October incorporated into the U.S. bargaining position the "build-down" concept, which called for retiring older weapons as a corollary to modernization with the aim of reducing the total number of warheads over time. The Soviet Union, which had linked INF and START talks all along, rejected the modified proposal and, at the end of the negotiating round on Dec. 8, refused to agree to a resumption date for START.

Agenda for Geneva

As the date for the Geneva talks approached, the United States and Soviet Union had not altered their basic positions on either strategic or intermediate-range missiles. Officially, these remained as irreconcilable as they were when the two sets of talks were interrupted at the end of 1983.

New Talks on Offensive Weapons

Some observers speculated that the format to be followed in Geneva, establishing an "interrelationship" between the two categories of offensive weapons as well as strategic defense, could offer a means of breaking the stalemate. By merging the negotiations on INF and strategic forces, it was said, the two sides might satisfy Moscow's insistence on including the British and French INF arsenals — totaling some 140 missiles armed with 420 warheads — in NATO's overall weapons count. These would seem less significant if the entire Euromissile issue were to be considered in the context of the 10,000 or so strategic weapons possessed by both sides.

Gromyko seemed to indicate that a merger might be acceptable. "Earlier we conducted talks separately on strategic arms and on intermediate-range arms — and the two sides then agreed to try to conduct them this way because it might be easier this way to find accords — while it has now become absolutely clear that it is impossible to hold talks and to try to reach agreement on strategic armaments without solving also the question of intermediate-range weapons," he said during his Jan. 13 interview on Soviet television.

Whether or not this statement reflected Soviet interest in the merger idea, Reagan administration officials reportedly were opposed. The inclusion of INF with strategic weapons may give the NATO allies, who were closely involved in the INF talks, too great a say in the formulation of the U.S. position on strategic weapons. Given the West Europeans' strong desire for an arms control agreement between the superpowers, it was said, the United States would come under pressure to make concessions on strategic weapons.

The administration appeared determined to continue its buildup of these weapons and to be wavering on its promise to abide by the terms of the unratified SALT II treaty. Reagan said in 1981 that the United States would not exceed the limits the treaty imposed on strategic weapons so long as the Soviet Union did likewise. But the administration's report on Soviet non-compliance charged Moscow with several treaty violations, and Reagan on Jan. 26 for the first time indicated the United States was considering ignoring SALT II when a new, 24-missile-bearing Trident submarine — the *USS Alaska* — was put to sea in October 1985. Under the treaty's terms, the administration would have to retire an older, 16-missile Poseidon submarine or dismantle eight land-based Minuteman II ICBMs when the Trident was completed. Adelman of the Arms Control and Disarmament Agency had said recommendations would be made to the White House in October on whether to continue to abide by SALT II.

Meanwhile, weapons systems in all three areas of the American nuclear triad were being modernized. In addition to the Trident, which was quieter and thus more difficult to detect than older submarines, the sea leg of the triad was soon to be reinforced by the long-range, highly accurate D-5 (also called the Trident II) submarine-launched missile. The Tomahawk cruise missile also was slated for deployment on board some 100 surface ships and submarines by the end of the decade. The stealth bomber, designed to evade detection by enemy radar, and air-launched cruise missiles incorporating stealth technology also were expected to be completed by the early 1990s. The MX, whose fate was to be considered as the talks got under way, was only one of several new developments strengthening the land-based missile force.

Strategic Defense Initiative

Judging from the barrage of Soviet criticism, the Soviet Union was expected to concentrate its negotiating stance on preventing the SDI from proceeding beyond the research stage. Announcing the program on March 23, 1983, Reagan hailed the SDI concept as nothing less than visionary: "What if free people could live secure in the knowledge that their security did not rest upon the threat of instant U.S. retaliation to deter a Soviet attack, that we could intercept and destroy strategic ballistic missiles before they reached our own soil or that of our allies?" The purpose of SDI, he said, was to strengthen deterrence. The feasibility of such a non-nuclear defense system was expected to be determined by the early 1990s.

According to official descriptions, SDI would constitute a "layered defense" using different technologies to destroy attacking missiles during each phase of the ballistic trajectory. An ICBM could be destroyed during its "boost phase" shortly after launch, during the "post-boost phase" before the warheads were released, in the "mid-course phase" while the released warheads were soaring through space, or during the "terminal phase" as they re-entered the atmosphere. A panoply of exotic-sounding weapons utilizing lasers and mirrors and based both on the ground and in space — hence the "Star Wars" connection — were envisioned.

SDI supporters, including Kampelman, insisted that it not be used as a "bargaining chip," to be dispensed with in return for Soviet concessions. "Strategic defense would compensate for the inevitable difficulties of verification and for the absence of genuine trust by permitting some risk-tak-

ing in [arms control] agreements," Kampelman and two co-authors wrote in a controversial article published in the *New York Times Magazine* shortly after his appointment to the Geneva talks. "This is another reason why strategic defense should not be traded in the forthcoming negotiations in return for promises that can be broken at any time."

Repeating the concerns expressed by some American scientists, Soviet officials and academics condemn SDI out of hand. ". . . Its creation will certainly increase the danger of the first (pre-emptive) strike and the probability of making wrong decisions in a crisis situation," a group of Soviet scientists wrote in a study issued in 1984. "That is why strategic stability will be diminished, although the two sides will retain a rough parity in their strategic armaments." Another Soviet commentator predicted that SDI would escalate the arms race. "The other side cannot shut its eyes to these war preparations, of course," arms control analyst Alexei Fedorov wrote. "It will do everything to make the Pentagon realize that [Soviet] ballistic missiles have not become 'a heap of junk' while the U.S. offensive strategic potential hangs over it like the sword of Damocles."

Some observers believed that the Soviet Union planned to resume testing and deployment of its anti-satellite (ASAT) systems. Like SDI, ASAT involved space weaponry. But while SDI would use space- and ground-based weapons to destroy attacking missiles, ASAT would destroy only satellites, including SDI satellites and existing communications and spy satellites. The Soviet Union established its ASAT program in the early 1970s. But after the United States began developing its own ASAT system, Russia in 1983 proposed a ban on further ASAT development. Between October 1984 and February 1985 the Soviets did not mention such a ban, leading some observers to believe they wanted to develop their system to counter SDI.

Because the terms of the 1972 ABM Treaty prohibited the eventual testing and deployment of the space-based components of SDI, negotiators involved in the space weapons category of talks in Geneva were expected to discuss this as well as the alleged Soviet violations of that treaty. Meanwhile, some administration officials were openly discussing an approach to arms control that made it difficult to understand why the negotiators should bother to meet in Geneva at all. In an article published by *Foreign Affairs* just as the agenda for the March talks was announced, ACDA Director Adelman wrote in support of "arms control without agreements." According to this approach, each side would develop a strategic defense system, such as SDI, with the expectation that the other would do the same. President Reagan envisioned such a development when he offered to share SDI technology with the Soviet Union: if both sides constructed a viable strategic defense, he said, perhaps both would then dismantle their nuclear arsenals once and for all.

6

The Economic Dilemma

When Ronald Reagan captured the presidency in 1980, he mounted the most serious assault on federal spending and tax policies in nearly 50 years. And his reelection in 1984, by an overwhelming landslide, gave him the best chance of any president since World War II to consolidate his gains and bring about a major realignment in American politics.

The "Reagan Revolution" challenged the trend, begun in the 1930s and extended almost continually until the 1970s, toward growing government intervention in the economy. Reagan, calling for steep cuts both in taxes and domestic social spending, sought to curtail the government's role as economic manager and guarantor of social equity. At the same time, he provided for an unprecedented peacetime military buildup and edged the country toward a more assertive foreign policy.

The policy's foundation was a novel formulation of economic policy, which pulled together disparate elements in the Republican Party — traditional fiscal conservatives, tax-cutting neo-conservative activists and free-market theorists — into a ruling coalition that some believed could supplant Democratic domination of postwar policy making. With deft lobbying, imaginative use of congressional procedures, and effective use of television to appeal directly to the American people, Reagan achieved changes in policy many had thought impossible.

The president's strength was not unlimited, however. For some of his key victories, he relied on defectors from Democratic Party ranks. After scoring big wins during his first year in office, Reagan had a tougher time with Congress and had to spend much of the remainder of his first term defending his accomplishments rather than trying to extend them.

At the end of his first term, Democrats continued to control the House of Representatives by a wide margin, and Republicans felt far from secure in their hold on the Senate. While the economy had managed to weather the worst recession since the Great Depression of the 1930s, worrisome deficits and deteriorating U.S. competitiveness in international markets clouded the economic future. They also threatened to drive a wedge between the old-line traditional fiscal conservatives and the younger activists, who together formed the main pillar of Reagan's support.

Whether the president could consolidate his grip on policy making — and hence assure a new era of conservative control — remained an open question as the president began his second term in January 1985. Much would depend, it was agreed, on whether time would confirm Reagan's promise that his brand of conservatism offered a brighter economic future than the policies of the past would.

Setting the Stage

To a large degree, Reagan won the presidency because traditional economic policies were not working to bring about growth without inflation. Based on the teachings of British economist John Maynard Keynes, postwar economic theory had assigned to the government an ever-larger role in regulating the pace of economic activity.

Keynes maintained that government could bring about optimal economic performance by controlling the level of total demand for goods and services in the economy. He said unemployment results from inadequate demand for goods and services. To cure that, he recommended increasing individual income, either by cutting taxes or raising government spending.

Inflation, according to Keynesian theory, results when demand exceeds the economy's capacity. To cure inflation, the theory recommended taking steps to reduce income, either by raising taxes or cutting spending.

As the postwar era wore on, Keynesian prescriptions worked well against unemployment. But they increasingly fell short in controlling inflation. Presidents and Congress generally found it easier to pursue policies that were likely to result in inflation than to risk producing the social conflict that comes with high unemployment. That may be because unemployment, although it affects fewer people, causes more severe hardship than fairly modest inflation spread out among most people. "Inflation has served as a vent for distributional strife, an escape hatch through which excess demands are automatically channelled," wrote analyst Fred Hirsch.

found it difficult to restrain demand. Inflationary pressures grew in the late 1960s, when President Lyndon B. Johnson and Congress balked at raising taxes or cutting back "Great Society" spending to pay for the Vietnam War. Later, President Richard Nixon overheated the economy to help ensure his re-election.

Moreover, beginning in the 1970s, the economy began to experience a new kind of inflation, which Keynesian economics had not anticipated. Poor harvests pushed up food prices. Then, the Arab oil embargo sent oil prices soaring, and that drove up prices for a myriad of related goods.

Economic policy makers were at a loss to deal with these problems. If they did nothing, higher energy prices would reduce purchasing power. And the resulting fall in demand would lead to a rise in unemployment. But if they tried to offset the loss in income by pumping more dollars into the economy, they ran the risk of fostering inflation because then there would have been more dollars available to buy the same limited supply of goods.

Most economists preferred bolstering income rather than letting the increase in oil prices touch off a potentially severe recession. Even if that produced more inflation, they said it was a price worth paying. "There's no sense in shooting ourselves in the foot to show how much we care about inflation," said economist Arthur Okun in 1979. "Inflation is a terribly serious problem, but it's not going to be cured by deep recession. Or if it is, the cost may not be worth it."

By the late 1970s, the economy seemed badly out of balance. Years of stimulative economic policy, coupled with an accommodative approach to oil shocks, had produced ever-worsening inflation. The unpredictable rise in prices undermined voters' confidence at home and sent the dollar plummeting in international money markets.

While the U.S. economy had managed to weather the worst recession since the 1930s during President Reagan's first term, U.S automobile manufacturers continued in 1985 to struggle against formidable international competition.

Moreover, the rate of new capital investment in the United States was lagging behind that of most Western industrial nations — also partly the result of inflation, which encouraged consumption over investment. The investment lag was especially worrisome because high energy prices made investment doubly important by rendering many plants and production processes that relied on cheap energy obsolete.

"The new reality ... is the re-emergence during the 1970s of the economics of scarcity — a progressive imbalance between the demands we have been placing on our economy and our capacity to satisfy them," wrote Alfred Kahn, a Cornell University economist who served as President Jimmy Carter's inflation adviser.

Carter gradually came to the conclusion that inflation was the nation's primary economic problem. But he could only turn to conventional medicine — a bitter dose of austerity, slow growth and stagnant or declining standards of living. "There is no way we can avoid a decline in our standard of living," Kahn said in 1979. "All we can do is adapt to it."

That view proved politically unpalatable. "To materially reduce standards of living as compelled by low productivity is unthinkable for a Democratic government in peacetime," declared Sen. Jacob K. Javits, R-N.Y. (1957-81).

'Reaganomics'

Reagan picked up the banner of prosperity just as Democrats gloomily were telling Americans they had to settle for a lower standard of living. He said the nation could fight inflation and achieve greater prosperity at the same time. The key, he said, was to diminish the role of government in the economy.

"The people have not created this disaster in our economy," he said in announcing his candidacy for president in 1979. "The federal government has. It has outspent, overestimated and overregulated. It has failed to deliver services within the revenues it should be allowed to raise from taxes."

After his election, the new president directly challenged the postwar faith in government intervention in the economy. The American economic system, he said, "has never failed us." But we have failed it "through a lack of confidence and sometimes through a belief we could fine-tune the economy and get a tune to our liking."

"Reaganomics," as the new president's economic views came to be known, rested on several principles: taxes and government spending should be cut sharply; the government should focus on creating a healthy long-term economic environment rather than on trying to smooth every swing of the business cycle; wages and prices should be set by market forces — meaning that any suggestion of using wage and price controls to rein in inflation should be dropped and that deregulation of transportation, banking and other industries should be continued; and finally, price stability should be ensured through firm control of the money supply.

Supply-side Economics

Supply-side economics, an untested new doctrine popular among some young conservatives, provided the rationale for cutting taxes despite the fear of inflation. Supply-siders argued that Keynesian tax cuts had mistakenly concentrated on increasing consumers' purchasing power. They said cuts should be designed instead to create incentives to save and invest, produc-

ing an increase in the supply of goods and services that would avert price increases.

The fulcrum of economic activity, according to supply-siders, is the marginal rate of taxation, the rate on the last dollar earned. The higher the marginal tax rate, the less incentive a person has to work rather than be idle, or to save rather than consume, they maintained. By reducing marginal tax rates, supply-siders concluded, the government could encourage more work and savings, in the process increasing output without inflation.

Reagan economists said the effects of a cut in marginal tax rates would be felt at all levels of income. But they said the cut in marginal rates would be effective because the biggest benefits would go to people in the upper income brackets, who can afford to save and invest more. Tax cuts that redistribute income to poor people are more likely to increase consumption because people in low tax brackets cannot afford to save, they said.

Liberals said that argument merely rationalized a program designed to benefit the well-to-do. But Reagan replied that the nation had grown tired of Democratic programs designed to redistribute income. "The taxing power of the government must be used to provide revenues for legitimate government purposes," he said. "It must not be used to regulate the economy or bring about social change."

Conservative Activism

Reagan also tapped traditional conservative objections to heavy domestic spending. David Stockman, who was to become his budget director, complained in 1980 that the federal budget had become "an automatic coast-to-coast soup line that dispenses remedial aid with almost reckless abandon."

That sentiment struck a responsive chord with an American public facing the threat of economic stagnation and declining living standards. While federal programs to help the most needy maintained a fair level of support, others that aided the working poor — people with some job but a very low income — proved particularly vulnerable.

Significantly, Reagan heeded a group of young neo-conservatives who said tax cuts should take priority over spending reductions. Young conservatives such as Republican representative Jack Kemp of New York complained that the GOP in the past had consigned themselves to the status of political outsiders because they placed too much emphasis on balancing the budget rather than on cutting taxes. The defeat four years earlier of President Gerald R. Ford, who made spending reductions a prerequisite to tax cuts, underscored Republican frustration. "As Republicans, we must rid ourselves of the perceived political idolatry of balanced budgets," Kemp said. "Republicans must not be bookkeepers for Democratic deficits."

The same idea was advanced by Irving Kristol, a popular conservative polemicist. "When in office, liberals ... will always spend generously, regardless of budgetary considerations, until the public permits the conservatives an interregnum in which to clean up the mess — but with liberals retaining their status as the activist party," he wrote. "The neo-conservatives have decided that two can play at this game — and must, since it is the only game in town. ... They vigorously advocate [increased defense spending and] tax cuts, with the budget remaining a secondary consideration."

Monetarism

Reagan embraced one other idea that had been outside the mainstream of economic thinking for much of the postwar period — monetarism. Developed by conservative economist Milton Friedman, monetarism held that economic stability without inflation best could be ensured by holding the rate of growth in the supply of money to the rate the economy can physically achieve.

Monetarists said that the level of economic production is determined by physical factors the government cannot greatly influence over the long run. They said Keynesian attempts to increase demand by giving consumers more purchasing power might work in the short run but eventually would merely produce inflation by adding to the supply of money without being able to affect long-term productive capacity. "Inflation is always and everywhere a monetary phenomenon," Friedman said.

Monetarism had important effects on Reagan's economic approach. It put prime responsibility for fighting inflation on the Federal Reserve Board. Moreover, it freed Reagan from traditional Republican worries about large deficits. That is because monetarists held that deficits would not cause inflation, so long as the Fed prevented the supply of money from increasing faster than the economy's potential.

Economic Performance

President Reagan's first year in office was as successful as the nation had seen from a president in 20 years. The centerpiece of his program — personal income tax rate reductions totaling 25 percent over three years and accelerated depreciation allowances that let businesses write off the cost of investing in plants and equipment more quickly — won congressional approval.

Moreover, the president and his allies won substantial reductions in dozens of domestic social programs. The key to their victory involved using a little-known congressional budgetary procedure called "reconciliation" to force enactment — in a single bill requiring just one vote — cuts in dozens of programs. It was, said House Budget Committee Chairman James R. Jones, D-Okla., "clearly the most monumental and historic turnaround in fiscal policy that has ever occurred."

Victory came at a cost, however. To win support for the tax cut — and keep Democrats from claiming it as their own — Reagan had to agree to many expensive "sweeteners," including provisions to index the tax code to offset the effects of inflation, deductions for married couples and for non-itemizers making charitable contributions, and others. To win support from key conservative Southern Democrats, he also accepted special tax breaks for oil producers. All together, these provisions swelled the loss to the Treasury to a staggering $749 billion over five years.

While winning support for his big increases in military spending, Reagan got fewer cuts in domestic spending — $130.6 billion over four years — than he originally proposed.

Recession

It soon became clear that steep tax cuts and less substantial spending restraint would result in growing deficits. The outlook worsened when the Federal Reserve's return to strict monetary restraint brought on renewed recession, undermining federal revenues even further.

The recession, which Reagan blamed on his predecessors, was the most severe of the postwar period. Coupled with projections that the congressional tax cuts would send deficits soaring above $100 billion, it unnerved financial markets. Reagan was forced to return to Congress with a package of additional budget cuts and "revenue enhancements" — a euphemism for tax increases.

Lawmakers, stung by heavy administration pressure for the initial tax and budget bills, rejected the new proposals in 1981. But in 1982, they passed an administration-supported bill to raise almost $100 billion in revenues by closing tax loopholes and beefing up tax compliance.

Ironically, the recession helped the president fend off counter-attacks against key provisions of his 1981 tax cut. Some proposed delaying the cuts until the deficit outlook improved, but supply-siders such as Kemp argued that a recession was no time to raise taxes.

True to his word, Reagan successfully resisted stopgap spending measures to pull the country out of recession. He let the Comprehensive Employment and Training Act, the Democratic public jobs program of the 1970s, expire. And he blocked new proposals for public works spending. The closest the administration came to new recession-fighting spending was to boost funds for highways and mass transit. But that was financed completely by an increase in gasoline taxes and was widely seen more as a response to a real need for road building and bridge repairs than to the recession.

Relations between the administration and the Federal Reserve were prickly. Fed chairman Paul Volcker said the administration's large deficits contributed to driving up interest rates. That caused the White House some embarrassment. But Volcker, careful to avoid treading on more sensitive political ground, refused to tell Congress whether it should reduce red ink by raising taxes or cutting spending.

The administration, for its part, said the Fed contributed to economic troubles by failing to contain sharp fluctuations in the money supply. But, despite some rumblings in Congress that the Fed should be forced to bring interest rates down even at the risk of incurring new inflation, Reagan made no serious move to reduce the central bank's independence.

Apologia

The recession hurt Republicans at the polls in 1982. In his 1983 budget message to Congress, the president admitted that the promised supply-side miracle of rapid growth without inflation had not materialized. The Fed's successful fight against inflation had pushed interest rates to unusually high levels, severely hurting economic production.

"The process of economic adjustment to non-inflationary growth has been far more prolonged, costly and disruptive to financial markets and business activity than originally projected," Reagan said.

Relations between Reagan and Capitol Hill turned nastier in 1983. Democratic gains in the 1982 elections made Congress less pliable, but Reagan was still in a position to block actions he did not like. Little was accomplished on the legislative front in 1983.

Meanwhile, high interest rates and economic stagnation had sent the value of the dollar soaring, driving up the cost of U.S. exports and bringing in a flood of cheap imports. Pressures mounted for protection from imports in numerous industries. Moreover, many developing countries neared the brink of default on their debt, undermining confidence in the U.S. banking system. U.S. banks also suffered severe loan losses as the slowdown of inflation sent many businesses into bankruptcy.

These developments worried the Fed, and in November 1982, with inflation significantly slowed, it began easing the monetary reins. By mid-1983 the economy was surging.

When Reagan eased his assault on federal spending programs in 1984 — a move derided as election-year maneuvering — lawmakers rejected his proposals and adopted a three-year $150 billion deficit "down payment." It included $50 billion in tax increases.

That barely put a dent in deficits, which were projected to total about $600 billion through fiscal 1987. But at least by 1984 the economic picture had brightened. Reagan approached the 1984 election in an enviable position. Unemployment was down, inflation was very modest and interest rates — though still high by historical standards — were easing.

1984 Issues

Democrats attacked the Reagan record on two fronts in the 1984 election. First, they raised the issue of "fairness." They said Reagan's tax cuts had helped the rich, while his spending reductions hit mainly the working poor.

That view was supported in a 1984 study by the Urban Institute. It reported that in the four years since 1980 disposable income of the poorest one-fifth of all American families had declined by 7.6 percent after inflation, while the income of the top one-fifth had risen by 8.7 percent. The study said the Reagan tax cuts had not helped the poor at all, but that they raised after-tax income by 2.8 percent for the middle class and by 6 percent for the wealthy.

The study said Reagan spending cuts had hit mainly the working poor. People completely dependent on the government for support still had a "safety net" of federal support, it said, but those partially dependent had suffered severe setbacks.

The Democrats' second line of attack was against the enormous budget deficits projected as a result of the Reagan administration's mix of sharp military spending growth and tax cuts. They warned that heavy government borrowing to finance the deficits would drive interest rates up, stifling business investment and choking off the economic recovery. And they argued that, by sending the value of the dollar so high against foreign currencies, domestic industries were losing their competitive edge in international trade.

Walter F. Mondale, the 1984 Democratic candidate, made raising taxes a cornerstone of his candidacy. He charged that Reagan was not being honest with Americans if he did not admit the need for higher taxes. Reagan, however, said he would op-

Reagan Attempts to Relieve...

The most formidable trade issue facing President Reagan in his second term was this: the imbalance between U.S. exports and imports that exceeded $101 billion in 1984. The Commerce Department reported that this figure was more than twice as high as the 1983 trade decifit.

The robust economic recovery appeared, however temporarily, to be able to handle the usually worrisome trade deficit. The growing economy, high domestic interest rates, relatively low inflation and political stability combined to make U.S. investments attractive to foreign investors. Foreign investment in turn brought a steady flow of capital into the United States.

The strong dollar made U.S. products expensive on the world market, hurting exports, but allowed foreign-made products and commodities to sell at bargain prices in the United States, keeping inflation low.

As long as the recovery remained strong, many economists said, the overall consequences of the trade deficit could be borne. But many warned that unless the recovery spread abroad, spurring foreign demand for U.S. exports, and unless the government cut domestic spending, reducing its need to borrow and relieving pressure on interest rates and the dollar, trade deficits would continue to mount and economic growth could stall.

Meanwhile, export-sensitive industries — textiles and steel, for example — were clamoring for help. And some trade interests were pointing to practices of other nations to promote exports of goods and services, and crying foul.

Modified Free Trade

The Reagan administration maintained that the best way to promote international trade, and so reduce the U.S. trade deficit, was to discourage protectionist barriers such as tariffs and quotas. Promoting free trade was a main presidential theme at the annual economic summit meetings of the industrialized nations.

The administration's support for free trade, however, had been questioned by some observers. "Here's an administration that issued a white paper on free trade and has made a number of free trade decisions," a spokesman at Consumers for World Trade, a non-partisan trade group, noted. "Yet when you look at the facts, you also see a long list of protectionist decisions."

A Mixed Record

On litmus tests of free trade sentiment, Reagan's record was mixed. In support of free trade, he turned down an International Trade Commission (ITC) recommendation to restrict copper imports. He reduced barriers on Korean and Taiwanese shoes, rejected restrictions on Japanese machine tools and backed the Caribbean Basin Initiative, which removed duties on certain exports from Central American and Caribbean Basin nations.

On issues pending in late 1984, he backed legislation to extend for 10 years the Generalized System of Preferences, the arrangement that lifts duties on many goods produced in developing nations. He opposed domestic content legislation, which would require fixed amounts of U.S. parts and labor in foreign cars sold in the United States,

... the Growing Trade Deficit

arguing that it would raise car prices and reduce the range of inexpensive cars available in the United States. He also disapproved of steel quota legislation.

Reagan called for a new round of multilateral trade talks to liberalize trade. Yet he backed legislation to continue bilateral talks with the United States' largest trading partner, Canada, and began formal negotiations to establish a free-trade zone with Israel. Some observers, such as Sen. John H. Chafee, R-R.I., wondered whether this stance departed from the multilateral approach, which had contained protectionist pressures since World War II.

Reagan also approved a variety of tariffs and quotas for Japanese autos and motorcycles, sugar, textiles and steel used in specialized products such as jet engines.

The split between Reagan's free trade and free enterprise statements and actions extended to his positions on farm exports. He ended the grain embargo to the Soviet Union and signed a five-year agreement for further shipments to the Soviets. Administration officials successfully negotiated lower barriers on U.S. beef and citrus fruit shipments to Japan. The administration succeeded in preventing the Europeans from restricting U.S. corn gluten exports and taxing U.S. vegetable oil.

Yet Reagan's decision in 1983 to impose quotas on textiles led the Chinese to cancel several hundred million dollars worth of U.S. wheat purchases. The president supported two types of government intervention in trade: "blended credit," which lowers interest rates on loans to foreign purchasers of U.S. farm products by combining private and government-backed loans, and bonuses such as the extra wheat in a subsidized flour sale to Egypt.

Some administration officials argued that Reagan conceded somewhat on free trade to deflect pressure for even more protectionist measures. They pointed out that a rapidly changing and perplexing worldwide economy presented difficulties any administration would find hard to resolve.

But some protectionist pressures came from within the administration itself. On the sensitive issue of the export of high-technology products that could have military applications, the administration was split between the business-minded Commerce Department and Defense Department hard-liners who feared that sophisticated goods could make their way to the Soviet Union and Eastern Bloc nations.

Reagan expanded the Defense Department's authority to review some types of export licenses for high-technology products but favored retaining most enforcement powers within the Commerce Department. Reagan also had mixed foreign policy and trade policy objectives. He tightened quotas on Nicaraguan sugar to pressure the Nicaraguan government to stop backing guerrillas fighting to destabilize other Central American nations.

Compounding Reagan's difficulty deflecting protectionist pressures was the administration's lack of an on-going trade initiative. Observers such as I. M. Destler, a senior fellow at the Washington-based Institute for International Economics, noted that presidents in the 1960s and 1970s could use global trade talks to mobilize export interests and deflect industry demands.

pose a tax increase — except as a "last resort." His overwhelming electoral victory in November 1984 appeared to confirm the political wisdom of that stand.

Second-term Outlook

The president began his second term in firm control of the economic policy debate. Elected by an overwhelming majority, he was the first president given the chance of another term in 12 years.

He had survived politically despite a severe recession. He claimed, along with the Federal Reserve, credit for cooling inflation. Moreover, Reagan had changed the terms of debate about economic policy in Washington. He had brought the nation through a recession without significant emergency spending legislation. And he had so cut federal revenues that new spending programs were unthinkable. In fact, the prospect of further spending cuts, needed to reduce the menacing $200 billion annual deficits, appeared fairly strong.

Large deficits threatened to keep interest rates high and possibly to stall the economic recovery. Partly because of the strong value of the dollar, American factories continued to lose ground to foreign competitors.

Tackling the Deficit

Deficits posed political, as well as economic, dilemmas. To reduce spending further, the government would have either to slow the president's military buildup or slash domestic programs that had strong middle-income constituencies. Neither would be attractive, especially for a Republican administration.

In February 1985 President Reagan submitted for congressional consideration his 1986 budget proposals. Members of the House and the Senate, Democrats and Republicans alike, reacted against the president's call for a 5.9 percent inflation-adjusted increase in defense spending coupled with deep cuts in domestic programs. Yet the budget proposals brought home a sobering message to legislators about the bleak prospects for controlling federal deficits. It had become clear that lawmakers would have to accept many of the administration's spending cuts — or propose other politically unpalatable alternatives — to make a dent in deficits projected by the Congressional Budget Office to grow to almost $300 billion by the end of the decade.

The administration's deficit-reduction plan called for many cuts that had been proposed in prior budgets and rejected by Congress. However, the fiscal 1986 budget also called for deep new reductions in programs that had remained relatively unscathed in previous budget-cutting efforts.

Among the programs slated for elimination were a number that largely aided middle-class taxpayers and powerful interest groups that were not likely to give up their benefits without a fight. The budget proposed terminating general revenue sharing for state and local governments, the Small Business Administration, the direct-loan programs of the Export-Import Bank, the subsidy for Amtrak rail passenger service, the Job Corps, Community Services Block Grants and Urban Development Action Grants.

It also called for large reductions in farm price supports and lending programs, Medicare and Medicaid, housing aid, nutrition programs and student loans. The budget proposed a 5 percent pay cut for federal workers and a 10 percent across-the-board cut for non-defense administrative expenses. It made relatively small cuts in a number of the programs that were part of the so-called "social safety net." This was done, according to budget director Stockman, in recognition of the fact that large cuts were made in these programs over the previous four years.

No changes were proposed for Supplemental Security Income, veterans' pensions or the earned income tax credit for poor working families, nor for Social Security. Food stamp funding would remain about the same, with $56 million in savings assumed from a proposal to require able participants to join work programs.

In defense of the domestic spending cuts, Stockman maintained at a briefing for reporters that a one-year across-the-board "freeze" of domestic spending, as proposed by some, "simply won't solve the problem. . . . We have to do more."

"I have no doubt that political resistance and the political opposition to many elements of the budget will be strong," he said. "But the fact is there aren't any alternatives." He said that Reagan's 1984 re-election was a mandate against new taxes and justified the administration's defense spending request as necessary to fulfill agreements between the administration and Congress over the previous four years to strengthen national defense.

Stockman noted that the president's budget blueprint hit the $50 billion deficit-reduction target that Federal Reserve chairman Paul A. Volcker had said was the minimum needed to convince financial markets that the government was trying to get its fiscal house in order. The budget director said that failure by Congress to act on the deficit quickly would pose an "acute threat to the best economic performance . . . we've had in 25 years. . . . The day of reckoning has arrived."

Reforming the Tax Code

Taxes, too, would be on the agenda during the second Reagan term. During his re-election campaign, President Reagan called for an overhaul and simplification of the tax code. Serious doubts about wholesale reform were based on a number of premises. One was that Congress would simplify and reform the tax code only if public support was strong enough to counter the special interests who liked the tax code

the way it was. Another was that tax changes would be combined with efforts to solve Congress' No. 1 problem: the federal deficit. But any increase in taxes to reduce the deficit likely would weaken the necessary grass-roots support for reform.

As Barber B. Conable Jr., N.Y., the retiring senior Republican on the House Ways and Means Committee, saw it in 1984, the average American would sit down before any tax changes were to be acted on and figure out what they would do for him or her. "If the bottom line is tax reduction, that is tax reform," he said. "If the bottom line is his taxes went up, that is not reform. That is fraud." With a $200 billion federal budget deficit, he said, it would be hard to avoid the latter.

Some White House aides reportedly were concerned that Reagan might have backed himself into a corner during the election campaign by vowing repeatedly not to raise taxes, since almost all tax-overhaul plans mean higher taxes for some people.

The Treasury Department released its tax proposal in November 1984, but Reagan appeared reluctant to take a stance on the plan. This proposal was written under the direction of Treasury Secretary Donald T. Regan, who switched jobs with Reagan's White House chief of staff, James A. Baker III, in early 1985. Reagan expressed some doubts about the Treasury plan, which proposed to eliminate special tax breaks and to lower rates.

Baker said in an appearance before the House Ways and Means Committee in February that President Reagan would present a specific proposal to Congress some time around the beginning of May. Baker also reiterated Reagan's remarks, made in his Feb. 6 State of the Union address, supporting lowered individual income tax rates, with a top rate of 35 percent or less, and the elimination of taxes for individuals at or around the poverty level. The existing top individual rate was 50 percent.

He said the administration was committed to retaining the home mortgage interest deduction, opposed tax changes that would raise more revenues than the existing system and supported lower corporate tax rates while maintaining investment incentives. He said that corporations might have to pay higher taxes if rates for individuals were to be lowered.

"Absent compelling reasons to the contrary," Baker said, "the tax system must not be used to favor one taxpayer over another, to favor one industry over another, to favor one form of consumption over another or to favor one investment over another."

One member of Congress warned that the longer the administration took to move on tax reform, the more time special interests, each with its own "compelling reasons," would have to work against it.

7

The Domestic Agenda

The nation's domestic agenda in 1985 was shaped almost entirely by consideration of the huge federal budget deficits. The biggest rift between Congress and the Reagan administration was not expected to be over whether the cuts should be made, but rather what their composition should be. *(Background on economic policy, pp. 57-68)*

In his fiscal 1986 budget request, President Reagan proposed to raise overall government spending only slightly but also to continue a trend of the previous four years that shifted expenditures from domestic programs to national defense. Domestic programs, many of which were near and dear to constituents' hearts, made up about 60 percent of the federal budget in 1985; this share would drop to 52 percent by 1990 if the president's program were enacted. Members, both Republican and Democratic, had told administration officials that the entire range of government spending — including defense and Social Security, which the president had promised not to cut — had to be "on the table" at budget negotiations.

Numerous issues were sure to enter the fray over which domestic programs should be cut. Chief among them in 1985 was agricultural policy, as American farmers were buffeted by declining land values and international competition. Others of perennial concern were: welfare, education, energy and environment.

Reagan Aims to Reshape Farm Policy

Within weeks of Reagan's second inauguration, the magnitude of the farm problem prompted proposals for change from his agricultural advisers. On Feb. 22, 1985, the administration officially asked Congress to eliminate or radically curtail the economic network of income supplements, production controls and loans that defined the way much of American agriculture had operated since the 1930s. The legislative vehicle, the Agricultural Adjustment Act of 1985, had, except for the year, the same title as the Depression-era farm law it would repeal. The name underscored Reagan's desire to reverse course from the New Deal, when the federal government set itself up as the major force in determining how much farmers should produce and what they should be paid.

Release of the administration's sweeping farm proposal came at a time when Congress was already knotted in debate over the economic status of American farmers and the appropriate role of the federal government in agriculture. Four years of

More than 10,000 farmers gathered in St. Paul, Minn., to protest farm foreclosures and their general economic plight.

low profits, caused by global trade problems, high domestic interest rates on loans and collapsing land values, had created a severe agricultural credit problem. The crisis was most acute in the Midwest.

The credit crisis was viewed as a symptom of larger, systemic problems in agriculture, problems that Agriculture Secretary John R. Block had designed the austere bill to cure. The administration's proposal was meant to put U.S. agriculture on a "market-oriented" track, by providing minimal aid to farmers and thereby, indirectly, forcing lower market prices for their goods.

Conflicting Views

For members of Congress who had to review the expiring farm programs, early 1985 was a disquieting time. Their task was to write a four-year authorization of these aid programs in the face of conflicting claims that the programs themselves were destroying much of American agriculture

— and that nothing else looked better.

Farm groups were in disarray. Some sided with the Reagan administration, urging drastic cuts in spending and radical redesign of the farm support program. Yet others asserted that this was the very worst time for change because farmers were so broke that they needed more help, not less. To emphasize their plight, thousands of Minnesota farmers streamed into the state capital in January 1985 to protest farm foreclosures and their general economic plight.

Back in Washington, new players, with competing agendas, had joined the fray. Environmental groups and executives of powerful agricultural corporations such as Pioneer Hi-Bred Inc. and Cargill Inc. said that the environmental and economic problems of farming were too important to leave the solutions to farmers alone.

If the political situation was confusing, so was the problem at its center. It was clear that much of American agriculture and the businesses that depended on its health were in severe financial trouble, despite the fact that the federal government had been pumping record amounts of money into the rural economy since 1982.

Farm programs reauthorized in 1981 were estimated then to cost $11 billion in the following four years. But they swiftly soaked up that amount in 1982 and, in 1983, costs jumped to $18.9 billion.

That was the year the Reagan administration handed out an additional $9 billion worth of surplus commodities to farmers through the Payment in Kind (PIK) program to encourage cut backs in production. USDA officials put the four-year cost of those programs, through 1985, above $50 billion.

Even with such hefty subsidies, about 15 percent of the nation's 600,000 commercial farms — those with annual sales of more than $40,000 — had in 1985 precarious debt-to-asset ratios of 70 percent, a level of debt that meant almost certain failure in existing market conditions. The farm machinery industry was running at half its peak capacity of 1979; other agriculture-related businesses had suffered comparable reverses.

The basic problem was surplus: farmers producing much more than sodden global markets could absorb. American agriculture grew by leaps and bounds in the 1970s, believing that ever-expanding international markets would sop up all that U.S. farmers could grow. For a number of complex reasons, that was no longer the case and there were even unnerving hints of other nations selling their surplus crops in the United States.

Farm surpluses hurt farmers because they kept market prices low — often lower than what it cost a farmer to grow a crop or raise livestock. The problem was compounded by farmers' high level of indebtedness, at crushingly high interest rates.

Farming had become a high-capital business, but farmers in significant numbers were not earning enough to pay off their loans. In the first half of 1984, three agricultural banks failed; in the second six months, 22 went under, according to the Independent Bankers Association (IBA). The bankers' group believed that the pace would continue to accelerate. What made the credit problem acute, according to IBA's Weldon Barton, was the declining value of farm loan collateral — land.

In Iowa, for example, where farm land values had plummeted 37 percent since 1981, "we're dying," declared Sen. Tom Harkin, D-Iowa. The credit situation in the Midwestern heartland was ominous. Yet the economic status of individual farms was far from uniform, meaning that help desperately needed by some would prove a windfall for others. Some mid-sized farms had managed to stay clear of expensive debt and were quietly holding their own. Texas land values were rising, Barton reported. A tiny minority of highly capitalized, high-tech spreads dominated markets while scooping in million-dollar subsidies from Washington.

Reagan's Proposals

The administration chose to attack these problems with a plan of extreme austerity. Agriculture Secretary Block said that farms had been failing for almost 50 years "with almost the same intensity, regardless of farm policies pursued. It's time to start something different."

The proposal was meant to put American agriculture in fighting trim to compete with the stark realities of cut-rate Argentine wheat, Brazilian soybeans and Canadian pork. The administration argued that U.S. farm goods were laboring under two devastating economic burdens, both of which could be addressed by farm program cuts. Spending cuts, the argument went, would help reduce the federal deficit. That in turn could help lower the value of the dollar against other currencies. The highly valued dollar effectively added 30 percent to the price foreign buyers paid for U.S farm goods. Farm programs, according to this theory, had artificially inflated prices of U.S. commodities, and that inflationary effect had heated up global production.

Members of Congress may have agreed in principle with much of this argument. But more directly exposed to the political fallout of farm problems and program cuts, they showed little agreement on how to proceed.

"America's farm policies aren't working — it's time to change them," Sen. Jesse Helms, R-N.C., announced in a November 1984 press release. Helms, chairman of the Senate Agriculture Committee, declared that "it is now painfully clear that U.S. agriculture is subject to global business conditions. As a result, present farm policy has become ineffective and disastrously costly."

At the other pole, House Agriculture Committee Chairman E. "Kika" de la Garza, D-Texas, believed that the only thing wrong with existing farm programs was inept management by an administration hostile to their basic purposes. He said their costs were minimal compared with the overall budget and that agriculture had, in the past few years, already endured painful reductions in program spending. De la Garza also maintained that American farmers could not go head-to-head with cheap foreign competition — not without federal aid. "If you make the American farmer compete with the least common denominator, he's broke, he's gone, he's out of business."

The divergence between Helms and de la Garza mirrored divisions throughout the farm community, illustrated by comments at a December conference sponsored by the National Agricultural Forum, Resources for the Future and other organizations.

"The acts of the general Depression should have been voted out in World War II," declared June L. Sekoll, who identified herself as a New York dairy wife and editor of *Country Folks* magazine. "Every time we have a crop of poor managers ... we give them a shot in the arm" with federal aid, Sekoll said. That process, she concluded heatedly, "increases the competition for those of us who have never gone to the government for loans."

Yet Floyd Walgren, a Nebraska corn grower, describing the harsh disruptions in rural lives and businesses caused by farm failures, said that "right now is probably the poorest time we have ever had to make the transition" away from government support for agriculture.

Jim Brophy, a Colorado farmer and vice president of the Rocky Mountain Farmers Union, faulted existing policies for pressuring farmers, regardless of environmental consequences, to plant as much land and treat it as intensively as possible with agricultural chemicals to get the highest yields.

Members were acutely sensitive to such conflicting views. But many were preoccupied with the larger questions of the nation's deficit and the administration's announced goal of slashing farm program spending as part of an all-out attack on the deficit.

Getting the Government Out

The administration's new plan differed from previous "omnibus" farm bill reauthorizations in that it was intended to be a permanent law. For years Congress had written multi-year amendments to so-called permanent farm law, dating to the Agricultural Adjustment Act of 1933, which was recodified and substantially amended in 1938 and 1949. The amendments were the "omnibus" farm bills of 1981, 1977, and 1973 and also revisions to them that had come almost annually.

The old laws mandated very high farm price supports and restrictive regulation of how much farmers were permitted to grow. The administration's plan proposed to repeal most of the old laws. Virtually no one in Washington, including Block, expected that Congress would pass the administration bill intact.

Hardly any member of Congress disagreed with the long-term goal of "getting the government out of agriculture," one of the most durable slogans of farm politics. But few believed the troubled financial status of many farmers in 1985 would permit the governmental withdrawal that the agriculture bill envisioned.

The bill assumed that reductions in per-unit prices would be made up by greater volumes of sales. It would sharply reduce the commodity loan rates that had traditionally set minimum market prices. And it would virtually end a system of income supplement payments to farmers, known as deficiency payments, by phasing them down to the same level as loan rates.

The administration also wanted to end authority for two types of grain reserves. Farmers often argued that the existence of such reserves tended to depress market prices. One reserve provided loans for farmers at favorable rates if they held crops off the market until prices rose to specified levels. The other reserve was meant to stock wheat and grain for emergency, humanitarian aid abroad. For humanitarian aid, the administration bill proposed only to earmark stocks held by the Commodity Credit Corporation, which managed farm price-support programs.

The administration argued that the protective and expensive array of existing farm programs had perversely harmed global demand for U.S. farm goods and that only by stripping away many of these programs could U.S. farmers again compete aggressively for crucial foreign markets.

Equally important to the administra-

tion, though, was reducing the record high costs of farm programs. Like entitlement programs for the poor, such as food stamps, farm program costs went up when the farm economy was in trouble, because more people turn to the programs for help.

Agriculture Department officials said that under their plan farm programs would cost $20 billion to $35 billion in fiscal years 1987 through 1991, compared with estimated four-year costs of existing programs at $60 billion to $85 billion. Although these savings estimates were constructed from forecasts of factors such as market prices, demand and farmers' plantings, USDA departed from past practice and withheld these forecasts. Agriculture Department officials also declined to express in dollars the level of support that would be offered farmers by programs such as commodity loans, whose rates would be determined by new formulas based on market prices.

Reagan Vetoes Credit Bill

A high-speed drive to get extra loan money to farmers to finance their spring plantings crashed when President Reagan killed an emergency farm credit bill, vetoing it March 6, 1985, in a nationally televised appearance. In his veto message on the credit bill, Reagan asserted that severe financial problems afflicted only a small minority of farmers and that "96 percent do not have liquidity problems."

The vetoed bill would have added $1.85 billion to a $650 million loan-guarantee program, provided $100 million to reduce interest rates on private loans guaranteed by the program, revised some eligibility rules for the guarantees, and allowed farmers to get early advances on crop loans that they normally receive in the fall.

Reagan criticized the measure as "a massive new bailout that would add billions to the deficit," while coming too late to offer any help to farmers. Advocates of more farm aid had said that action by early or mid-March was essential, to enable farmers to get crops in the ground on time. Tying the bill to larger budget questions, Reagan said Congress "failed" its first major test of bringing spending under control.

Welfare Programs and The Fairness Issue

The growth of social welfare programs began to dominate discussions about American domestic policy as early as the mid-1960s. Conservatives condemned the steady expansion of these programs, asserting they had placed an unacceptable burden on the U.S. taxpayer while doing little to alleviate the long-term problems of the poor. Dissatisfaction with welfare helped propel Reagan into the presidency in 1980, and he moved quickly to slow the rate of growth in domestic spending.

From the beginning, Reagan maintained that his budget-cutting efforts were aimed only at those low-income individuals who were able to obtain substantial incomes by combining their earnings from work with federal cash assistance and "in-kind" benefits. The poorest individuals — the truly needy — would be spared from the budget ax. "Those who through no fault of their own must rely on the rest of us, the poverty-stricken, the disabled, the elderly, all those with true need, can rest assured that the social safety net of programs they depend on are exempt from any cuts," said Reagan in February 1981.

But during Reagan's first term, advocates of social welfare programs asserted repeatedly that Reagan's policies were unfair to the poor. The destitute maintained their eligibility for means-tested entitlement programs, such as Aid to Families with Dependent Children (AFDC), food stamps, housing assistance and Medicaid, but critics contended that many of the poor had their benefits reduced by direct cutbacks, deferred increases and hikes in rents and other fees. Opponents also said that the "working poor" whose benefits were eliminated were thrust back into dire poverty.

A study by the Congressional Budget Office (CBO) released in August 1983 found that 40 percent of the budget savings were coming from reductions in benefits to households with incomes of less than $10,000 a year. In addition, during the same month, the Census Bureau reported that the nation's poverty rate had increased in 1982 to 15 percent, the highest level in 17 years.

The issue of "fairness" to the nation's needy was central to the Democratic presidential campaign against Reagan. Presidential contender Sen. Gary Hart, D-Colo., said, "The Reagan record reflects an insensitivity to the needs of poor Americans that is unique in the post-Depression era." But, election results indicated either that most American voters agreed with the president's approach to these problems or that other issues were more important.

In 1985 the president again attempted to slow the growth of federal health care expenditures by targeting Medicaid for major spending curbs. But in contrast to previous years, the president sought only modest fiscal 1986 reductions in federal welfare programs, which had borne the brunt of social spending cuts in the initial budgets of his first term.

Reagan also asked states to help control federal spending. The fiscal 1986 budget called for an overhaul of federal financing of state administrative expenses for Medicaid, food stamps, and AFDC, the principal federal-state welfare program. A grant for each program would be provided to cover states' administrative expenses, which currently were financed as an open-ended entitlement. Fiscal 1986 administrative expenses would be frozen at 1985 levels.

Medicaid Cap Proposed

The president proposed a cap on federal contributions to Medicaid, the federal-state program that paid medical bills for welfare recipients and certain other low-income families. A different cap plan had provoked one of the most bitter budget battles in Congress in 1981, with the administration losing badly. Medicaid, with about 22.5 million people enrolled, was projected to cost the federal government about $23.7 billion in fiscal 1986 outlays, and states about $19.3 billion. Federal matching rates ranged from 50 percent to 78 percent of program costs. What the administration wanted in 1981 was to limit to 5 percent the rate of federal Medicaid spending growth in the following year. The fiscal 1986 budget sought to hold fiscal 1986 spending at $22.2 billion, an actual reduction from fiscal 1985. To help states get through the year, a one-time pool of $300 million would be available.

Beginning in 1987, the administration wanted federal Medicaid spending increases to be limited to the general rate of inflation for health care, as measured by the Consumer Price Index. If total program costs grew faster than that rate, states would have to make up the difference. To help states control costs, the budget proposed giving them more latitude in collecting private insurance payments and in determining eligibility for program benefits.

Welfare Benefits

Reagan's 1986 budget once again attempted to make Aid to Families with Dependent Children benefits and other types of welfare conditional on work by recipients. Every year since 1981, the president had proposed some form of "workfare," requiring states to make it mandatory for able-bodied welfare recipients to work in exchange for their benefits.

In 1981 Congress voted to allow states to set work requirements but did not make it mandatory; about half the states did this.

The budget also called for requiring unwed minors with children to live with their parents in order to qualify for AFDC. That proposal was included by the Senate in a 1984 deficit reduction bill but was dropped in conference. The change was intended to eliminate what the administration saw as an "incentive for minor parents to leave home and use AFDC to establish financial independence."

Food Stamps and Child Nutrition

As part of his fiscal 1986 budget the president called for a work requirement from food stamp recipients. He also proposed making middle-income children ineligible for federally subsidized school meals and the cancellation of a July 1, 1986, cost-of-living increase for child nutrition programs.

With these changes, outlays for food aid in fiscal 1986 would total $18.3 billion, compared with $18.6 billion for fiscal 1985. The food stamp program would consume $11.9 billion, providing benefits to 20.1 million people. Enrollment was expected to decline slightly, by about 120,000 people, because of improved economic conditions. The administration estimated that its mandatory work requirement, similar to one sought for welfare recipients, could save $56 million — either by giving beneficiaries work experience that will help them get jobs, or by driving some recipients out of the program. Meanwhile, Reagan was asking $318.9 million more in fiscal 1985 funds for the food stamp program.

For child nutrition programs, including meals for children in schools and day-care programs, outlays would be $3.4 billion, down from $3.8 billion in fiscal 1985.

The administration wanted to cancel federal subsidies for meals served to children whose family incomes exceeded 185

Reagan's Policies on Abortion...

In his 1984 State of the Union address, President Reagan called on Americans to "come together in a spirit of understanding and helping" and find "positive solutions to the tragedy of abortion." Throughout his first term, the president championed a constitutional amendment and bills to outlaw abortion, none of which were passed by Congress.

But the president gave little encouragement to federal programs to deter unwanted pregnancies or to provide pregnant women with alternatives to abortion. As soon as he took office in 1981, the president sought cuts in the government's three main programs related to pregnancy prevention and assistance for pregnant women.

Aside from a basic desire to reduce the budget, part of the reason, according to administration officials, was profound discomfort with government involvement in family planning programs. Some of Reagan's staunchest supporters believed the government should have no role in providing services or information on sex education or contraception.

Abortion has been legal nationwide in the United States since the Supreme Court's 1973 *Roe v. Wade* decision, which established the right of a woman to have an abortion based on an implied right of privacy in the Constitution. Beginning in 1973, the number of abortions reported each year averaged about 1.5 million; about one-third were performed on teenagers.

Since 1977 federal funding for most abortions for poor women was prohibited except to save the life of the pregnant woman. The funding ban was upheld by the Supreme Court, as were similar state laws. However, 15 states and the District of Columbia continued to fund abortions for poor women.

Defining alternatives to abortion proved to be almost as controversial as the debate over abortion itself. At bottom were questions of the proper role of government, religious tenets and the country's shifting morality. The continuum of possibilities began with preventing an unwanted pregnancy and extended to the provision of services to a woman during pregnancy and to the child afterward.

No matter how good the alternatives, many advocates of legalized abortion contended that abortion must always be available. "Even if you had perfect contraception, there would always be a need for abortion as a backup," said William Hamilton of Planned Parenthood.

Reagan and his allies in the anti-abortion, or "pro-life," movement disagreed with that view. And some of the pro-life forces also had reservations about federal government programs to reduce the number of abortions. Judie Brown, president of the American Life Lobby, for example, believed that the federal government should have no role in family planning; rather that family and community resources should provide advice.

The Catholic Church, another major element of the anti-abortion movement, saw the issue as part of a larger social problem. Cardinal Joseph Bernardin of Chicago said,

...and Family Planning Alternatives

"The Catholic position on abortion requires — by the law of logic and the law of love — a social vision which joins the right to life to the promotion of a range of other rights: nutrition, health care, employment and housing."

Congress refused to go along with Reagan's cuts in two of the three programs that provided alternatives to abortion. But the president was initially successful in cutting by almost one-fourth the money available for the government's major family planning program, Title X of the Public Health Service Act of 1970. Title X provided support for more than 5,000 clinics, run by hospitals, health departments, Planned Parenthood affiliates and other agencies. For several years, the Reagan administration requested no funding specifically for family planning, but rather proposed a block grant for states to use for a variety of health matters, including family planning. Congress refused and continued to earmark Title X funds for family planning services. Critics pointed to the increasing numbers of illegitimate births and abortions and charged that the programs were a clear failure. Defenders said that without these services, the statistics would have been even worse.

There had been two new federal initiatives related to abortion alternatives since 1981, neither coming from the administration. One was the Adolescent Family Life Program proposed by Sen. Jeremiah Denton, R-Ala. Established in 1981, the program was expected to exhaust nearly $15 million in fiscal 1985 on 59 demonstration projects to discourage teenagers from engaging in sexual activity, while encouraging those who did become pregnant to carry their pregnancies to term. No abortion counseling was permitted. In 1985, this program was under challenge in the courts. The other initiative, known as the Child Health Assurance Program (CHAP), was enacted in 1984 as a modification of Medicaid, the federal-state health program for the poor, and required state coverage for first pregnancies.

One defender of legalized abortion, Henry A. Waxman, D-Calif., chairman of the House Energy and Commerce Subcommittee on Health and the Environment, supported Denton's program and worked with some abortion opponents for the Medicaid change. "I respect the anti-abortion position that many people hold," he said. "I have always found it incredible," he added, "that an administration opposed to abortion would also oppose family planning—which is the only federal program that could directly help reduce the number of unwanted pregnancies."

Administration officials disagreed. Marjory Mecklenburg, deputy assistant secretary at Health and Human Services, believed Reagan had a commendable record on the issues related to abortion. "Not only does the president favor protection of the unborn, but he is also concerned about alternatives to abortion," she said. "It is the administration's view that some categorical service programs such as family planning and maternal-child health programs are best administered by the states through block grants," Mecklenburg said.

Reagan's 1986 budget proposed further cuts in programs providing lunches to schools and day-care centers.

percent of the federal poverty level ($18,870 for a family of four). Advocates of food aid defended these subsidies, saying that without the participation of all children they could not afford food service for any students, so that poor children would lose access to free or reduced-price meals.

Administration officials said the budget provided enough money, $1.48 billion, to serve the existing caseload of three million people in a nutrition program for low-income pregnant and nursing women, infants and young children (WIC). In 1984, however, the Appropriations committees said that $1.5 billion would be needed to sustain a caseload of that size.

Other Welfare Programs

The 1986 budget would freeze spending for many other social service and anti-poverty programs at fiscal 1985 levels. Among them, grants to help low-income people pay their energy bills would continue to be funded at $2.1 billion. The administration resurrected a proposal ignored by Congress in 1984 to finance energy aid from a fund set up with fines paid by oil companies for overcharging.

Reagan asked $5.4 billion in budget authority, $714 million less than in 1985, to support state social services and several programs assisting children, families and the aged.

Education Cuts Focus On Student Loans

Forced by Congress to live with an Education Department he would have liked to abolish, President Reagan Jan. 10, 1985, named William J. Bennett to the agency's top post. Bennett, who was chairman of the National Endowment for the Humanities, was an outspoken advocate of improving educational quality and revitalizing the traditional humanities curriculum in schools and colleges. Bennett succeeded T. H. Bell, who officially left the Cabinet Dec. 31, 1984, after a tenure marked by frequent criticism from conservatives.

In announcing Bennett's nomination, a White House spokesman said the president had asked for a new study of the future of the Education Department. At Bell's recommendation, Reagan in 1982 proposed downgrading the department into a federal education foundation, but the idea was ignored by Congress.

Meanwhile the administration proposed funding cuts, taking special aim at college student loans. Saying that middle-income college students should rely less on the government to foot their tuition bills, President Reagan proposed a $15.5 billion Education Department budget for fiscal 1986 that would shrink student-aid rolls by 20 percent. (Approximately half of the nation's college freshmen received some form of government aid.) The sum requested for the department was about 14 percent lower than the record-high $18 billion Congress appropriated for fiscal 1985.

Student aid made up almost half the Education Department's budget. The largest programs were Pell grants for the neediest students and Guaranteed Student Loans (GSL). The department was also responsible for administering three other programs in which aid was distributed by colleges: Supplemental Educational Opportunity Grants, College Work-Study and National Direct Student Loans.

The proposed reductions in student aid would include a $4,000 annual ceiling and a ban on subsidized loans to students whose families earned more than $32,500. These were only part of far broader changes envisioned by the administration. According to the president's budget, all student aid except GSL eventually would be replaced with a single grant program to be administered by the states.

Student Loan Controversy

Because of its size, the loan program was a particularly tempting target for budget-cutters. The private capital lent under the program also was the largest source of financial aid for college students. Although the federal government did not directly provide loan capital under the program, it encouraged banks to make loans to students by paying a fee, known as a "special allowance," to supplement the below-market interest rate charged to students, which was 8 percent in 1985. The government also paid all interest on loans while borrowers were in school and for a short grace period after they left college and reimbursed banks for defaults.

Private lenders were expected to provide some $7.9 billion in guaranteed loans to students in fiscal 1985, while federal costs were projected to total some $3.7 billion. That federal tab was up sharply from the $480 million spent in fiscal 1978, the last year before Congress enacted the Middle Income Student Assistance Act of 1978, which allowed all students, regardless of income, to receive federally subsidized loans.

Even after Congress in 1981 reinstated an eligibility test for students whose families earned more than $30,000, the program continued to provide aid to many middle-income families. The Office of Management and Budget (OMB) said that about 30 percent of the loans went to students whose families earned more than $32,500 a year.

Gary L. Jones, under secretary of education, said the college-aid overhaul would

Tuition loan programs came under scrutiny during Reagan's second term.

mark "a major philosophical shift by returning to the traditional emphasis on parent and student responsibility for financing college costs." The College Board calculated average costs for the 1984-85 school year at a private university at $9,022 and at a public university at $4,881. Many protested that a cap on aid would deny education at private schools to all but the wealthy. But Jones said students could draw on a range of other sources to supplement the $4,000: their families, state scholarship programs and financial aid from their college.

Also, the administration proposed a $25,000 family-income cap to be eligible for all other forms of Education Department aid — grants, direct loans and work-study

subsidies. OMB estimated that about 5 percent of all Pell grants and more than 20 percent of campus-based federal aid went to students with family incomes over $25,000.

Newly installed Education Secretary Bennett added fuel to the fire at a Feb. 11, 1985, news conference by saying some students could cope with federal aid cuts by simply forgoing luxuries such as stereos, cars and vacations. Critics charged that his remarks showed disdain for students and insensitivity to the financial circumstances of federal aid recipients.

Defending the administration's proposed $4,000 annual cap on federal aid to students, Bennett said the federal government should give top priority to ensuring that the neediest students have access to some form of higher education. He questioned if there was a further federal responsibility to help students pay for the college of their choice regardless of its cost.

"I don't know of any proposed cut that more clearly defines the current philosophical debate than does that applied to student aid," said Rep. Pat Williams, D-Mont. "The president's savings at the expense of middle-income students will be spent by the Pentagon in 24 hours."

The budget would let all students borrow under an existing program, known as "PLUS," which would provide federally guaranteed loans — but entirely unsubsidized — of up to $4,000. PLUS loans would not be counted toward the $4,000 cap on aid. The Education Department said that about 10 percent of the aid recipients in 1982-83, or 480,000 students, received more than $4,000 a year.

Student Loans and the Banks

The last time Congress took a whack at student loan spending, it was the students who bore the burden. In 1981, for example, Congress authorized banks to charge borrowers a 5 percent fee to be deducted from their loans. It also established a financial-need test for aid applicants with more than $30,000 in family income and limited the amount students could borrow to their demonstrated financial need. In 1985 a raft of proposals to force some belt-tightening among banks and state loan agencies was included in the administration's student-loan budget.

One such proposal would require state student-loan agencies, which serve as intermediaries between banks and the federal government, to absorb a larger share of default costs. Administrative cost allowances to the agencies also would be eliminated. Another would curb subsidies currently paid to banks to ensure an adequate return on student loans. The "special allowance" fluctuated with Treasury bill rates and was considered excessive by some critics. The administration wanted to fix the rate and provide a lower subsidy during the years a borrower was in school. In a related recommendation, the budget proposed tying the interest paid by students to the rate paid on 91-day Treasury bills, estimated to average 8.65 percent in 1985, instead of the fixed rate of 8 percent.

With federal government subsidizing the interest rate and reimbursing banks for defaults, OMB called the loan program a "banking bonanza" and charged that financial institutions were making excessive profits at taxpayers' expense. However, past efforts to curb student loan subsidies to financial institutions had met with stiff resistance from banking lobbyists who carried a powerful trump card: if Congress were to go too far in changes that add to the cost or complexity of student loans, the banks could refuse to make the loans.

But the administration contended that bankers were crying wolf and that the loans were particularly attractive investments for banks because, among other things, they were fully guaranteed against default by the government. "I don't want to be too cynical, but I think any change we've proposed in GSL has always been met with the charge that the banks will drop out of the program," said Gary L. Bauer, deputy under secretary of education. "In the past, it has been adjusted and the banks have not dropped out."

Other Education Issues

The 1986 Reagan budget proposed funding major elementary and secondary education programs at close to fiscal 1985 spending levels. However, the administration would drop 38 relatively small categorical education programs, many of which the president sought unsuccessfully to eliminate during his first term, including immigrant education, the Women's Educational Equity Act, aid to libraries and a portion of the impact aid program for school districts that educate children of federal employees.

Compensatory education for disadvantaged schoolchildren would get $3.6 billion, which was $49 million less than in fiscal 1985, reflecting administration proposals to curb spending for education aid for the children of migrant workers.

The budget provided the same overall amount for vocational education as in fiscal 1985 — $738 million — but added $32 million to basic grants to states and cut an equal amount from grants for consumer and homemaking education. The administration also asked Congress to finance a new program to improve mathematics and science education at $100 million — the same amount provided in fiscal 1985, the first year of the program. But the budget asked Congress to rescind the $75 million it provided for fiscal 1985 for another new program, grants to magnet schools involved in desegregation efforts.

Of the higher education programs that provided grants to colleges, rather than financial aid to their students, only a handful would survive. College aid programs slated for elimination included: the Fund for the Improvement of Postsecondary Education; international education and foreign language study grants; and campus construction grants.

What Ever Happened To the Energy Crisis?

President Reagan in January 1985 nominated John S. Herrington, a White House assistant for personnel, to head the Energy Department. Herrington replaced Donald P. Hodel, who moved to the top job at the Interior Department. Hodel's shift back to Interior, where he had served as under secretary during Reagan's first administration, rekindled discussion that the Energy Department might be abolished and its functions taken over by Interior. Such a plan would coincide with the president's desire to limit sharply the government's role in setting energy policy.

While the president was unable to kill the Energy Department during his first term, he made considerable cuts in staff, shifted money from programs involving conservation and renewable energy sources to nuclear power, and cut back on data gathering by the department. These moves and their continuation during the second Reagan term confirmed what many had suspected: the "energy crisis," at least as far as the White House was concerned, was a dead issue.

Energy policy had been *the* issue of the 1970s — a national concern that President Jimmy Carter had called "the moral equivalent of war." Falling oil prices and the Reagan administration's reluctance to intervene in the energy marketplace put the issue on a back burner. But, though the crisis atmosphere was gone, for key members of Congress the concern remained.

"We're all so fat, dumb and happy again," said Sen. James A. McClure, R-Idaho, the chairman of the Senate Energy and Natural Resources Committee. In June 1984, as oil tankers were being sunk in the Persian Gulf during the Iran-Iraq war, McClure could not muster a quorum of his committee to consider a bill requiring preparations for an oil shortage.

"I feel frustrated that nobody is aware of the fact that the problem is still there, like a sleeping vampire that waits to rise," said Rep. John D. Dingell, D-Mich., chairman of the Energy and Commerce Committee and the most influential remaining member of the group that steered energy legislation through Congress in the 1970s. Energy "has ceased to be a political question," he said.

Reagan's Energy Plans

For his second term, Reagan put together a modest, production-oriented legislative agenda aimed at making it easier to build nuclear plants, speeding decontrol of natural gas, and increasing the use of coal. Congress, however, was still oriented toward emergency planning and conservation.

The president's fiscal 1986 budget for the Energy Department called for sharp cuts in domestic programs, leaving the agency dominated more than ever by defense activities. The budget proposed a 36 percent reduction in civilian energy spending. Activities related to the development and production of nuclear weapons would increase 10 percent and would account for $8 billion of the proposed $12.5 billion Energy Department budget. Despite administration discussions about merging the Energy and Interior departments, the suggestion was not reflected in the 1986 budget.

Strategic Petroleum Reserve

The total budget request was 13 percent below that for fiscal 1985, but the reduction depended on a halt in the stock-

To most Americans, long lines to buy gas in 1973 and 1979 represented energy problems at their worst.

piling of oil in the Strategic Petroleum Reserve (SPR), for which Congress appropriated $2.05 billion in fiscal 1985. Small savings would come from elimination of the Solar Energy and Energy Conservation Bank, and substantial cuts in other areas such as conservation, coal research and development, and wind technology.

While the SPR moratorium had congressional support, most of the other proposed cutbacks had been considered and rejected by Congress in the past. Another new idea, to accelerate the repayment of construction debts by four federal hydroelectric power supply systems, would raise consumer rates substantially and probably provoke opposition on Capitol Hill.

The administration proposed an indefinite moratorium on filling the SPR after fiscal 1985 and suspension of storage facility construction. The Energy Department estimated that at the end of fiscal 1985

there would be 489 million barrels of oil in the reserve — the equivalent of 108 days of net imports. Although short of the original 750 million-barrel goal, this amount was deemed adequate by the administration because of changes in consumption patterns and other market conditions.

Hydroelectric Power

In the area of hydroelectric power the administration proposed significant changes in the way the Bonneville Power Administration and three other federal electric power agencies would repay their construction debts. Repayments would be accelerated and interest rates raised to market levels. Existing rates dated from the time the projects were started. The changes would increase revenues by $1 billion, to be paid by electric power customers; some rates could rise by as much as 48 percent. Sen. Mark O. Hatfield, R-Ore., chairman of the Appropriations Committee, denounced the idea Jan. 31 as a "dismal, unconscionable program" that would have "a devastating impact" on his region.

Conservation, Research Cuts

The administration sought cuts in federal support for research and development in energy conservation. Conservation grants, which went to pay for weatherizing schools, hospitals and the homes of low-income people, would also be reduced. The administration also proposed that these grants, along with the low-income energy assistance program of the Department of Health and Human Services, be supported by fines paid by oil companies for violating oil price controls in effect during the 1970s. A similar proposal in the 1985 budget was ignored by Congress.

Except for defense programs, the administration proposed substantial cuts in the Energy Department's budget for research and development. Research into fossil energy and solar and renewable energy would be cut. Spending for these programs was far below the levels when Reagan took office. Solar, renewables and fossil energy programs were appropriated at $2.7 billion in fiscal 1981; requests for fiscal 1986 amounted to only one-fifth of that. Despite its longstanding support for nuclear power, the administration recommended a reduction in research into nuclear fusion.

Facing the Future

There would be a battle on Capitol Hill if the president tried to merge the Energy and Interior departments, as congressional opposition was still strong. But in early 1985 energy enjoyed a low profile. The Energy Department was "like the Maytag repairman," said Robert C. Odle Jr., the Energy Department's congressional liaison. "We don't get calls very often, and we think that's terrific."

This attitude infuriated many who tried to deal with the energy problems of the 1970s. They continued to believe that another crisis was almost inevitable, and that the administration should be preparing for it.

"Because we are doing nothing in the way of intelligent planning, we will have to address all the problems when the crisis next returns to curse us — and it will — in an atmosphere of panic and outrage," said Dingell. "That is an appallingly bad way to legislate."

Environmental Laws Up for Renewal in Second Term

By early 1985, 10 of the nation's major environmental laws had expired or were scheduled to do so. Congress had completed work on only one of them, the Resource Conservation and Recovery Act, which regulated the disposal of hazardous waste.

Continued congressional inaction would leave most of the other nine laws unchanged, but still in effect. Even with funding authority technically expired, environmental programs usually could be carried over from year to year with appropriations bills. *(Box, pp. 86-87)*

The prospect of continued inaction on environmental laws was in some ways a relief to groups pressing for stringent pollution control. When President Reagan took office in 1981, environmental lobbyists feared he would push Congress to relax numerous regulatory statutes enacted in the 1970s, which was a goal of the 1980 Republican Party platform. That appeared feasible early in 1981, when the president commanded a working majority in Congress — at least on economic issues — of Republicans and conservative Sun Belt Democrats. By March 1981, Reagan had proposed drastic cutbacks in the politically popular federal program of grants for construction of local sewage systems. By the end of the year, Congress had voted those reductions, along with cuts in the budget of the Environmental Protection Agency (EPA) that were part of broader domestic cuts.

But environmentalists and their legislative allies dug in their heels on other issues before the 97th Congress. With surprising ease, they managed to stave off administration proposals to relax both the Clean Air Act and the regulatory provisions of the Clean Water Act. And in the 1982 elections, environmental groups gained new strength on Capitol Hill as Democrats picked up 26 seats in the House and held their own in the Senate. Emboldened by such success at the polls, they went on the offensive in the 98th Congress, seeking to beef up laws on air and water pollution and toxic waste disposal and cleanup.

But the environmentalists soon discovered the same time-honored truth the Reagan administration had learned the hard way: it is easier to hold the high ground than to capture it, to defend the status quo than to change it. "We have enough influence to keep bad things from happening," one veteran environmental lobbyist said, but he conceded that 1985 was more likely to bring continued "stalemate" than progress from his organization's point of view.

Some environmental lobbyists expressed private dismay over the legislative stalemate. The laws that remained on the books threatened to become increasingly out of touch with the times. The 1972 Clean Water Act, for example, required EPA to set up a "pre-treatment" program for regulating the discharge of pollutants by industry into municipal sewage systems. More than a decade later, EPA had not come up with a workable program.

Leaving the unworkable parts of the law on the books could lead to administrative chaos. Even more dangerous, from the perspective of environmentalists, was that it might lead to selective enforcement — or undermine the laws completely.

But there were areas where everyone concerned agreed that action was needed. A good example was acid rain. In 1981, clean-air debate centered on industry proposals for relaxing the existing law. By 1984, acid rain had become the dominant air-quality issue in Congress. Total national emissions of sulfur dioxide, the main cause of acid rain, stood at about 26 million tons per year in 1980, down from about 30 million tons in 1970 when the Clean Air Act was passed. Environmentalists urged a drastic tightening of existing smokestack controls that would reduce annual emissions by another eight million to 12 million tons per year.

The "superfund" — the hazardous-waste cleanup law — was another example. Virtually no one in Congress could be found arguing that the $1.6 billion, five-year program should be halted or trimmed back. The issue was whether its renewal for another five years should be at a $5 billion or a $10 billion funding level.

EPA Budget

Reagan's fiscal 1986 budget would leave most of the EPA unscathed and add more spending to control toxic pollutants. The president proposed $4.67 billion in budget authority for EPA overall. EPA's operating budget request, the indicator of its regulatory effort, would be $1.368 billion for fiscal 1986, up slightly from the $1.308 billion level enacted for 1985.

In a Feb. 4, 1985, briefing on the budget, EPA Administrator Lee M. Thomas said the EPA's 8 percent increase from fiscal 1985 levels was "all the more significant when placed in the context of the overall freeze that has been imposed on many federal agencies and departments." But William Drayton, an environmental lobbyist who served as EPA's chief budget officer during the Carter administration, noted the agency's proposed $1.37 billion operating budget was scarcely more than the $1.35 billion appropriation for fiscal 1981. When inflation was taken into account, that represented a drop in real-dollar spending, Drayton said, while EPA's responsibilities had increased dramatically.

Thomas pointed to steep increases in proposed spending for EPA's two programs to control hazardous wastes: the superfund program and a separate program to regulate disposal of such wastes under the Resource Conservation and Recovery Act (RCRA), which Congress reauthorized in 1984.

The budget provided the first public glimpse of the proposal Reagan was expected to send Congress for renewal of the superfund program. The president asked $900 million in fiscal 1986, up from $620 million for 1985, with figures for later years pointing toward a $5.5 billion effort for 1986-90. That was more than the $5 billion the administration asked for in 1984, but less than was authorized in a $10.2 billion measure passed last year by the House and a $7.5 billion version reported by the Senate

Nine Environmental Protection Laws...

In 1985 nine major environmental laws required action by Congress because their funding authorizations had expired or would expire.

Superfund

This 1980 law, officially the Comprehensive Environmental Response, Compensation and Liability Act (PL 96-510), set up a $1.6 billion fund to pay for prompt cleanup of abandoned hazardous-waste dumps and toxic spills. It also made dumpers and dump owners legally responsible for paying cleanup costs. The law authorized the Environmental Protection Agency (EPA) to use the fund for immediate cleanup and then go to court for the slower process of recovering costs. In 1983 complaints about how the EPA carried out the superfund law prompted congressional investigations that led to the firing of Rita M. Lavelle, the superfund director, and the resignation of EPA administrator Anne M. Burford.

Toxic Substances Control Act

Enacted in 1976 after five years of debate, this law (PL 94-469) expanded federal regulation of industrial and commercial chemicals and for the first time required pre-market testing for those considered potentially dangerous. The act was renewed for two years (1982-83) in a 1981 law (PL 97-129), with no substantive changes.

Clean Air Act

The nation's principal air-pollution control law, the Clean Air Act was enacted in 1970 (PL 91-604) and substantially amended in 1977 (PL 95-95). Its funding authorization expired in 1981, as Congress found itself buffeted by conflicting pressures. The Reagan administration and several industries sought to relax the law, while environmentalists wanted new controls on acid rain and toxic air pollutants. Unwilling to pay the high political price needed to settle the quarrel, Congress opted for inaction. It imposed a moratorium on moves by the EPA to punish cities that failed to meet legal deadlines for cleaning up their air, and it pushed the problem of reauthorization under the rug.

Clean Water Act

Funding authorization for the regulatory part of this law (PL 95-217), which controlled water pollution by requiring permits for any discharge into a waterway, expired Sept. 30, 1982. The House on June 26, 1984, approved a compromise revision of the law (HR 3282), but a Senate version (S 431) never reached the floor. Authorization for politically popular sewage-plant construction grants was scheduled to expire Sept. 30, 1985. While the 1984 House bill more than doubled the program's current $2.4 billion size, the Reagan administration could seek to eliminate it.

FIFRA

The Federal Insecticide, Fungicide and Rodenticide Act (PL 92-516), which was the main law regulating the registration, labeling and use of pesticides, was due for re-

... Awaiting Action by Congress

authorization in 1981. The last major overhaul of the act came in 1978 (PL 95-396). Congress cleared a simple one-year reauthorization (PL 98-201) of the pesticide control law in 1983. A reauthorization bill would face disputes among pesticide makers, environmentalists, labor, farm and health groups. Controversies included whether stricter state registration laws could pre-empt federal requirements, whether individuals should be able to sue to stop violations of the law, and whether information filed by companies with the government on the health effects of pesticides should be released to the public.

Safe Drinking Water Act

This 1974 law (PL 93-523) gave EPA the power to set maximum allowable levels for chemical and bacteriological contaminants in drinking water systems serving more than 25 customers. Congress enacted a three-year reauthorization (PL 96-63) in 1979, which expired at the end of fiscal 1982. Efforts to reauthorize funding for the law foundered in 1984.

Ocean Dumping Act

This law, which is Title I of the Marine Protection, Research and Sanctuaries Act of 1972 (PL 92-532), set up a program to regulate the dumping of industrial waste, municipal sewage sludge and other materials in the ocean. Funding authorization expired in 1982. The House passed reauthorization bills in 1982, 1983 and 1984, but the Senate did not act on them.

Coastal Zone Management Act

This 1972 law (PL 92-583) established a federal-state planning program to balance preservation of coastal natural resources such as fishing grounds with economic development efforts such as offshore oil and gas drilling. The act was amended in 1976 to authorize a $1.2 billion program of federal aid to coastal states to help them offset the effects of energy development. Congress drastically cut authorization levels for the program, however, in 1980 (PL 96-464).

Endangered Species Act

Originally enacted in 1973, this law (PL 93-205) made it a federal offense to buy, sell, possess, export or import any species listed as endangered or threatened. It also prohibited federal projects from jeopardizing listed species or their habitat. Congress enacted a three-year reauthorization of the act in 1982 (PL 97-304), reaffirming the basic outlines of the program, but streamlining its enforcement. Lawmakers rejected Reagan administration proposals for greater consideration of economic costs of listing species and set tightened deadlines in an effort to force the administration to speed up listing decisions. Western water developers were expected to seek relaxation of provisions that could block projects in the Colorado River basin, but some environmental groups wanted further tightening of the law.

Reagan announced that he wanted EPA's superfund, which was designed to clean up toxic waste dumps, renewed in 1985.

Environment Committee.

For the RCRA program, the budget sought a 44 percent increase — $236 million, up from about $164 million appropriated in 1985. Program growth would actually be even greater, because some $28 million in fiscal 1985 funds came to RCRA from other programs. Environmental groups and some members of Congress maintained that even this steep rise in spending on toxic-waste control was not enough to do the job. They noted that the 1984 RCRA legislation called for many new regulatory attacks on the waste problem. For example, it required EPA to control leaking underground storage tanks, small quantities of hazardous wastes, and the blending of such wastes with fuel oil. It also required the agency to ban land disposal of many liquid and solid toxic wastes. EPA estimated that about 70 new regulations would have to be issued as a result of the 1984 law.

Superfund

Superfund renewal was the one law Congress was most likely to act on in 1985 because it was the one that could not be put off. Its taxing authority, not just authorization for appropriations, was due to expire Sept. 30, 1985. The superfund came mostly from a special tax on petrochemicals, and without a continued inflow of funds the cleanup work could not continue for long. Renewal also appeared to be a political necessity. Toxic dumps tended to create groups of scared and angry voters demanding action, and there are toxic dumps in virtually every state.

In 1981-83, when Anne M. Burford headed EPA, the administration hoped to avoid any renewal of the superfund law. Following congressional charges that the agency was derelict in enforcing the law — a controversy that culminated in Burford's resignation — President Reagan changed his mind. As 1984 began, he announced he did want the law renewed — but not until after the election. The House nonetheless passed a bill (HR 5640) in August that extended the cleanup fund for five more years and increased it from $1.6 billion to $10.2 billion. The Senate Environment Committee in September approved a more modest $7.5 billion version, but that bill never reached the Senate floor. Environmentalists blamed the administration pleas for delaying the bill.

Clean Air Act

When legislation relaxing the Clean Air Act was drafted by the administration in June 1981, Rep. Henry A. Waxman, D-Calif., chairman of the House Energy Subcommittee on Health and the Environment, released it early to the press and denounced it. The administration first delayed and then abandoned its promise to propose specific amendments to the law, instead sending to Capitol Hill a set of 11 general principles. This was one of the first legislative proposals the administration made on the environment, and the outcry Waxman set off was loud enough that it was also one of the last.

By 1984 Waxman went on the offensive, pressing to report out a clean-air bill that actually strengthened existing law by imposing controls on acid rain. He came within a single vote of winning in subcommittee. Waxman was planning another legislative initiative in 1985. In response to more than 2,000 deaths after poisonous gas escaped from a chemical plant in Bhopal, India, Waxman wanted to force EPA to regulate hazardous air pollutants. EPA had the discretion, but not the requirement, to do so. Waxman had lost earlier fights on the issue, one of many left unresolved in the general stalemate over the Clean Air Act. His plan was to try to move a hazardous air pollutants bill separately.

"In some cases the status quo is what the environmentalists want to defend," Waxman said, "and in others the agenda is to move forward with new legislation. Acid rain is not being addressed by the present law and we need legislation. Toxic air pollutants are not sufficiently being addressed with this EPA and under present law, and so we need legislation.

"The whole Clean Air Act otherwise is a reasonably good one, which should be modified slightly, but from my perspective I'd rather leave the present law in effect than to gut it as the Reagan administration would have had us do, and probably still would if they had their opportunity," he said.

Interior Budget Request

In contrast to EPA, the Interior Department's budget authority would be slashed under the new budget from some $6.602 billion in fiscal 1985 to $5.635 billion for fiscal 1986. The biggest cuts would be in two areas: acquisition of land for parks and wildlife refuges and construction of Western water projects.

The president proposed two user-fees. One would raise entrance or camping fees for national parks and wildlife refuges. Such fees defrayed about 7 percent of the operation and maintenance cost of those facilities, and the administration wanted to raise that to a 25 percent share. The other proposal would bring grazing fees on public lands closer to market value. During Reagan's first term, Congress blocked a similar move to raise park fees.

Another proposal would deduct federal costs for oil and gas leasing and for timber sales before splitting proceeds from such activities with the states. Such a move would cost the states some $50 million annually in lost oil and gas revenues alone. *(Box, Timber sales, pp. 90-91)*

The 15 percent overall reduction in the Interior Department budget affected all 10 of its major bureaus, but almost two-thirds of the cuts came from three agencies: the Bureau of Land Management (BLM), the National Park Service and the Bureau of Reclamation. Most of BLM's cut would come as a result of a proposed land swap with the U.S. Forest Service. Most of the $239 million cut in the Park Service's budget came in two slices: $135.9 million less than fiscal 1985 for land acquisition and $61.6 million less for construction. The budget proposed a three-year moratorium on land acquisition for the National Park System and National Wildlife Refuge System, as well as on grants to the states for their own acquisition programs. Reagan requested only $13 million to buy lands for parks and refuges in 1986, down from $210 million appropriated for fiscal 1985.

Recreation land acquisition had been a bone of contention between the Reagan administration and Congress since 1981,

Congress Expected to Review . . .

The Reagan administration's sale of timber in the national forests to private loggers was an issue that Congress was expected to tackle in 1985. For much of the winter of 1984-85, the question of whether the Treasury was getting a fair return for this timber had been debated across the Western states. The argument shifted to Congress in February 1985 when hearings began on the timber sales program. The U.S. Forest Service had to determine how much timber should be cut during the next decade in the 155 national forests it ran.

One conservation organization, the Wilderness Society, decided to make timber sales an issue, and the society's 130,000 members and $6.5 million annual budget made it possible to mount a weighty lobbying effort. The Wilderness Society estimated that U.S. taxpayers lost $2.1 billion over a 10-year period from "below-cost" timber sales — sales where the Forest Service spent more to produce and sell the timber than it received in return from logging companies. A society report charged that environmental consequences such as soil erosion and damage to drinking water, fisheries and wildlife habitats were being subsidized by the government. The Forest Service disputed that assessment.

Behind the issue of below-cost timber sales was a more basic debate over the proper balance between conservation of the national forests for future generations and exploitation of them to benefit the economy. The National Forest System was built on the idea that profit alone should not dictate the cutting of publicly owned timber resources. Like the laws and policies that govern it, the forest system was assembled bit by bit over almost a century. It was developed only after vast tracts of forest had been cleared for settlement and agriculture and more land cleared for the timber to build and fuel a growing nation. One of the earliest components was more than 13 million acres that President Benjamin Harrison set aside as national forest "reserves" during his term in 1889-93.

The cornerstone was laid when Congress passed the Forest Management Act of 1897 that set out both forest conservation and timber production as goals. President Theodore Roosevelt added more than 100 million acres to the system from 1901-09. The system grew to about 191 million acres, and Congress over the decades passed numerous laws prescribing how it should be managed.

In response to the building boom that followed World War II, sales of timber took a huge jump. That brought about legislation that stated as policy that forests were not for the single purpose of timber production, but also for outdoor recreation, grazing, watershed, fish and wildlife. The law also directed the agriculture secretary to seek a sustained yield of those resources, the highest output that could be sustained in perpetuity without harming the productivity of the land.

But stating multiple use and sustained yield as goals left plenty of room for disagreement over how to manage each forest. Congress tried to establish mechanisms with new laws, one in 1974 and another in 1976, mandating planning activities in 10-year cycles at the national, regional and local levels. And 1985 was the year for the Forest Service to issue the first major wave of final forest plans required under the 1976 law, including setting aside land the service believed unsuitable for commercial timber

... Timber Sales Under Reagan

production. The Wilderness Act of 1964 established another option for use of national forest: designating an area as wilderness.

A 1984 study by the General Accounting Office (GAO) found that the Forest Service had indeed sold timber in many cases for less than the costs of putting it up for sale. But that was not the whole picture. The Forest Service emphasized that the overall timber sale program made money for the Treasury — even in 1983 when the timber harvest was especially low because of a housing slump. From 1978 to 1983, officials noted, costs of the sales totaled $2.9 billion and timber harvests brought in revenues of $4.3 billion.

The timber industry argued that not all costs and benefits can be counted in dollars. In districts where logging was the dominant industry, timber sales could mean the difference between a viable local economy and a disaster area. Moreover many of the costs charged to timber production also produced other things people wanted from the forests, such as recreation. A logging road built for timber production could be used by hikers and fishermen years later.

A January 1984 analysis by the Congressional Research Service (CRS) said, "The difficulties in accurately assessing the receipts, benefits, expenditures and costs make this issue exceptionally complex." The study pointed out that sales generated indirect receipts for the federal Treasury through the taxes paid by logging companies and their employees. Some harvests, it added, were intended to replace an aging, low-quality stand of trees with a vigorous new stand — increasing receipts far in the future. Other harvests were intended to thin out stands while they were growing, bringing some revenue immediately but also a future payoff. Still other sales were likely to help control insect and disease epidemics, reducing possible losses from nearby stands.

To get logs out of remote and often mountainous forests, new roads frequently were needed. Roughly a third of the total cost of an average Forest Service timber sale was spent on these roads, which become federal property. Environmentalists worried that too many roads were being built too fast into virgin forests. They said that logging roads could have harmful environmental impacts, especially when poorly sited, designed and built. One problem was a snowballing cycle of erosion that fills streams with silt and makes them useless for valuable fish such as salmon and steelhead.

But road building was in many cases the key factor that determined whether a forest area became commercial timberland or wilderness protected from logging. To qualify for consideration as a wilderness, a forest area in most cases had to be roadless. Once Congress designated an area as wilderness, road building was legally prohibited. Some environmentalists charged the Forest Service with plotting to push thousands of miles of new roads into roadless forest areas to forestall any future consideration of them as wilderness. But the Forest Service cited statistics showing declining road construction since the mid-1970s.

Critics in the Wilderness Society and elsewhere, however, said the real issue was not the total miles of road built but the mileage built into previously roadless areas.

when the president proposed a moratorium on further land acquisition by the Park Service, the Fish and Wildlife Service, the U.S. Forest Service and the Bureau of Reclamation, saying the government should concentrate on better maintenance and improvement of the lands it already had. For fiscal 1982-84, Congress had appropriated substantial funds for acquisition despite Reagan's opposition.

In the 1984 election year, the president proposed resuming park land purchases; Congress gave him far more than he asked for. In 1985, a post-election year, Reagan went back to his old moratorium proposal. He also halted a five-year park improvements program a year earlier than planned, for savings of $24.5 million.

8

Reagan's Judicial Legacy

Long after Ronald Reagan leaves the White House, the men and women he chose to serve as judges and justices will be interpreting the Constitution and applying the nation's laws. Reagan's judicial appointments could well be his most lasting legacy: laws can be repealed, and policies reversed, but appointees to federal judgeships serve for a lifetime.

Few were more keenly aware of this aspect of presidential power than Walter F. Mondale, Reagan's opponent in 1984, who had watched as vice president while Jimmy Carter transformed the federal judiciary with his appointment of a record number of liberal judges. Echoing the words of the Democratic platform, Mondale warned the nation that Reagan in a second term could reshape both the Supreme Court and the lower federal courts "not just for his own term — or even for the rest of his own lifetime — but for the rest of ours and for our children's."

Reagan's first term provided ample evidence of the way in which a president's use of the appointment power can affect the course of the courts. With the single nomination of Sandra Day O'Connor in 1981, Reagan shifted the balance of power within the Supreme Court. By choosing a committed conservative to replace a moderate justice who often swung between the liberal

and conservative sides on the court, Reagan created a strong conservative foursome able to attract at least the one more vote necessary to become a majority on most issues.

Influence of Federal Judgeships

President Carter did not have the opportunity to name a member of the Supreme Court — the first full-term president in history to be denied that chance — but he left behind him a large and influential corps of moderate-to-liberal federal judges. He appointed 262 federal judges, more than any president in history, primarily because Congress during his term approved creation of 152 new judgeships, which he filled. (In 1985 there were 571 federal district judges and 156 appeals court judges, a total of 727 posts.)

In 1984 the tension between federal appeals courts dominated by Carter appointees and the newly conservative Supreme Court was dramatically apparent in the frequency with which decisions of those appeals courts were overturned by the high court. But scarcely had that tension become clear before signs of its easing began to appear, as Reagan placed his own conservative judges on the bench.

In his first term Reagan appointed 166 new federal judges, most of them affluent white Republican men. Although he did not appoint as many women and Hispanic judges as Carter, he did place 16 women in lower court judgeships and eight Hispanics in judicial posts. He appointed only two black judges during his first term.

In the first year of his second term, Reagan might be asked to name another 100 federal judges, helped along by the 98th Congress, which approved legislation in 1984 creating 85 new posts. By the end of his fifth year in office, then, Reagan could have surpassed Carter's record number of appointments. Assuming all Carter's nominees were still in office, the 727 judicial posts would then be divided among 262 Carter appointees, 266 Reagan appointees and only 199 judges named by earlier presidents. By the end of his second term, it was plausible that Reagan would have replaced so many of those more senior federal judges that an absolute majority of the federal judges in the country would owe their posts to their Republican loyalties.

Although nominations to federal district and appeals court judgeships rarely draw much public attention, they are in many ways just as significant for the individual citizen as Supreme Court appointments. Federal district judges handle civil and criminal cases every day, affecting the lives of citizens far more directly than the nine Supreme Court justices. District court decisions are reviewed, if appealed, by the judges who sit on the 12 circuit courts of appeals. Most appeals court rulings are final. Only a fraction of them are reviewed by the Supreme Court.

The White House was careful to ensure that most of these nominees shared the administration's belief in judicial restraint, but the strength of the new judges' commitment was untested as of early 1985. Conservatives had tended to use "judicial activism" as a pejorative describing the tendency of the Warren court, above all, to reach out to expand the rights of underprivileged

groups and individuals. "Judicial restraint" was used as the antithesis of "judicial activism."

Conservative judges, however, could be just as activist in working to attain their ends as liberal judges, and it was not known whether Reagan's conservative judicial nominations would result in a diminished role for federal judges in setting the course for the nation. If it did, it would mark a sharp change from the decades after the historic 1954 decision of *Brown v. Board of Education,* when increasingly activist federal judges participated in the functions of other branches of the government to an unprecedented degree.

In the early 1960s federal judges began to monitor the operations of public school systems attempting to end racial segregation, supervise the administration of state prisons and mental institutions and participate in drawing new electoral maps for state legislatures and Congress.

Legacy of Power

Nowhere is the power of a president's judicial legacy greater than on the Supreme Court. In 1975, 30 years after the death of Franklin D. Roosevelt, one of his appointees, William O. Douglas, still sat on the U.S. Supreme Court. The existing court's most liberal member, William J. Brennan, was named to his seat in 1956 by President Dwight D. Eisenhower.

In his second term, Reagan could anticipate naming at least one — and perhaps as many as four — Supreme Court justices. Not since Eisenhower had one president named five justices. As Reagan was sworn in for his second term, five of the sitting justices were 75 years of age or older, well beyond the milestone of 70 — the average age at which death or serious illness had caused justices to leave the court in the 20th century.

A shift in the high court's philosophy

The members of the U.S. Supreme Court: from left to right, Harry A. Blackmun, Thurgood Marshall, William J. Brennan Jr., Chief Justice Warren E. Burger, Sandra Day O'Connor, Byron R. White, Lewis F. Powell Jr., William H. Rehnquist, and John Paul Stevens.

was long anticipated by certain conservatives. Richard Nixon campaigned against the liberal Supreme Court led by Chief Justice Earl Warren. Soon after he entered the White House in 1969, Nixon nominated an outspoken conservative appeals court judge, Warren E. Burger, as Warren's successor.

In the next three years, Nixon named three more conservative justices, Harry A. Blackmun, Lewis F. Powell Jr. and William H. Rehnquist, to replace retiring members of the Warren court. In 1975 President Gerald R. Ford chose John Paul Stevens, a moderate appeals court judge, to succeed Douglas, who retired in poor health.

By 1976, only four veterans of the Warren court still sat on the bench: Brennan, Potter Stewart, Byron R. White and Thurgood Marshall. Two of them — White and Stewart — had disagreed with some of the Warren court's major decisions.

Despite these changes the court of the 1970s continued in the path set by the Warren court, adhering to the letter, if not the spirit, of most of its major pronouncements. The anticipated shift to the right did

not come. Indeed, in some areas of the law, particularly in cases involving the rights of women, the court of the 1970s went far beyond the court of the 1960s.

In his 1983 book, *The Burger Court: The Counter-Revolution That Wasn't,* former Supreme Court reporter and *New York Times* columnist Anthony Lewis wrote: "There has been nothing like a counter-revolution," during the 1970s. "It is fair to say, in fact, that the reach of earlier decisions on racial equality and the First Amendment has been enlarged. Even the most hotly debated criminal law decision, *Miranda,* stands essentially unmodified." But, even as the book was being printed, the counter-revolution was under way. In the 1983-84 Supreme Court term, the conservative core of the court took control.

By mid-1984 the court had voted to modify the landmark *Miranda* decision, to open substantial holes in the wall between church and state, to amend the rule denying prosecutors use of illegally obtained evidence and to limit the power of federal judges to use affirmative action in remedying past discrimination. The Supreme Court

The Justices

After Potter Stewart's retirement and Sandra Day O'Connor's confirmation, the court's membership was unchanged for the rest of Reagan's first term. By 1984 it was one of the oldest courts in history; the average age of the justices was 70.

Reagan, re-elected at age 73, could look to the court and see five justices who were his seniors. No one gave any sign of considering retirement.

The members of the court during this period were:

Chief Justice Warren E. Burger, named to that post by President Nixon. Burger, born in 1907, marked his 15th anniversary as chief justice in June 1984.

Justice William J. Brennan Jr., born in 1906, appointed by President Eisenhower in 1956.

Justice Byron R. White, born in 1915, appointed by President Kennedy in 1962.

Justice Thurgood Marshall, born in 1908, appointed by President Johnson in 1967.

Justice Harry A. Blackmun, born in 1908, appointed by President Nixon in 1970.

Justice Lewis F. Powell Jr., born in 1907, appointed by President Nixon in 1971.

Justice William H. Rehnquist, born in 1924, appointed by President Nixon in 1971.

Justice John Paul Stevens, born in 1920, appointed by President Ford in 1975.

Justice Sandra Day O'Connor, born in 1930, appointed by President Reagan in 1981.

seemed to have moved into a posture of committed conservative restraint.

When Bruce Fein, a close observer of the Supreme Court and a former general counsel of the Federal Communications Commission in the Reagan administration, was asked what had prompted the long-awaited counter-revolution to arrive, he answered succinctly: "Sandra Day O'Connor!"

Stewart: Man in the Middle

O'Connor's impact on the court was due in part to the character of the man she replaced, Potter Stewart, in part to her own background, beliefs and abilities and in part to the same shift in public perceptions and values that had placed Ronald Reagan in the White House for two terms.

There were only two firm alliances within the Supreme Court during the last half of the 1970s. Chief Justice Burger and Justice Rehnquist almost always voted together on the conservative side of an issue; they were almost always counter-balanced by Justices Brennan and Marshall, who came down just as regularly on the liberal side.

The power at the court lay somewhere in the middle, with the five other justices — Stewart, White, Blackmun, Powell and Stevens. Whichever side won three of their votes became a majority — sometimes the liberals won, sometimes the conservatives, and sometimes there was so much disagreement within the court that it was difficult to know who had prevailed. Even when the justices agreed on how to decide a particular case, they frequently disagreed on why.

Early in 1981 the *Harvard Law Review* noted that since Chief Justice Burger arrived at the court in 1969, there had been more plurality opinions — opinions on which fewer than five justices agreed — than there had been in the entire previous history of the court. This meant that the justices could not agree on the reason for the decision, leaving unclear guidelines for those (police officers, for example) who must act on the decision. In six of the cases argued and decided with full opinion in the 1980-1981 term, Potter Stewart's last, a majority of the court failed to agree on the reasoning for the court's eventual decision. Frequently the court was described as *fragmented, splintered* or *leaderless.*

Throughout his 23-year career on the court, Stewart was a "swing vote," the "man in the middle" between the staunch liberals and the firm conservatives. His position on capital punishment illustrates this stance. When the court in 1972 held that virtually every capital punishment statute in the country was unconstitutional because it allowed judges and juries far too much discretion in deciding upon whom to impose this ultimate sentence, Stewart agreed. His description of the court's reasoning was most often quoted. He explained that the laws at issue allowed such random imposition of the sentence of death that capital punishment thus imposed became "cruel and unusual in the same way that being struck by lightning is cruel and unusual."

Four years later, however, as the court upheld some of the modernized death penalty laws enacted by states in the wake of the earlier decision, it was Stewart who set out the court's view that the Constitution permits capital punishment, that "the punishment of death does not invariably violate the Constitution."

O'Connor: A Different Justice

O'Connor, a woman of practical experience and firmly held beliefs, did not take Stewart's place as a swing vote. From the first, she allied herself with Burger and Rehnquist, forming a trio that demonstrated a steadily increasing attraction for Powell, White and Blackmun.

Before coming to the court, O'Connor had served in all three branches of state government. After several years as an assistant attorney general in Arizona, she was appointed and then elected to the state senate, where she became majority leader. In 1974 she moved into the judicial branch, becoming a superior court judge and in 1979 a judge on the state court of appeals. Both the political skills honed in those years and the practical knowledge gained from such close association with the everyday workings of state government were commodities in short supply on the U.S. Supreme Court.

From her own experience, O'Connor was well aware of the difficulties faced by police, lawyers and judges when they try to comply with confusing and unclear directives from the nation's highest court. The men whom O'Connor joined on that bench all had been federal judges for at least a decade, independent of and isolated from the give-and-take of political debate. None of them could match the variety of government experience that O'Connor had enjoyed in a relatively short period of time.

And there was the generation difference. The court that O'Connor joined at age 51 was a panel of aging veterans, most of them old enough to be her father.

Although the extent of O'Connor's influence was impossible to measure, her arrival at the court clearly set off a realignment among the justices. Stevens voted more and more with Brennan and Marshall on the liberal side of a case, while Powell, with even more regularity, joined Burger, Rehnquist and O'Connor in a conservative foursome. Only White and Blackmun continued to function as swing men.

In the 1983-84 term, both White and Blackmun tended to side with the conservatives far more often than with the liberals. In 1983 White joined the liberals on one of every three closely contested issues, but by 1984 he was voting with them on only one of every four. Blackmun voted with the liberals twice as often in 1983 as he did in 1984.

Reagan Victories

This realignment within the court produced a remarkable string of conservative decisions in 1984. The court that in 1983 flatly rejected the Reagan administration's arguments for change in its position on controversial issues such as abortion and tax breaks for discriminatory private schools now endorsed White House arguments limiting affirmative action, relaxing federal regulation of business and enhancing the role of religion in American life.

This turnabout in the administration's fortunes came about in part because of a change in the issues and in part because of the administration's care in tailoring its arguments to the views of the court. In 1983 the solicitor general was asking the court to approve major changes in settled areas of law and public policy, changes sought primarily by conservative activists or big business. In 1984 the administration took its stand on less explosive issues, endorsing positions supported by a broader constituency in the nation at large.

The solicitor general emphasized, in every possible context, the belief that Reagan shared with a majority of the justices — that the role of the federal judiciary was a limited one, that judges should leave policy making to the political branches of the government. Rarely did the administration challenge a Warren Court precedent head-on. Instead it argued that the primary reason for those rulings had been attained — that church and state were clearly separate, that police and prosecutors now routinely acted to guarantee the rights of criminal suspects. The administration argued that some lower court judges, however, were taking these precedents one step too far — and that the court should halt that trend.

The theme of judicial restraint was a popular one, and the justices joined right in with the tune. Time and again the nation's most powerful judges curtailed the author-

ity of other federal judges to enforce federal and state laws, insisting that the judiciary defer to the "political" branches of the government.

"Federal judges — who have no constituency — have a duty to respect legitimate policy choices made by those who do," the court declared in a clean air dispute resolved late in June 1984. A few days later, as the court backed the administration's power to limit travel to Cuba, it reiterated the statement of an earlier court that foreign relations were "so exclusively entrusted to the political branches of government as to be largely immune from judicial inquiry or interference."

Many of these victories came at the expense of federal appeals court judges who saw their rulings emphatically reversed and often vigorously criticized by the Supreme Court.

Judicial Tension

Politicians have always assumed — and lawyers have always denied — that Democratic presidents appoint liberal federal judges and Republicans, conservative ones. The tension that emerged in 1984 between the Supreme Court and several federal courts of appeals seemed to validate the political assumption.

President Carter appointed 56 of the 121 active judges on the nation's 12 courts of appeals. He chose moderate to liberal judges, among them more blacks (38), more women (40) and more Hispanics (16) than had ever before served on the federal bench.

After O'Connor joined the Supreme Court in 1981, seven of the nine sitting justices had been named by Republican presidents. Only White and Marshall had been appointed by Democrats.

In the 1983-84 term, the Supreme Court reversed two of every three lower court rulings it reviewed, most of which came from the federal appeals courts —

where a majority of the judges had been named by Democratic presidents. Time and again in 1984, the court replaced a lower court's liberal reading of the Constitution or the laws with its own more conservative views.

The worst win-loss records before the court in that term were those of the U.S. Court of Appeals for the District of Columbia and the 9th U.S. Circuit Court of Appeals. The latter is based in San Francisco and hears appeals from nine Western states plus Guam and the Northern Mariana Islands. On both these courts, judges appointed by Democratic presidents decisively outnumbered Republican nominees.

The Supreme Court reversed every one of the eight decisions it reviewed from the U.S. Court of Appeals in the District of Columbia. Long a bastion of liberalism — and the one on which Chief Justice Burger had served, usually in dissent, before moving to the Supreme Court — the District Court of Appeals was composed of 11 judges, seven named by Democratic presidents.

A similar pattern of reversals was seen in the 9th Circuit Court, the nation's largest with 23 judges. Twenty-seven of this court's decisions were reviewed fully by the Supreme Court; 23 were reversed outright; only one was upheld without qualification. Until late 1984, 16 of the 23 judges on the 9th Circuit bench were placed there by Democratic presidents, all but one chosen by Jimmy Carter.

A similar, but less striking, correlation appeared when one examined the reversal rates of appeals courts on which there were more Republican than Democratic appointees. A prime example was the 7th U.S. Circuit Court of Appeals, composed of two Democratic appointees and seven Republican ones. The Supreme Court reviewed five of this court's decisions in 1984, and it affirmed three.

Tipping the Balance

By the end of his first term, Reagan had named 31 appeals court judges. But in 1985 he was to fill at least 24 more appeals court seats, thanks to the 1984 law creating that many more new appellate judgeships.

As of September 1983, 70 Democratic appointees and 58 Republican selections sat on the nation's appeals courts. The addition of 24 more Reagan nominees would tip the overall balance decisively and could have a definite impact on the character of several of the individual circuit courts.

Once again the U.S. Court of Appeals for the District of Columbia Circuit provided a clear example of the impact of carefully selected judicial nominees. As of January 1985 that court consisted of 12 seats, including one newly created and still vacant seat. The 11 judges included two named by President Lyndon B. Johnson, one named by President John F. Kennedy, and four named by President Carter — for a total of seven Democratic appointees.

One Nixon appointee sat on that court — and three chosen by President Reagan. Two of these three ranked high on the list of possible Reagan selections for the Supreme Court: Robert H. Bork and Antonin Scalia. Already their votes and their views, along with those of Kenneth W. Starr, Reagan's other selection for that court, have sufficiently diluted its unmitigated liberalism so that it no longer was considered the nation's most liberal appeals court, a reputation it had enjoyed for several decades.

Precedent: The Judicial Brake

Despite the opportunity for President Reagan to appoint a dramatic number of new federal judges to his liking, a major brake on any sudden changes in the nation's law by these judges was their general reverence for precedent, or established law. This element, often referred to as the doctrine of *stare decisis* (let the decision stand), was in the view of Anthony Lewis one major reason that there was no judicial counter-revolution in the 1970s.

"Conservative judges — meaning those who are more cautious in lawmaking — are naturally committed to the doctrine of *stare decisis*. It follows logically that they should respect a precedent once established, even though they opposed that result during the process of decision," writes Lewis.

Only "a few judges today are prepared to break boldly — radically — from prevailing constitutional doctrines," Lewis continued. But one, William Rehnquist, was sitting on the Supreme Court. "Rehnquist really goes back to first premises in his opinions and is willing to rethink doctrines in terms of a personal constitutional ideology," Lewis observed. He could be joined by others on the court who were "as ready as he is to uproot established doctrine," Lewis wrote.

But Sandra Day O'Connor was not one of those. When the Supreme Court in 1984 approved the first exception to the 1966 Miranda rule, which said that police and prosecutors may not use evidence obtained from the suspect before he was warned of his rights, O'Connor criticized the majority's view: "Were the Court writing from a clean slate, I could agree with its holding. But *Miranda* is now the law and, in my view, the Court has not provided sufficient justification for departing from it or for blurring its now clear strictures."

And so even among the conservatives on the court, there was tension produced by differing views of the importance of maintaining stability and preserving precedent. So long as the conservatives had to remain unified to prevail as a majority, this tension would be dormant on most issues. If the conservative majority became larger, it would not be unlikely for an open split to develop within it.

In 1984 the court's conservative trend was evident in decisions concerning the rights of the accused, separation of church and state, states' rights and abortion.

Crime, Church and State

Throughout the 1970s the court demonstrated an increasing receptiveness to the arguments of police and prosecutors on questions of criminal law. That trend accelerated in the early 1980s. In 1984 the justices approved three major exceptions to Warren Court rules that had been unamended for almost two decades. In each case the Reagan administration backed the exceptions approved by the court.

In a 5-4 decision, the court allowed a "public safety" exception to the *Miranda* rule, permitting police to ask a suspect a question — "Where's the gun?" — in the interest of protecting the other people in the area, before they advised him of his rights.

The court also approved two exceptions to the much-criticized exclusionary rule denying state prosecutors the use of evidence that police had obtained in violation of a suspect's constitutional rights. In 1984 the court, 7-2, permitted use of such evidence if it inevitably would have been discovered anyway — or, in a 6-3 decision, if it was obtained by police acting in "good faith." In 1985, the court was being watched closely for any sign that it intended to enlarge these exceptions, particularly the good faith exception to the exclusionary rule.

In its 1984 decision the court seemed to confine that exception to situations in which police conducted a search with a warrant that they believed was valid but, through a technicality, turned out to be invalid. Whether the court was willing to apply this sort of exception to a search not authorized by any warrant was a question of great concern to those involved in criminal justice.

Criminal cases always constitute the largest single category on the court's argument schedule, but in the early 1980s the number of First Amendment cases — free speech, free expression, freedom of the press, freedom of religion — multiplied noticeably. In the 1984-85 term, better than one case in 10 argued before the court involved the First Amendment.

A dramatic shift in the court's view of the proper relationship between church and state occurred in the early 1980s. The Warren Court, which forbade prescribed school prayer and many varieties of state aid to parochial schools, emphasized the wall of separation that the First Amendment erected between church and state.

That wall stood relatively unbreached through the 1970s. But in the 1980s the court approved the historic practice of opening legislative sessions with prayer, a state's provision of an income tax deduction for parochial school tuition and the right of student religious groups to conduct meetings on state university property.

Early in 1984 the court declared that the First Amendment required "accommodation" — not "separation" — of the interests of religion and government. That announcement, which came as the court permitted city officials to include a nativity scene in a holiday display, seemed to herald a new era in the application of the First Amendment's guarantees of religious freedom.

In 1985 the court had ample opportunity to expand on its new doctrine of accommodation. For the first time in more than 20 years, the court was expected to decide a case concerning prayer in public schools. From Alabama came the case of *Wallace v. Jaffree*, which called for the justices to decide whether the First Amendment was offended by a state law permitting a moment of silence for meditation or silent prayer in state public school classrooms each school day. The Reagan administration urged the court to permit this sort of "moment of silence" law as an appropriate

accommodation of religious interests in American life.

The court was also to decide whether the same First Amendment that permitted the use of a crèche in a city holiday display required city officials to permit a citizens' group to erect a crèche in a city park during the Christmas season.

States' Rights, Abortion

In two other areas the court's strong conservative voices, Rehnquist and O'Connor, put the majority on notice that change could be just around the corner. In February 1985 the court divided 5-4 to overturn a 1976 decision (also reached 5-4) and declare that nothing in the Constitution specifically limited the power of Congress to tread on state's rights in exercising its broad power to regulate commerce.

In *Garcia v. San Antonio Metropolitan Transit Authority*, the court applied federal minimum wage law to employees of state and local governments. Nine years earlier, the court had found this an impermissible intrusion into state affairs. In dissent Rehnquist and O'Connor each took the extraordinary step of declaring their confidence (as the youngest members of the court) that this decision too would be overturned soon and that the court would once again limit the power of Congress to interfere in state affairs.

O'Connor's views on abortion were the subject of intense but unproductive scrutiny during her confirmation hearings in 1981. Less than two years later, when the court reaffirmed its commitment to *Roe v. Wade*, its 1973 decision denying states the power to ban abortion as criminal, O'Connor dissented. She pointed out for the first time from the high court bench a major logical flaw in *Roe v. Wade*, which the majority would have to mend if it was to preserve the principle of that ruling.

In *Roe v. Wade* the court held that states could ban abortions performed late in pregnancy, after the point at which the fetus was "viable" — that is, it could survive outside the womb. As medical science steadily advanced, it became possible to keep alive infants born earlier and earlier in a pregnancy, O'Connor pointed out. Unless the court restructured the logic supporting *Roe v. Wade,* states would be able to ban abortion earlier and earlier in pregnancy, effectively negating the right of choice that *Roe v. Wade* had provided women.

9

Cabinet Profiles

In selecting the Cabinet secretaries for his second administration, Ronald Reagan adhered to the dictum "if it ain't broke, don't fix it." For the most part, his new Cabinet was made up of men and women who had been in office since 1981 or who had replaced the original members months or years earlier.

This relative stability contrasted vividly with Jimmy Carter's mid-term Cabinet shuffle. Following a widely praised July 1979 televised address in which Carter decried America's "crisis of confidence," the president accepted the resignations of five Cabinet secretaries — and it was evident that three were leaving at his direction. Carter's successor, however, reportedly disliked firing anyone and did so during his first four years only with great reluctance.

As Reagan began his second term, six of his original Cabinet-level appointees remained in the same job: John R. Block, Agriculture; Malcolm Baldrige, Commerce; Caspar W. Weinberger, Defense; Samuel R. Pierce Jr., Housing and Urban Development; William J. Casey, Central Intelligence; and David A. Stockman, Office of Management and Budget.

Several other members of the first-draft team stayed on but in different positions. The president announced in January 1985 that Treasury Secretary Donald T.

Regan would switch jobs with trusted White House chief of staff James A. Baker III. And to succeed Labor Secretary Raymond J. Donovan, who resigned in March 1985 to stand trial on charges of larceny and fraud, President Reagan nominated William E. Brock III, U.S. trade representative since 1981.

Several of Reagan's first appointees left his administration to take new jobs. Energy Secretary James B. Edwards departed Washington in November 1982 to become president of the Medical University of South Carolina, leaving behind him the department he had promised to dismantle. Edwards never intended to stay the full four-year term, hoping instead that Congress would approve the department's demise. Reagan replaced Edwards with Donald P. Hodel, under secretary of the interior.

In late 1982 Transportation Secretary Drew Lewis, who was widely regarded as one of Reagan's most able Cabinet members, resigned to become chief executive officer of Warner Amex Cable Communications Inc. The first woman to head a Cabinet department in the Reagan administration, Elizabeth Hanford Dole, succeeded Lewis. Richard Schweiker, who had the tough job of secretary of health and human services in a time of budgetary restraint, resigned in January 1983. His stated reason for leaving was to become president of the American Council of Life Insurance. President Reagan's second woman Cabinet appointee, former representative Margaret M. Heckler, R-Mass., took over the sprawling department from Schweiker.

Jeane J. Kirkpatrick, who had served with Cabinet rank as Reagan's United Nations representative since January 1981, left her post as Reagan's second term began to return to teaching at Georgetown University in Washington, D.C. Kirkpatrick reportedly wanted another foreign policy job with the administration, but none was offered. Vernon A. Walters succeeded her.

While some appointees left their posts voluntarily, others departed or worked under a cloud of controversy. Reagan somehow managed to remain aloof from most of these problems, giving rise to the nickname, "Teflon president." Troubles did not seem to stick to him.

Alexander M. Haig Jr., who abruptly resigned as secretary of state on June 25, 1982, was the first to leave under fire. The volatile Haig had come under increasing criticism from some high administration officials, including Defense Secretary Weinberger, over various foreign policy issues. Haig was succeeded by George P. Shultz, an economist, business executive, and veteran Cabinet official.

Interior Secretary James G. Watt resigned on Oct. 9, 1983, thereby avoiding an almost surefire no-confidence vote in the Senate because of his abrasive style and unpopular natural resource policies. Several Democrats forced a delay in the confirmation of William P. Clark as Watt's successor, because of concern over administration policies under Watt rather than doubts about Clark's qualificiations.

In October 1984 Labor Secretary Donovan became the first incumbent Cabinet officer to be indicted on criminal charges. Donovan asserted he was innocent of the charges concerning financial dealings of his construction company before he joined the Cabinet. Nevertheless, he resigned his post March 15, 1985, to stand trial.

Reagan's longtime confidant and adviser, Edwin Meese III, who had been counselor to the president during the first administration, ran into trouble when he was appointed by Reagan to head the Justice Department. Only after a 13-month wait — longer than for any other Cabinet nominee in recent history — was Meese confirmed by the Senate as attorney general on Feb. 23, 1985. He was first nominated in January 1984 to succeed William French Smith, who wanted to return to private law practice in California. Meese's confirmation ran into a snag when questions arose about some of his personal financial transactions. The controversy centered on whether Meese helped get federal jobs for people who provided him financial assistance.

Below the Cabinet level, Reagan encountered other setbacks among the team he pulled together to run the government. The Environmental Protection Agency (EPA) suffered a major scandal in 1983 over the misuse of "Superfund," leading to the resignation of administrator Anne Gorsuch Burford and the return of the first EPA administrator, William D. Ruckelshaus. The well-respected Ruckelshaus, who was expected to help restore integrity to the agency, was unanimously confirmed.

The long-planned change of command at the Justice Department was one of several top-level job shuffles that occurred as President Reagan began his second term:

● The administration announced that Energy Secretary Hodel would replace Interior Secretary Clark, who said he wanted to return to his California ranch. John S. Herrington, White House personnel director, was to succeed Hodel.

● The president nominated William J. Bennett, chairman of the National Endowment for the Humanities, to succeed Education Secretary Terrel H. Bell, who resigned Dec. 31, 1984.

● Ruckelshaus resigned as EPA administrator, and Reagan nominated Lee M. Thomas, a top Ruckelshaus assistant, to succeed him.

Following are profiles of the Cabinet-level appointees as of April 8, 1985:

James A. Baker III
(Treasury Secretary)

Secretary of the Treasury James A. Baker III, former White House chief of staff, was the first new Cabinet member to be confirmed by Congress after President Reagan began his second term. The Senate vote was unanimous, 95-0. Baker replaced Donald T. Regan, who left Treasury to take over Baker's White House job.

The job exchange was generally well received on Capitol Hill. Republicans saw it as reinvigorating the administration for the president's second term, and Democrats anticipated little change in policies.

During his four years as a crucial player in backroom negotiations with Congress, Baker had earned a reputation for legislative expertise that often forged political compromises needed to enact administration policies. He had been especially useful as a bridge between a sometimes ideological president and House and Senate Republicans trying to win a majority of votes in a diverse, two-party Congress.

As the manager of campaigns for President Gerald R. Ford and Vice President George Bush, Baker also had built a reputation as a keen political strategist. And he had won congressional admiration since 1981 for his willingness to negotiate with Democrats and Republicans alike. These skills were expected to be put to the test in anticipated battles over reduction of the federal deficit and simplification of the tax code.

Early Life

Baker, 54 at the time of his appointment, had spent most of his professional life as a corporate attorney in Houston. He graduated from Princeton University in 1952 and received his law degree from the University of Texas Law School in 1957, after spending two years in the Marine Corps.

In 1970 Baker began a long political relationship with his Texas friend George Bush by helping to manage Bush's unsuccessful bid for a U.S. Senate seat. Baker first worked in national politics as a deputy chairman of President Ford's 1976 election campaign. In 1978 he launched a losing bid for the GOP nomination for Texas attorney general, and in 1980 he was campaign chairman for Bush until Bush dropped out of the race for the Republican presidential nomination.

Baker worked for the Reagan-Bush campaign and, in November 1980, was named Reagan's chief of staff, a move that stunned partisans who had questioned Baker's conservative credentials. While Baker had his differences with conservatives during Reagan's first term — especially because of his willingness to compromise with those on Capitol Hill — he continued to have the backing of the conservative who mattered most, President Reagan.

Outlook for Treasury

As an experienced corporate lawyer and a veteran of the Commerce Department during the Ford administration, Baker was expected to bring a useful mix of talent and expertise to his Treasury post. He was a proven gambler, whose victories had reached across political ideologies to form a popular consensus.

Although he had no economics degree, Baker had decided attitudes toward what may be the crucial issue during Reagan's second term — the federal deficit. He had often endorsed an across-the-board budget freeze, only to see the president side with Defense Secretary Caspar W. Weinberger in sparing deep cuts in the military budget.

He also was likely, according to close friends, to work for low interest rates, which he saw as a way toward economic growth. He was said to support the idea of simplifying the tax code but reject the Treasury Department's proposal to eliminate special depreciation and investment tax credits the existing code allowed business.

When during his confirmation hearings committee members expressed doubts about the feasibility of the Treasury tax reform proposal, Baker repeatedly told the senators that the plan would be changed and that it was only a starting point toward that simplification.

Other than that, Baker gave few concrete details about his intentions toward the deficit, tax simplification or interest rates. But he was clear on two points: that President Reagan's priorities would be deficit reduction and tax simplification and that his views on those areas would be those of the president's. Beyond that, he was likely to remain the pragmatist, building consensus and working behind the scenes to get the president's programs across.

Malcolm Baldrige
(Commerce Secretary)

President Reagan's secretary of commerce, Malcolm Baldrige, a survivor from Reagan's original Cabinet, was equally at home in a corporate suite or in the saddle. A successful businessman — the chairman of the board and chief executive officer of Scovill Inc. of Waterbury, Conn., and a board member of several other companies — Baldrige also was a member of the Professional Rodeo Cowboys Association and a prize-winning steer roper. The non-controversial nominee had been confirmed by the Senate 97-1.

Although not well known in Washington in 1981, Baldrige was widely respected in business circles and had strong Republican Party credentials. In 1980 he was chairman of the Bush for President Committee in Connecticut, one of the few states Bush won over Reagan.

Baldrige was credited with launching Scovill, formerly a brass manufacturing concern, on an ambitious program of product expansion and diversification that transformed it into a "mini-conglomerate" with sales of $941.6 million in 1979, according to Scovill board member Robert Kilpatrick. The manufacturing company included well-known trade names such as Hamilton Beach appliances and Yale locks.

Decentralized Management

At the time of his selection, Baldrige said his management style was "very uncluttered and decentralized, with accountability as well as authority shared down to the lowest level."

Friends and associates said businessman Baldrige showed a willingness to make difficult decisions and a dogged determination to chip away at tough problems. They cited his ability to take a hard look at some of Scovill's less profitable ventures and to divest the company of them.

During Reagan's first term, Baldrige was credited with keeping the peace with other Cabinet members, namely U.S. Trade Representative Bill Brock, where touchy turf struggles could have ignited. To avoid this, Brock and Baldrige instituted a system of having one overlapping interagency committee feed into another. This helped eliminate much of the procedural haggling on which traditional Washington thrives.

An often-silent member of a bipartisan working group of members of Congress and administration officials appointed by the president to study the deficit problem during 1984, Baldrige went along with the president by saying that the way to cut the deficits was to reduce expenditures not raise taxes.

He said that the extraordinarily high level of business cash flow, particularly during 1984, and the budget surpluses of the states and municipalities could help prevent federal borrowing from crowding out private credit needs — a threat particularly strong to small businesses.

According to congressional sources, Baldrige faltered in legislative affairs — particularly in failing to get House action on an export trading company bill.

GOP, Midwestern Roots

Baldrige's roots in the Republican Party went back to his father, H. Malcolm Baldrige, who was a Republican House member from Nebraska in 1931-33.

Baldrige himself was very active in party politics. A delegate to the Republican National Convention in 1968, 1972 and 1976, Baldrige was Connecticut co-chairman of United Citizens for Nixon-Agnew. He also was a member of the National Republican Finance Committee.

Despite his Connecticut base, Baldrige had strong ties to the Midwest. Born in Omaha Oct. 4, 1922, Baldrige worked on a Nebraska ranch during the summers. He traveled East to attend the Hotchkiss School in Connecticut and Yale University, where he was graduated in 1944.

After serving in the Army in World War II, Baldrige joined Eastern Co. as a foundry foreman, rising to become president in 1960.

He left Eastern to join Scovill as executive vice president in 1962, becoming president and chief executive officer in 1963 and chairman and chief executive officer in 1969.

Besides his direction of Scovill, Baldrige was a director of AMF Inc., IBM Inc., Bendix Corp., Connecticut Mutual Life Insurance Co., Eastern Co. and Uniroyal Inc.

William J. Bennett
(Education Secretary)

Forced by Congress to live with an Education Department he would have liked to abolish, President Reagan named William J. Bennett to the agency's top post. Bennett succeeded Terrel H. Bell, who officially left the Cabinet on Dec. 31, 1984, after a tenure marked by frequent criticism.

Bell's departure was welcomed by many of the administration's conservatives, who charged that he had not pursued with enough vigor key items on Reagan's agenda, including tuition tax credits and abolition of the department. Such critics were generally pleased by Bennett's selection.

In announcing Bennett's nomination, a White House spokesman said Reagan had asked for a new study of the future of the Education Department. At Bell's recommendation, Reagan in 1982 had proposed downgrading the department into a federal education foundation but the idea was ignored by Congress.

Bennett, former chairman of the National Endowment for the Humanities (NEH), had been an outspoken advocate of improving educational quality and revitalizing the traditional humanities curriculum in schools and colleges.

"He has the capacity to be a great secretary of education," said Sen. Edward M. Kennedy, D-Mass., "and the times demand that we have the best." But Sen. Paul Simon, D-Ill., voiced concern that Bennett would not be a strong advocate within the administration for education spending, as Bell had been.

After assurances from President Reagan that he would not seek abolishment of the Education Department, the Senate unanimously confirmed Bennett on Feb. 6, 1985.

Champion of the Humanities

Before becoming chairman of the NEH in 1982, Bennett, 41 at the time of his appointment, was president of the National Humanities Center in North Carolina. He earlier had taught philosophy and law at a number of universities. A graduate of Williams College in Massachusetts, he received a law degree from Harvard Law School and a doctorate in philosophy from the University of Texas at Austin.

At the NEH, he emphasized the traditional core of humanities study in literature, history, the classics and philosophy. In November 1984 Bennett issued a report on the liberal arts that aired his deep disenchantment with college humanities teaching, which he said left too many students "lacking even the most rudimentary knowledge about the history, literature, art and philosophical foundations of their nation and civilization."

Bennett's policies at the NEH had been applauded by intellectuals and educators who favored a return to the academic basics. But some critics saw Bennett's views as reflecting a trend toward elitism, and they voiced concern that the endowment had given short shrift to newer academic fields such as women's studies and black studies.

Philosophical Biases

Questions during Bennett's confirmation hearing focused largely on his views on civil rights and on the administration's expected proposals to curb sharply federal aid to middle-class college students.

In his opening statement, Bennett committed himself to "full enforcement" of civil rights and other laws administered by the Education Department. "At the same time, I will make every effort to prevent the department from being needlessly meddlesome or intrusive," Bennett added.

He restated his much-publicized opposition to the use of hiring quotas and preferential treatment to advance women and minorities. Bennett cited that conviction when he refused in 1984 to submit a report on NEH hiring goals required of all federal agencies by the Equal Employment Opportunity Commission. "I do not think we should count by race," Bennett said. "We should move to a colorblind society."

Soon after Bennett's confirmation, a controversy erupted over cuts in federal aid for college students. At a news conference Feb. 11, the newly installed education secretary added fuel to the fire by saying some students could cope with federal aid cuts by simply forgoing luxuries such as stereos, cars and vacations. Critics charged that his remarks showed disdain for students and insensitivity to the financial circumstances of federal aid recipients. Bennett maintained that the federal government should give priority to the neediest students, and he questioned if there was a further federal responsibility to help students pay for the college of their choice regardless of its cost.

John R. Block
(Agriculture Secretary)

During Reagan's first term, the Illinois farmer and state official chosen to be secretary of agriculture was forced to grapple quickly with the need to balance the perennial demand of farmers for higher price supports against pressures from budget-conscious Reagan economic advisers to cut farm credit and other federal subsidy programs.

John R. Block described himself as a "free market man" who believed high prices for farm goods — not price supports — were the best guarantee of high farm income. He said during his confirmation hearings in 1981 that he felt food was a "valuable tool" to "promote greater stability in the world . . . and peace." But he said he would be "very reluctant" to impose any embargo because, in "turning the faucet on and off, we will fail in our effort to create better relations with other countries."

Major farm groups and the National

Governors Association said Block had been unusually able and aggressive in his former post as director of the Illinois Department of Agriculture. The governors' group and Sen. Robert Dole, R-Kan., strongly backed Block's nomination.

Understands Farmers' Problems

Block, 49, often said he understood farmers' problems because he was a farmer himself. In Senate testimony in 1984 he said that high interest borrowing, along with a drop in farm land values and other farm-economy difficulties, had been responsible for the squeeze felt by many small farmers.

In fact, Block, who owned 3,000 acres of mostly hog and corn farms in Illinois and other jointly owned farm land in Illinois and Minnesota, admitted owing $8 million in 1984 on his properties. He had had to use his equity in 940 acres of farm land in southeast Minnesota to help underpin some loans made from the First National Bank of Minneapolis. Block also was forced to sever ties in 1985 with an Illinois business partner whose financial problems may have posed a threat to Block's farming business.

Block's private problems came to light as the agriculture secretary was outlining the Reagan administration's controversial farm bill in January 1985. The basic federal farm law, the Food and Agriculture Act of 1981, which was to expire in October 1985, was up for revision and faced a divisive struggle in Congress because few members could agree on when and who should make sacrifices called for in the administration's proposal.

The administration's primary aim, Block said, was to create a safety net of supports for farmers that would be based on free market prices, rather than on government estimates of the cost of producing a crop. But the administration's proposals, coming from a farm recession, were expected to face stiff opposition from members of farm states and other lobbyists.

Farm Policy Background

Block, a 1957 graduate of the U.S. Military Academy at West Point, left the Army in 1960 to take over his family's farm near Galesburg, Ill. He expanded it to 3,000 acres from 300, raised hogs and soybeans and was a former board member of the Illinois Farm Bureau. When Block was appointed state agriculture director in 1977 he was a strong advocate of revisions in Illinois' conservation law. The program he drew up was voluntary and relied on financial incentives to reward farmers for protecting land from erosion. It had fewer "teeth" than environmental groups would have liked, but one Illinois Farm Bureau representative praised it as a good start on a serious problem.

Block also played a major role in setting up a 1980 state conference on the problem of conversion of prime farm land to non-farm uses such as shopping centers or industrial development. After the conference, Illinois governor James R. Thompson ordered state agencies to evaluate the impact of their actions on farm land use.

Block also pushed for development of state trade promotion offices abroad to act as "middlemen" for sales of Illinois farm products and the production of gasohol. A physical fitness buff, Block had competed in the Boston Marathon.

William E. Brock III
(Labor Secretary)

In a move that could help repair frayed White House ties with organized labor, President Reagan nominated William E. Brock III, U.S. trade representative, to be secretary of labor. The Senate unanimously confirmed the nomination in April 1985. During hearings, Brock stated that his top priorities would include job creation through economic growth. He succeeded Raymond J. Donovan, who resigned March 15 to stand trial.

While Donovan came to the Cabinet in 1981 an unknown in Washington circles, Brock's credentials included 14 years in Congress and a successful stint as chairman of the Republican National Committee. The nomination drew praise from both business and labor, including some union officials whose relations with the Reagan administration had been in the deep freeze.

"While we have not always agreed [with Brock], he has earned our respect," said AFL-CIO President Lane Kirkland. "We look forward to a new and constructive relationship with the Labor Department."

Filling the Void

President Reagan moved quickly to fill the top Labor post, which was vacated by Donovan after a New York Supreme Court judge refused to dismiss charges concerning financial dealings of his construction company before he joined the Cabinet. Donovan took a leave from his post after he and some of his former business associates were indicted in October 1984.

Throughout Donovan's tenure, the Labor Department's budget cuts and allegedly lax enforcement of labor laws came under steady criticism from union officials, most of whom opposed Reagan's re-election in 1984. Speaking of tensions between the White House and labor, Brock told reporters, "We've had some very difficult times and we have a lot of communicating to do. But that's precisely what I would like to do."

While Brock was not expected to bring a shift in labor policies, one union lobbyist said, "He's the best you can hope for. There's a feeling that at least there will be more of an open door at the Labor Department."

Trade Job

Brock's departure from the trade representative's office came at a time when many of his efforts to strengthen the agency and the administration's trade powers were falling into place. He won new authority in 1984 to negotiate pacts to lift trade restraints between the United States and other nations. The first such agreement, with Israel, was submitted to Congress in early 1985.

He also helped defeat efforts within the administration to create a Department of Trade, which would have combined parts of Brock's office and the Department of Commerce.

Key to these victories was a strong working relationship with lawmakers such as Senate Majority Leader Robert Dole, R-Kan., former chairman of the Finance Committee. Brock also earned the respect of conservatives within the administration who had complained when he was named trade negotiator in 1981 that he had been slow to back Reagan's presidential candidacy and had refused to use funds from the Republican National Committee to oppose the Panama Canal treaties.

But Brock smoothed over these objections. He became a chief architect of Reagan's plan to restrict auto and steel imports and pressure the Japanese for trade concessions.

Congressional Career

A Tennessean, Brock began his career in Congress with four House terms, 1963-1971. He went to the Senate in 1971 after defeating Democratic incumbent Albert Gore. He built a generally conservative voting record in Congress, earning a 91 percent career support rating from the U.S. Chamber of Commerce. He voted in support of the AFL-CIO's position about 14 percent of the time during his Senate service.

Brock lost his Senate seat in 1976 to Democrat Jim Sasser, whose campaign portrayed Brock as a country-club Republican who represented the banking and insurance industries.

As chairman of the Republican National Committee from 1977-81, Brock earned respect for his organizing skills and for his efforts to broaden the party's base. "One of Brock's strong priorities was to reach out to groups and people that were not traditionally involved in the party," said Senate Labor Committee Chairman Orrin G. Hatch, R-Utah. "That record and that ability could serve him well as secretary of labor."

Brock, 54, was graduated from Washington and Lee University in 1953. After a three-year stint in the Navy, he returned to work in his family's candy manufacturing business before running for the House.

Elizabeth Hanford Dole
(Transportation Secretary)

Elizabeth Hanford Dole, formerly President Reagan's assistant for public liaison, was appointed on January 5, 1983, to head the Transportation Department. She was the first woman in the Reagan administration to head a Cabinet agency. Former United Nations representative Jeane J. Kirkpatrick also held Cabinet rank at the time.

Dole replaced Drew Lewis, who resigned Dec. 28, 1982, to head Warner Amex Cable Communications Inc. Married to Senate Majority Leader Robert Dole, R-Kan., Elizabeth Dole once said of her career and marriage: "There's a lot of interest, but no conflict."

As an assistant to the president, Dole had been responsible for meeting with special interest groups, defusing criticism and building coalitions for the administration. Members of Congress, congressional aides and lobbyists gave Dole high marks, describing her as extremely capable, hard working, charming — and a good politician. They noted that Lewis, regarded as one of Reagan's most capable Cabinet heads, also had little transportation experience.

Washington Background

As a member of the Federal Trade Commission (FTC) from 1973 to 1979, Dole was known for her consumer orientation and a healthy skepticism about the usefulness of government regulation. She resigned from the FTC to work in her husband's unsuccessful presidential campaign in 1976 and later campaigned for Reagan and chaired a task force for him on human services. Dole was deputy director of the White House Office of Consumer Affairs in 1971-73 and executive director of a presidential consumer affairs commission in 1968-71.

Confirmation Hearings

It was clear during her confirmation hearings that members of the Senate Commerce Committee were in favor of Dole's nomination. But they also expressed concerns about various transportation issues — from trucking regulation to aid for Amtrak and local highway projects. They frequently mentioned their concerns without demanding answers from Dole.

As expected Dole stuck to the administration position, such as supporting further deregulation of the trucking industry, and did not give any indication of new transportation policies. She often said an issue needed more study before she could give a detailed answer.

Some members seemed to want assurances from Dole that she would support further deregulation, while others on the panel said deregulation resulted in less service for rural and small-to-medium-sized communities. "We will continue to pursue the process of deregulation whenever it serves the best interests of the public, but we will remain sensitive to the temporary dislocations that changes in regulatory policy can cause," she said. On Feb. 1, 1983, the Senate unanimously confirmed Dole's nomination.

Action Since Confirmation

As secretary of transportation, Dole adhered to two areas of commitment: deregulation and increasing transportation safety. In December 1983 she ordered a top-level review of her department's agencies to ensure that safety standards had not slipped as a result of changes brought by the deregulation of the airline, trucking and railroad industries. But critics cited the decreasing numbers of inspectors in the Department's Bureau of Motor Carrier Safety and the Federal Aviation Administration as indications that safety procedures had been relaxed.

Dole also had strongly supported the administration's response to a presidential commission's report on drunk driving, which recommended that federal highway funds be withheld from states in which the drinking age was below 21.

She also had shown support for standards that would call for automatic crash protection in automobiles. In June 1983 she welcomed a Supreme Court decision requesting that she review these standards. And on July 11, 1984, she announced a long-awaited rule concerning passive restraint systems in automobiles. The rule ordered automakers to install air bags or automatic seatbelts in all new passenger cars sold in the United States by 1989 unless a total of states representing two-thirds of the country's population passed legislation requiring the use of seatbelts before then.

Margaret M. Heckler
(HHS Secretary)

On Jan. 12, 1983, President Reagan nominated the second woman to his Cabinet as head of a government agency, Margaret M. Heckler. Heckler succeeded Richard S. Schweiker as secretary of health and human services (HHS).

Heckler, 51, a moderate Republican who lost to liberal Barney Frank, D-Mass., in the November 1982 election, was nominated the same week Elizabeth Hanford Dole was tapped to head the Department of Transportation.

Schweiker resigned to become president of the American Council of Life Insurance, a trade and lobbying organization for life insurance companies. His stated reason for leaving HHS was that the insurance group made him an offer too good to refuse, although there was speculation that he had tired of riding herd on the sprawling department while fending off attacks from constituency groups and the Office of Management and Budget (OMB).

Heckler, confirmed by a vote of 82-3 on March 3, waded head-on into several of the administration's most pressing problems: the financial difficulties of Social Security, Medicare and other inexorably growing social programs.

Record on Issues

Heckler attracted national attention in her first race for Congress in 1966 when she knocked off Joseph W. Martin, Jr., House Republican leader for two decades and the party's national chairman, in the GOP primary.

In Congress she pushed consumers', women's and Vietnam veterans' issues. When Reagan proposed eliminating veterans' storefront counseling centers, Heckler was one of his loudest critics. She energetically backed passage of the Equal Rights Amendment (ERA) in 1972, later pushed for an extension of the deadline for ratification by states and fought unsuccessfully against dropping ERA from the Republican platform in 1980.

Like Schweiker, she opposed federal funding for abortion, a position that swung the support of women's groups to Frank in the 1982 campaign.

Unlike Schweiker, Heckler brought to office no notable expertise in the programs she was to administer. During her eight terms in the House, she served on the Agriculture, Banking, Government Operations, Science and Technology, and Veterans' Affairs committees, but not the panels with legislative responsibility for HHS programs. Her penchant for changing committee assignments kept her low on seniority lists except on Veterans' Affairs, where she was the second-ranking Republican.

Heckler's reputation among congressional colleagues was uneven. When engaged in an issue, as when she helped defeat a new sugar price support pogram in 1979, Heckler could mobilize publicity and outside pressure groups effectively. She fought hard for a place on the Agriculture Committee, from which she launched her anti-sugar attack. But, apart from that dramatic success, she played little role in the panel's regular work.

Heads Largest Agency

Heckler was charged with leading the largest Cabinet agency, with 145,000 employees. Although she had demonstrated her authority over subordinate HHS officials, notably No. 2 man John Svahn, who left the agency to become President Reagan's assistant for policy development, her administrative abilities were largely untested. She had contentious political issues to face, chief of which was how to solve the problem of spiraling Medicare costs.

After taking office she concentrated on formulating new rules for payment of Social Security disability payments and doubled the amount of money devoted to finding a cure for acquired immune deficiency syndrome (AIDS) disease, which she called the nation's No. 1 health problem.

She also was credited with helping persuade President Reagan to back legislation to improve child-support payments and had supported proposals by HHS and White House staff to provide billions of dollars in new federal tax credits and deduc-

tions for working parents.

Heckler was born Margaret Mary O'Shaughnessy in Flushing, N.Y., on June 21, 1931, the only child of Irish-Catholic immigrants. She attended Albertus Magnus College and received her law degree from Boston College in 1953.

John S. Herrington
(Energy Secretary)

On Jan. 10, 1985, President Reagan nominated John S. Herrington, a former assistant to the president for personnel, to replace Energy Secretary Donald P. Hodel. Hodel was leaving the Energy Department to become interior secretary.

Herrington was a California lawyer and a veteran of past Reagan campaigns. He worked as assistant secretary of the Navy from 1981 to 1983 before becoming assistant to the president for presidential personnel. His wife, Lois Herrington, was an assistant attorney general.

In his confirmation hearings, Herrington acknowledged that he had little energy background. In his opening statement, he described his principal experience with energy in personal terms, saying he had waited in gas lines during the supply shortages of 1973 and 1979 and had insulated his home in an effort to conserve energy.

Under questioning by committee members, Herrington repeatedly admitted ignorance of particular laws, policy and problems. When asked whether he was familiar with fusion energy programs, Herrington replied: "I am not. I am far below the level of understanding to be able to tell the difference between fusion and fission." Most of the Energy Department budget is devoted to nuclear power research and nuclear weapons production.

Senators did not try to embarrass Herrington, shifting quickly from lines of questioning when he indicated ignorance of technical issues. Members appeared satisfied with his declaration that he had an open mind regarding matters he did not know about.

Several interest groups expressed dismay when Herrington's nomination was announced, saying his lack of expertise reminded them of James B. Edwards, a former South Carolina governor and oral surgeon who was Reagan's first energy secretary. But only one group, the Environmental Policy Institute, sent witnesses to testify. Its representatives did not oppose the Herrington nomination, instead using the occasion to express concern about several energy policies.

Other Energy Issues

Committee members used both Herrington's and Interior Secretary Donald P. Hodel's confirmation hearings to criticize energy spending cuts anticipated as part of the president's fiscal 1986 budget as well as any tax simplification plan that would eliminate tax breaks for conservation and for oil and gas exploration.

Herrington skirted the issue, saying that he had not been consulted in the preparation of the budget. Saying that it was no secret that the administration planned to propose a halt in the filling of the Strategic Petroleum Reserve, Herrington said that he had not yet formed an opinion on that idea.

When asked about ending tax incentives in the energy area, Herrington said he could see "a difference between eliminating business entertainment accounts and jeopardizing the energy security of our future."

Loyal to Reagan

Reagan's deputy press secretary, Larry Speakes, when announcing Herrington's nomination, said, "He knows the president's policies and desires and he has served effectively in the White House and the Department of Defense. And he is a specialist in personnel, administration and organization and he brings to the Energy Department a combination of the knowledge of civilian management and organization."

The president's announcement also emphasized that Herrington's first order of business would be to conduct a reorganization study of the department and its $12 billion budget, including the possibility of merging it with the Department of the Interior.

In his confirmation hearings, Herrington played down the idea of a possible merger of the two departments. "The president has nominated me to be a full-time secretary of energy, not a caretaker," he declared. "I have a totally open mind" on the merger issue, he said, adding that "nothing can be done without the full concurrence of this committee."

The Senate voted 93-1 to confirm Herrington on Feb. 6.

Donald P. Hodel
(Interior Secretary)

When Donald P. Hodel was sworn in as energy secretary on Nov. 5, 1982, he, like his predecessor James B. Edwards, was signing on for a job he was committed to eliminate. Although he supported President Reagan's proposal to merge most portions of the Energy Department into the Commerce Department, Hodel told a group of reporters he would launch no "major effort" to dismantle existing programs in the department.

More than two years later, when Hodel became slated to take over at the Interior Department, congressional fears arose that Hodel's former agency and his new department would merge. White House spokesmen said that Reagan had directed both Hodel and his successor as energy secretary, John S. Herrington, to study consolidation of the two departments after they were confirmed.

Soothing congressional concern, Hodel said in testimony Feb. 1, 1985, that he interpreted Reagan's instruction to mean that "if we could identify something that was not only good but would be perceived as good," he and Herrington would "make a recommendation" as to what Reagan's "options might be."

The Senate confirmed Hodel as interior secretary on Feb. 6, 1985, by a 93-1 vote.

Environmental Opposition

During confirmation hearings before becoming energy secretary, Hodel had been criticized by environmental groups for his activities as under secretary of interior, where he worked closely with the controversial interior secretary James G. Watt, and as administrator of the Bonneville Power Administration (BPA) from 1972 to 1977. "America does not need a second Watt in the Cabinet," Sierra Club president Denny Shaffer had written President Reagan.

However, spokesmen for the groups said they expected Hodel would be a more effective administrator than his predecessor and, unlike Edwards, a dentist and former South Carolina governor, Hodel had substantial experience in the energy field.

Much of the criticism of Hodel stemmed from his work as administrator of BPA, a large, federally owned agency that provides hydroelectric power from 30 dams to the Northwestern states. During Hodel's tenure, the BPA, like many U.S. utility companies at the time, predicted that the demand for power would far outstrip the supply by the early 1980s. BPA stopped selling cheap federal power to investor-owned utilities in 1973 and put public utilities on notice in 1976 that it would not be able to meet their additional demands after July 1983.

That warning, according to critics, led to an explosion of high-cost power plant construction. The Washington Public Power Supply Service (WPPSS) —nicknamed "WHOOPS" by its many critics — embarked on an ambitious program to construct five new plants, two of which were later canceled, forcing the project to write off billions of dollars in costs.

Back to Interior

While at the Energy Department, Hodel developed a reputation for political shrewdness and for having an efficient and pragmatic management style. In his two years as secretary he had been credited with becoming an effective and dedicated advocate of increased energy development.

At his new post at Interior, Hodel was expected to face several pressing issues, chief of which would be filling important job vacancies, including those of the assistant secretaries in charge of land, minerals and fish and wildlife and the directorship of the National Park Service.

Hodel also would have to decide on long-range policies for oil leasing on the Outer Continental Shelf, coal leasing on federal lands, surface mining policies, protection of the National Park System and creation of wilderness in Bureau of Land Management programs.

The lone dissenter to Hodel's confirmation, William Proxmire, D-Wis., conceded Hodel's qualifications but opposed his nomination because "the policies Hodel will pursue as secretary of the Interior are so dangerous." He pointed out that Hodel as under secretary had helped carry out the aggressive energy and resource development pursued by Watt.

Edwin Meese III
(Attorney General)

When President Reagan on Jan. 23, 1984, nominated his counselor Edwin Meese III to succeed William French Smith as attorney general, Meese's confirmation appeared to many as a foregone conclusion.

Yet, it was not until more than a year later, after being cleared of possible financial wrongdoing and proven ethically fit for the post, that Meese finally won Senate confirmation by a 63-31 vote. Earlier, Meese had barely won appoval on a 12-6 vote by the Senate Judiciary Committee.

Meese's confirmation ran into trouble in March 1984 when questions arose over whether he had helped get federal jobs for several people who had helped him in working out personal financial problems. At Meese's request, Smith asked a special three-judge panel to appoint an independent counsel, or special prosecutor, to investigate all allegations of possible wrongdoing by him. Jacob A. Stein, a Washington, D.C., trial lawyer, was named April 2, 1984.

After a five-month probe, Stein said in a Sept. 20, 1984, report that he had found "no basis" for prosecuting Meese for violation of a criminal statute. Because his investigatory mandate did not cover ethics issues, Stein made "no comment on Mr. Meese's ethics and the propriety of his conduct or an evaluation of his conduct for office."

Meese's nomination had been put on hold while Stein conducted his investigation. Although Congress was still in session when the counsel's report was issued, Senate Judiciary Committee Chairman Strom Thurmond, R-S.C., decided to put off any action on Meese's nomination until the new Congress was convened in 1985.

Final Confirmation

When confirmation hearings were taken up again in early 1985, Meese and his supporters contended that the Stein report had given the nominee a clean bill of health. But opponents said it was simply a starting point for questioning the ethics of his conduct, particularly his failure to disclose financial relationships with people he subsequently approved for federal jobs.

Two Meese financial transactions prompted detailed questions from the Judi-

ciary Committee. The first involved two loans totaling $60,000 that were arranged for Meese by John R. McKean, a San Francisco accountant who subsequently was appointed to the Board of Governors of the Postal Service. The other financial transaction involved California businessman Thomas J. Barrack, who put together a deal to buy Meese's home in La Mesa, Calif. Barrack subsequently obtained a position as an assistant secretary in the Interior Department.

Meese conceded to the committee that, as a result of the Stein probe, "I have a much higher level of sensitivity to matters now than I did when I arrived in Washington. . . . I would take pains to avoid the appearance [of impropriety]," he said. Sen. Joseph R. Biden Jr., D-Del., was not satisfied with Meese's answers, however. In an emotional exchange with Meese Jan. 30, Biden blasted the nominee for talking about "technicalities" instead of discussing broader ethical issues involved.

Meese replied that a "fair reading of the facts" showed that he had done "nothing intentionally wrong." But Meese said he hoped the hearings and his willingness to answer questions would help the public see that he was fit to be attorney general. He also promised to make regular, detailed financial disclosures.

Early Life

Meese graduated from Yale in 1953 with a degree in public administration and from the University of California Law School at Berkeley in 1958.

He spent eight years as deputy district attorney in Alameda County, Calif. He was named Reagan's legal affairs secretary in 1967, when Reagan became governor of California, and then served as Reagan's chief of staff until 1974.

Meese practiced corporate law from 1974 to 1977, then became a law professor at the University of San Diego, where he also served as director of the law school's Center for Justice Policy and Management.

Reagan's campaign adviser in 1980, he was named counselor to the president after Reagan took office. He was one of three to four men in the president's inner circle at the time. In his White House role, Meese helped shape administration policy on justice-related issues. Most recently, he was the prime force behind Reagan's successful effort to remake the Civil Rights Commission into an agency more receptive to the president's views on civil rights.

Samuel R. Pierce Jr.
(HUD Secretary)

Samuel R. Pierce Jr., President Reagan's secretary of housing and urban development (HUD), had made a lifelong habit of being "the first." Before he became Reagan's first and only black Cabinet appointee, Pierce broke barriers to become the first black named to a sub-Cabinet-level position in the Treasury Department, the first black to become a partner in a major New York law firm and the first black named to the boards of directors of two major U.S. corporations.

Pierce, a native New Yorker and lifelong Republican, had never had any direct involvement in housing issues. But supporters said his academic background, government experience and administrative abilities would serve him well in his management of one of the largest federal agencies.

Pierce was not opposed by anyone on the Senate Banking Committee, which considered his nomination, or in the full Senate, which confirmed Pierce by a unanimous 98-0 vote on Jan. 22, 1981. Pierce sailed through his confirmation hearings without a single buffeting question.

Earlier Career

Pierce was born in Glen Cove, Long Island, Sept. 8, 1922. His father was in the dry cleaning and real estate businesses.

During his undergraduate days at Cornell University, Pierce was a star halfback on the football team and was elected to Phi Beta Kappa in his junior year. After time out for service in the Army during World War II he received his undergraduate degree from Cornell in 1947 and a law degree from Cornell's law school in 1949. In 1952 he received a master's degree in tax law from New York University School of Law. He also did postgraduate study as a Ford Foundation Fellow at Yale Law School.

After finishing his education, Pierce served as an assistant district attorney for New York County and later as assistant U.S. attorney for the Southern District of New York. In 1955 he was named assistant under secretary of labor in the Eisenhower administration. He later became associate counsel and then counsel of the House Judiciary Antitrust Subcommittee.

Pierce returned to New York in 1957. Gov. Nelson A. Rockefeller, R, named him to the Court of General Sessions, which later became part of the New York Supreme Court. When the post became elective, Pierce ran for election but was defeated by a Democrat.

In 1961 Pierce joined the prestigious New York City labor law firm of Battle, Fowler, Stokes and Kheel, primarily as a labor mediator. He did another stint in Washington from 1970 to 1973, serving as general counsel of the Treasury Department in the Nixon administration.

Pierce served on the boards of directors of six major corporations — Prudential Insurance Co., General Electric Co., International Paper Co., U.S. Industries, First National Boston Corp. and the First National Bank of Boston. He was a trustee of the Rand Corp. and a governor of the American Stock Exchange.

In his confirmation hearings, Pierce said he would like to reduce the number of regulations that applied to housing programs and the amount of control HUD exercised over local governments. Pierce added that he did not think the federal government should prohibit local governments from enacting rent control ordinances. "HUD may find it can't economically go into an area if rents are set too low," he said. But he stopped short of saying HUD should not invest in communities with rent control policies.

As HUD Secretary

During Pierce's tenure, HUD suffered severe budget cuts. Critics said that the administration had nearly ended construction of housing for the poor and that Pierce had failed to speak out either for or against the budget slashing. He also was labeled inaccessible and unresponsive by constituent lobby groups.

In defense, Pierce cited as achievements made during his tenure: programs such as the Joint Venture for Affordable Housing, a $1.7 million demonstration project to make building construction less expensive by streamlining local building codes; helping to save community development block grants, urban development action grants and FHA insurance from the budget axe; and the placement of $139 million of HUD's money in 180 minority-owned banks.

George P. Shultz
(Secretary of State)

After secretary of state Alexander M. Haig Jr. abruptly resigned on June 25, 1982, President Reagan nominated George P. Shultz, an informal foreign policy adviser to Reagan, to the position. Shultz had never received formal training in the diplomatic arts but had wide experience in foreign affairs. He was president of Bechtel Group Inc., a worldwide construction and engineering firm based in San Francisco, when Reagan selected him for the post.

He was an original member of President Nixon's Cabinet, serving as secretary of labor from January 1969 to June 1970, director of the Office of Management and Budget from June 1970 to May 1972, and secretary of the Treasury from May 1972 to April 1974.

At Treasury, Shultz was the top U.S. official in trade matters. He represented the United States at meetings in Paris in March 1973 during an international monetary crisis and was the chairman of Nixon's Council on Economic Policy, coordinating international economic policy.

Shultz served Reagan as campaign adviser on economics in 1980 and was a member of the economic policy team during the transition period after the 1980 elections. He was mentioned prominently as a possible secretary of state when president-elect Reagan was making up his Cabinet after the 1980 elections. But in early December 1980 Shultz announced that he was taking himself out of consideration for a Reagan Cabinet post and had accepted the position of president at Bechtel.

Confirmation Hearings

Acting rapidly because of crises in the Middle East and U.S.-European relations, the Senate July 15, 1982, unanimously confirmed Shultz as secretary of state. But if inspired by an air of crisis in foreign affairs, the Senate's fast work was possible only because of the confidence Shultz exuded and evoked during the two-day hearings.

First, Shultz dispelled concerns raised by his years at Bechtel by pledging to sever all ties with the construction company and by promising that his Bechtel experience would not color his views on the Mideast.

Perhaps more central to his success, though, was the contrast between Shultz' calm, secure approach with Haig's combative, mercurial manner. Shultz proposed no dramatic departures from the policies Haig pursued, but he set out and defended his views in a judicious style that clearly soothed Democrats on the committee who were uneasy with Haig.

Foreign Policy Issues

Disputes over U.S. policy toward the Middle East and the Soviet Union had contributed to Haig's downfall and it was these issues that the committee probed most deeply with Shultz.

As expected, Shultz demonstrated a benevolent view toward the Arabs and a harder line than Haig had taken toward Israel's invasion of Lebanon, but he did so gently. And, as on questions of U.S.-Soviet relations, Shultz did not depart from Haig's basic line on Central American issues. But his less provocative tone and his emphasis on the need for economic development to remove the causes of turmoil in the region seemed to disarm Reagan's critics on the panel.

Shultz-Weinberger Debate

During his tenure, Shultz gained influence among the president's advisers. Reports indicated a growing tension between Shultz and Defense Secretary Caspar W. Weinberger. Shultz, for example, had urged retaliation against terrorist attacks. He also had led administration policy makers advocating the use of military troops in Lebanon and Grenada. Weinberger had been reluctant to send troops to those areas and reports had surfaced that the two advisers had differed in other policy areas, including arms control, the treatment of North Atlantic Treaty Organization allies, and the extent of U.S. intervention in Central America.

Caspar W. Weinberger
(Defense Secretary)

To run the government's largest bureaucracy, President Reagan chose a close adviser with diversified experience in high-level government administration. Two of the most prominent qualities of Defense Secretary Caspar W. Weinberger were his reputed managerial prowess in a variety of roles and his loyalty to Reagan.

The overwhelming 97-2 vote for him in the Senate — despite his lack of experience on defense issues — reflected the senators' confidence in his record. The only votes against Weinberger, who on Jan. 20, 1981, became the first Cabinet nominee confirmed, came from North Carolina's two Republicans, Jesse Helms and John East, both from the party's right wing.

Helms told the Senate before the vote that Weinberger did not have the necessary resolve or vision for the job. And he criticized Pentagon appointees, particularly Weinberger's choice of Frank Carlucci as his deputy, for not having credentials that were sufficiently conservative.

On the other hand, Armed Services Committee Chairman John Tower, R-Texas, praised Weinberger's government experience, calling the Californian "highly qualified because he has the right instincts."

Early Career in Government

Born in San Francisco in 1917, Weinberger received his undergraduate and legal education at Harvard, served in the Army during World War II and began practicing law in San Francisco after the war.

He was a Republican member of the California Legislature from 1952 to 1958, then vice chairman and chairman of the Republican state central committee from 1960 to 1964.

After Ronald Reagan's election as governor in 1966, Weinberger served as chairman of a state commission on governmental organization and economics (1967-68) and state finance director (1968-69). It was during this period that he acquired the nickname "Cap the Knife," a reference to his flair for budget cutting.

In January 1970 Weinberger became chairman of the Federal Trade Commission (FTC), then in turmoil from the just-ended chairmanship of Paul Rand Dixon. In his brief tenure there, Weinberger won general acclaim for bringing harmony to the commission. He also became a favorite of liberals for staking out a more aggressively pro-consumer position than had been taken in the first year of the Nixon administration. After less than six months at the commission, Weinberger was tapped by Nixon as the deputy director of the newly created OMB.

Weinberger's OMB tenure coincided with the peak of the domestic turmoil over the Vietnam War. In 1970 Weinberger became a frequent spokesman for the administration's effort to reverse moves in Congress to cut defense spending. He pointed out that Nixon's fiscal 1971 defense budget of $76.8 billion was $6 billion less than the previous year's budget, largely because of the continuing withdrawal of U.S. forces from Vietnam.

In January 1973 Weinberger moved to the Department of Health, Education and Welfare. While there, he was one of three Cabinet officials simultaneously named White House counselors. In this capacity, the three counselors divided among themselves responsibility for oversight over all domestic policy.

Actions During Reagan's Presidency

During Reagan's first four years in office, Weinberger had been a consistent proponent of increasing funding to the military and had gained the president's support in sparing the Pentagon from across-the-board budget cuts.

In defending the president's 1986 fiscal year budget, which called for an 8 percent increase in defense spending, Weinberger maintained that the Soviet Union continued to outproduce the United States in weaponry. Weinberger was credited with substantially increasing the number of combat-ready U.S. military units and with what he termed the "revitalization" of the armed forces.

Critics asserted that the Reagan administration's actions had increased the risk of confrontation and that the Soviets would continue to increase their defense spending to keep up with the United States.

William J. Casey
(CIA Director)

President Reagan got off on the right foot with the American intelligence community by naming a 67-year-old lawyer and self-made millionaire, William J. Casey, as director of central intelligence.

Indeed, many prominent former intelligence officials were elated by the choice of Casey. They said they hoped he would be just the right tonic to fortify the anemic morale at the Central Intelligence Agency and in the U.S. intelligence community at large.

The non-controversial nomination was approved by the Senate Jan. 27, 1981, by a 95-0 vote.

William E. Colby, a former CIA director who was practicing law in Washington, said Reagan's choice was "a very good one" because Casey "has a unique background and one very appropriate for the job."

That background included:
- World War II service in the Office of Strategic Services (OSS), the CIA's wartime predecessor, working to infiltrate U.S. agents into occupied Europe.
- Successful careers as a tax lawyer, teacher, writer and businessman that had earned him a fortune.
- Long and close associations with establishment Republicans that led to his appointment to various posts in the Nixon administration in the early 1970s: chairman of the Securities and Exchange Commis-

sion, under secretary of state for economic affairs and president of the Export-Import Bank.

• A continuing, and highly visible, interest in intelligence matters, as demonstrated by his participation in groups such as the Veterans of the OSS and the Association of Former Intelligence Officers, plus service on President Ford's Foreign Intelligence Advisory Board in the mid-1970s.

• A brief but successful stint as Reagan's presidential campaign manager that earned him Reagan's respect and his ear — and got Casey the job he had coveted for years.

Such experience, concluded John Bross, a former OSS and CIA officer who knew him, made Casey an "ideal choice for this job."

OSS Service

Born on March 13, 1913, and raised in New York City, Casey earned an undergraduate degree from Fordham University in 1934 and a law degree from St. John's University Law School in 1937. He began practicing law the following year when he was admitted to the New York State Bar.

He was commissioned a lieutenant in the Navy when the war began in 1941, but poor eyesight confined him to a desk job in Washington. Through friends in legal circles, Casey came to the attention of Maj. Gen. William J. "Wild Bill" Donovan, the Wall Street lawyer President Franklin D. Roosevelt tapped to form and run the OSS. This led Casey into the OSS. Casey left the OSS with a reputation as a forceful manager who could make tough decisions with speed and see that they were carried out.

Casey was in and out of government after his war service. He worked in Thomas E. Dewey's 1940 and 1948 presidential campaigns, and he ran a foreign policy group during Vice President Richard Nixon's 1960 presidential campaign.

In 1966 Casey ran unsuccessfully for the House of Representatives. He worked

again in 1968 for Nixon, who put him on the Advisory Committee on Arms Control and Disarmament in 1969.

President Nixon named Casey to the Securities and Exchange Commission (SEC) on Feb. 2, 1971. After a sometimes stormy tenure as SEC chairman, Casey was named under secretary of state for economic affairs in 1973. However, when Henry A. Kissinger became secretary of state, Casey was named to head the Export-Import Bank.

Action During First Term

During Reagan's first term, Casey had been involved in policy disputes centering on the CIA's role in funding and directing rebellion against the Sandinista regime in Nicaragua. Congressional oversight committees complained that Casey had not kept them well informed. Yet Casey also had been considered popular at the CIA, winning budget increases as high as 20 percent. He was credited with revitalizing the agency, which had been widely criticized during the 1970s.

David A. Stockman
(OMB Director)

President Reagan's director of the Office of Management and Budget (OMB) — David A. Stockman, a former conservative, two-term Republican representative from Michigan — in 1981 was given his long-sought chance to arrest the growth of the federal government's "social pork barrel."

Weeding out and reforming the myriad federal programs providing benefits for black lung victims, lunches for school children and aid for alcoholics or distressed cities had been a goal of the then 34-year-old member of the House ever since he entered Congress in 1977.

This commitment to reduce the government's fiscal involvement in all walks of American life made Stockman one of the most activist — and controversial — OMB chiefs. And, unlike his predecessors, he had firsthand knowledge of Congress' spending habits and its six-year-old budget process.

In Congress Stockman worked steadfastly to oppose expensive new "entitlement programs" — those that by law must provide benefits for all who meet the eligibility requirements. He took over the reins of OMB armed with an inch-thick list of spending cuts he had prepared early in 1980 on the eve of a House debate on ways to balance the budget.

Early Training

Born Nov. 10, 1946, in Camp Hood, Texas, Stockman grew up in St. Joseph, Mich., where his father ran a fruit farm. He graduated from Michigan State University with a degree in American history and then enrolled in Harvard University's divinity school.

It was there that he came to the attention of Rep. John B. Anderson, R-Ill. (1961-81), who brought him to Washington in 1970 as his special assistant and two years later named him director of the Republican Conference, the policy-making committee of all House Republicans. During his tenure under Anderson, he was known as a liberal party member.

In 1975 Stockman returned to Boston to study at Harvard's prestigious John F. Kennedy Institute of Politics. He left academia for the trenches of electoral politics in Michigan, winning election to the House in 1976 with 61 percent of the vote. He was re-elected in 1978.

Despite his short tenure in the House, Stockman played a major role in the development of several pieces of key legislation: hospital cost containment, child health care, synthetic fuels development and the Energy Mobilization Board.

'Taken to the Woodshed'

Stockman got into hot water with the administration in late 1981 when it was revealed that the December issue of the *Atlantic* would quote him expressing doubts about the supply-side theory on which the administration's economic plan was based. This news was released at a time when economic indicators were providing clear signals that the economy had entered a recession. After a meeting with the president on Nov. 12, Stockman told a press conference that Reagan was "not happy" and "very chagrined" about his comments in the *Atlantic* article. He likened his meeting with the president to "a visit to the woodshed after supper."

Stockman admitted that his "poor judgment and loose talk" had done the president's program "a serious disservice." He had offered to resign, he said, but the president "asked me to stay on the team."

Vernon Walters
(U.N. Representative)

On Feb. 8, 1985, President Reagan nominated retired general Vernon A. Walters, an experienced envoy, linguist and former Central Intelligence Agency official, to succeed Jeane J. Kirkpatrick as chief United States delegate to the United Nations.

Kirkpatrick, an outspoken conservative within the administration, was leaving the post to resume her academic career. She had been a professor at Georgetown University in Washington, D.C., and a resident scholar at the Washington-based American Enterprise Institute before being appointed to the U.N. post. Although she had sought a high-level foreign policy job in the second Reagan administration, she apparently had not been offered the post she wanted.

Diplomatic Experience

Walters told reporters at the State Department after his nomination, "I will do my best to continue the superb work that

Ambassador Kirkpatrick has done in the United Nations to restore and enhance the position of the United States." The U.N. post was to continue to hold Cabinet rank, as it had with Kirkpatrick. Although Walters would attend National Security Council meetings related to the U.N., he would not be an official member of the council. Walters reportedly had wanted this post, along with the U.N. position.

The 68-year-old Walters had worked for five administrations in the previous 40 years and had been involved in missions in Europe, the Middle East, Africa, Asia, South America and Central America. An accomplished linguist, he spoke seven languages: French, Spanish, Portuguese, Italian, German, Dutch and Russian. He served as deputy director of the Central Intelligence Agency under presidents Nixon and Ford.

He played a minor part in secret diplomacy ending involvement in Vietnam and also took part in negotiations that led to the opening of U.S. ties with China. He was an aide to W. Averell Harriman at the Marshall Plan headquarters in Paris and worked as an assistant to President Dwight D. Eisenhower on many foreign trips.

In recent years he had been sent to Cuba to explore improving relations with Fidel Castro and in 1982 was sent to Argentina to explain why the United States was supporting Great Britain in the Falkland Islands conflict. After President Reagan offered him the job of roving ambassador in 1980, Walters reportedly had visited 100 countries and logged 10,000 miles a week as the administration's chief troubleshooter. In 1984 alone he was known to have traveled to El Salvador, Sri Lanka and several African countries. His secret mission to El Salvador reportedly involved voicing concern to rightest leader Roberto d'Aubuisson about rumors of assassination attempts against the U.S. ambassador, Thomas R. Pickering.

Military Background

Walters, the youngest of three children, was born on Jan. 3, 1919, in New York. After attending French and English Catholic schools, he dropped out at age 16 to work in his father's insurance company.

In 1941 he enlisted in the Army and within a year was promoted to a second lieutenant. His linguistic skills drew him the attention of high ranking officers and he rose rapidly through the ranks. During World War II he served as liaison officer with the Brazilian forces fighting in the United States Fifth Army in Italy. He was aide-de-camp to Gen. Mark Clark during the liberation of Rome.

After the war he was posted as military attaché in Rio de Janeiro and Paris and rose to become a senior officer of the Defense Information Agency. After 35 years in the service he retired as a three-star general. During the Carter years, he became a private consultant and author and published his memoirs, *Silent Missions,* on his dealings with many world leaders.

Clayton Yeutter
(Trade Representative)

On April 2, 1985, President Reagan announced his intention to nominate Clayton Yeutter to be U.S. trade representative. Yeutter was selected to replace William E. Brock III, who moved to the slot left open when Labor Secretary Raymond J. Donovan resigned.

The trade representative post carries with it Cabinet rank, and, although he would not be an official member of the National Security Council, he would attend its meetings on occasion.

Yeutter was to come to the trade job at a time characterized by strained relations with Japan, protectionist sentiment in Congress and a record U.S. trade deficit. For the most part the choice of Yeutter for the post was applauded. According to news reports, Yeutter had been a strong contender for the slot of agriculture secretary in the first Reagan term, but he was passed over for John R. Block because of some opposition in the Senate.

As president of the nation's top trading market and a veteran of trade and agriculture posts in the Nixon and Ford administrations, Yeutter brought with him experience in both the private and public sectors. Beginning in 1978 Yeutter held the post of president and chief executive officer of the Chicago Mercantile Exchange. During 1977 and 1978 he was a senior partner in the law firm of Nelson, Harding, Yeutter and Leonard in Lincoln, Nebraska. Yeutter had served as deputy special trade representative from 1975 to 1977 during the Ford administration. From 1970 to 1975 he worked at the Agriculture Department, ending his tenure there as assistant secretary for international affairs and commodity programs.

He was director of the University of Nebraska Mission in Colombia from 1968 to 1970 and executive assistant to the Nebraska governor from 1966 to 1968. He was a faculty member in the Department of Agricultural Economics at the University of Nebraska from 1960 to 1966. From 1957 to 1975, he operated a 2,500-acre farming, ranching and cattle-feeding enterprise in Nebraska. He was on the boards of ConAgra Inc., the U.S. Meat Export Federation, the Japan American Society of Chicago Inc. and the Chicago-Tokyo bank.

10

The White House

The American people gave Ronald Reagan their strong vote of confidence in November 1984, and in his second term the president no doubt hoped to capitalize on this support. Max L. Friedersdorf, Reagan's chief lobbyist, remarked in February 1985: "I think the president is really at the absolute peak of his popularity. It's a golden opportunity in the first session [of the 99th Congress] at least to get his programs." Reagan would rely on his own near-legendary powers of persuasion and on the strong backing of his experienced vice president, George Bush, to get what he wanted. But in preparation for his second four years Reagan made key changes in his senior White House staff that would bear significantly upon his chances for success.

Reagan's first-term chief of staff, James A. Baker III, who had been a crucial player in backroom negotiations with Congress, swapped places with Treasury Secretary Donald T. Regan. Regan had shown his loyalty for the president and was in accord with him on most issues, notably economic ones. Many observers praised the switch, saying the change would invigorate the White House staff, but others wondered whether Regan could work as effectively as Baker had with Captitol Hill.

Another top position on the president's team, chief White House lobbyist, was

filled in 1985 by Friedersdorf, an experienced and effective legislative strategist. His return to the slot he had held in 1981 was expected to beef up the White House lobbying staff. Because Regan apparently was less familiar with the ins and outs of legislative strategy than was Baker, the White House required a skilled individual to guide administration lobbying.

Also newly installed in the West Wing were Patrick J. Buchanan as director of communications and Edward J. Rollins as presidential assistant for political and governmental affairs.

Other changes in the chemistry of the White House would result from the absences of Edwin Meese III, the president's closest aide for many years and his counselor during the first term, and Michael K. Deaver, another unusually close aide who had served as Reagan's deputy chief of staff. Meese moved to the Justice Department, where he was attorney general, and Deaver planned to leave the administration to open a public relations firm in Washington, D.C., in May 1985.

Several hundred additional people worked on the White House staff to support the president's foreign and domestic policies, control the federal bureaucracy, lobby for his programs in Congress, conduct his relations with the media, brief him on sensitive foreign intelligence operations, provide him with expert advice on the laws of the land and settle political problems within his administration.

Following are biographical sketches of President Reagan, Vice President Bush, and top White House staffers.

Ronald Wilson Reagan
(President)

When he became president in 1981, Ronald Reagan already had lived a long and eventful life. Movie star, television spokesman and governor of California, Reagan was a well-known figure to most Americans even before he began his pursuit of the presidency. Like Dwight D. Eisenhower and few other presidents, Reagan's national fame predated his political career.

Entertainment Experience

Along with gaining him notoriety, Reagan's 30-year career in the entertainment business also shaped his abilities and outlook. Years of experience as an actor and television host helped hone Reagan's talent for getting his message across. The consummate master of political television, he was unmatched in his ability to communicate directly to the people.

Reagan's approach to issues and the way he discussed them also reflected his time as an actor. He referred frequently to movies and their plots and expressed a view of the world in which, as in Hollywood, the line between right and wrong was sharply drawn. "We have been . . . told there are no simple answers to complex problems," Reagan once said. "Well, the truth is there are simple answers, just not easy ones."

Reagan grew up in modest surroundings in several small towns in rural northern Illinois. Born Feb. 6, 1911, in Tampico, Ill., he was the younger of two sons of John and Nellie Wilson Reagan. His father was an alcoholic Irish-Catholic who had trouble keeping a job; his mother was a Protestant of Scottish descent who loved the theater. When Reagan was nine, the family settled in Dixon, Ill.

After graduating from Eureka College, a small liberal arts institution near his home, Reagan began working as a sports announcer for a Davenport, Iowa, radio station. He developed a national reputation when the station joined the NBC network, which carried his football and baseball play-by-play throughout the Midwest.

Reagan was covering baseball spring training in California when an agent from Warner Brothers signed him to a film contract. In his 1937 movie debut, "Love Is On the Air," Reagan played a radio announcer who uncovered corruption in local government.

Over the next two decades, Reagan appeared in more than 50 movies. Although most of his films were not highly regarded by critics, he did have two notable roles — as George Gipp, a Notre Dame football player, in "Knute Rockne — All American," and as a small-town playboy who has his legs cut off in "Kings Row." But movies like "Bedtime for Bonzo," where he played opposite a chimpanzee, and "The Killers," in which he had his only villainous role, received less favorable responses from critics.

While in Hollywood, Reagan met and married another film star, Jane Wyman. Wed in 1940, the couple raised two children, Maureen and Michael. They were divorced in 1949. In 1952, Reagan married Nancy Davis, by whom he had two children, Patricia and Ronald. Reagan is the first divorced man ever elected president.

Reagan's career in politics began while he was still an actor. In 1947 he was elected president of the Screen Actors Guild, a major Hollywood labor union. He held that post for six years, working out several contract agreements with film studios. Reagan was the first former union chief ever to occupy the White House.

But Reagan's efforts in hunting down leftists in the film industry attracted more attention than his work as a labor negotiator. He was a strong supporter of the "blacklisting" of actors with alleged ties to the Communist Party, and in 1947 appeared before the House Un-American Activities Committee as a friendly witness in its investigation of communism in Hollywood.

During that period, Reagan's political views underwent a profound transformation. A Democrat for much of his life, Reagan had been a "near-hopeless hemophiliac liberal," as he put it in his 1965 autobiography, *Where's the Rest of Me?* As he struggled to purge his union, however, he gradually became much more conservative. By 1952, he was working for Eisenhower's campaign, while still a Democrat. Two years after he supported Richard Nixon's 1960 presidential campaign, Reagan became a Republican.

By that time, Reagan had all but abandoned his movie career in favor of television. His position as the host for the "GE Theatre" and corporate spokesman for General Electric from 1954 until 1962 gave him a political forum. It was an opportunity for Reagan to develop both his conservative political ideas and the set speech, with its anti-communist and anti-government themes, that he was to use so often during his rise to political prominence.

As California Governor

The turning point of Reagan's developing political career came in the fall of 1964, when he made a nationwide television speech seeking to revive Barry Goldwater's slumping presidential candidacy. In the speech, which marked his true arrival on the national political scene, Reagan spoke of the United States as "the only island of freedom that is left in the whole world."

Following that speech, several Califor-

nia businessmen approached Reagan, then host of "Death Valley Days," suggesting he run for governor. In a state where parties traditionally have held little influence, Reagan easily transformed his image from that of a television personality into a successful political figure.

Running for governor in 1966, Reagan handily defeated a GOP moderate, former San Francisco mayor George Christopher, in the party primary. He went on to crush his general-election opponent, incumbent Democratic governor Edmund G. Brown.

Reagan compiled a record as governor that was far more moderate than his conservative rhetoric. The highlights of his term generally fell into three areas: limiting government spending, cutting back on the welfare rolls and exercising more control over the massive state educational system. Reagan's supporters considered his efforts to overhaul the state welfare system to be his most successful endeavor as governor.

Almost immediately after his election as governor, Reagan took on national political importance. In 1968 he mounted a tentative campaign for president, switching from favorite-son status to a full-fledged candidacy two days before the Republican National Convention. He received 186 convention votes for president that year.

Leaving the California governorship in 1974, Reagan waged a determined campaign for the 1976 GOP nomination against President Gerald R. Ford. After fighting through a long primary season, the two candidates were almost even in delegate support. Reagan sought to expand his base by announcing in advance that moderate Pennsylvania senator Richard S. Schweiker would be his running mate. But he ended up losing to Ford by 60 votes at the convention.

After his 1976 defeat, Reagan maintained a high profile. He started a political action committee to distribute money to Republican candidates. He continued his active schedule of paid speeches, radio commentaries and newspaper columns until Nov. 13, 1979, when he announced his presidential candidacy for 1980.

George Herbert Walker Bush
(Vice President)

The man who once called Ronald Reagan's program "voodoo economics" had become by the election campaign of 1984 the chief drum-beater for Reagan's administration. Despite initial skepticism from Reagan himself and the outspoken hostility of some conservatives, Vice President George Bush managed to establish himself as a trusted White House team player.

Moreover, the 60-year-old Texan was able to maintain at least some of the expansion of vice presidential authority achieved by his predecessor, former vice president Walter F. Mondale. While Bush did not have quite the influence within Reagan's administration that Mondale had in Jimmy Carter's, he still had more clout than most earlier vice presidents.

Bush's impact on the administration had been most significant in the area of foreign affairs, both in terms of developing policy and in dealing directly with other governments. He also had been important in determining administration positions on issues such as regulatory reform and control of illegal drugs.

But it was Bush's tireless cheerleading for his boss that warmed the hearts of Reaganites. After traveling hundreds of thousands of miles making speeches for the administration's program and attaining a close personal relationship with Reagan, Bush effectively squelched any idea that he would not be on the ticket in 1984.

Bush's role could be even more important in a second term. When elected for his second term, Reagan was in good health, but he was entering his mid-70s; there was a statistically reasonable chance Bush would

occupy the White House even before the 1988 elections.

Active Vice President

A key moment in Bush's vice-presidential career came in March 1981, when Reagan, over the opposition of Secretary of State Alexander M. Haig, appointed Bush to be chairman of the Special Situation Group, the administration's crisis-management committee. Within a few days, Bush faced a major crisis — the wounding of Reagan in an assassination attempt.

After that, Bush was deeply involved in working out the administration's position on key foreign policy issues. When the Soviet-backed government of Poland declared martial law in December 1981, for example, Bush pushed for sanctions against the Soviet and Polish governments.

Bush also played a key role during the collapse of the Lebanese government in February 1984. With Reagan out of town and the U.S.-backed Lebanese army disintegrating, Bush took charge of deliberations that led to the withdrawal of U.S. forces from Beirut.

Reagan also used Bush as a sort of roving ambassador, sending him on missions that ranged from giving the government of El Salvador a warning on human-rights abuses to trying to mend relations with the Indian government.

Perhaps Bush's most significant mission came in February 1983, when he toured seven European countries. Bush's cogent presentation of Reagan's position on arms control helped quiet opposition to the installation of U.S. intermediate-range missiles on the continent. In February 1984, Reagan sent Bush to Moscow as head of the American delegation to the funeral of Soviet leader Yuri V. Andropov.

On domestic issues, Bush focused much of his energy on two task forces. One, on regulatory reform, completed its work in August 1983 with a report outlining proposals that it said would save government and business $150 billion over 10 years through changes in federal regulations. Another task force, on South Florida, sought to increase coordination among federal agencies trying to stem the illegal drug flow from South America.

Three times during his term, Bush made use of one of the few real powers granted to the vice president by the Constitution — the right to cast the deciding vote in case of a tie in the Senate. In 1983 he twice voted to save the administration's proposal to begin manufacturing lethal chemical weapons for the first time since 1969. Then in June 1984 he cast the deciding vote to preserve funding for the MX missile.

New England Roots

Although his career was based in Texas, Bush's roots were in New England and in the moderate Eastern Republican faction that once held sway in the party. His father, Prescott Bush, represented Connecticut in the Senate from 1952 to 1963.

The product of a wealthy upbringing, Bush graduated from Phillips Academy, an elite prep school in Andover, Mass. As a Navy pilot in World War II, he was shot down over the Pacific. He was rescued by a U.S. submarine that had raced a Japanese ship to get to him.

Returning from the war, Bush entered Yale University. After graduation in 1948, he moved to Texas to enter the oil business. His first jobs were as a warehouse sweeper and then salesman with an oil supply company of which his father was a director.

Backed by family money, Bush in 1951 helped start the Bush-Overby Development Co. Two years later, he co-founded Zapata Petroleum Corp., and in 1954 became president of Zapata Off-Shore Co. While living in Houston, Bush was active in local politics, becoming chairman of the Harris County Republican organization.

By 1964 Bush was ready to enter electoral politics. He won the Republican Senate nomination after a three-way primary and runoff but lost to Democratic incumbent Ralph Yarborough in November.

Bush then lowered his sights and in 1966 won election to the House from a newly created district in the affluent Houston suburbs. During his four-year House career, he voted a generally conservative line and defended oil industry interests on the Ways and Means Committee. But he also backed some civil rights and environmental protection legislation.

Bush tried again for the Senate in 1970. He had hoped to run again against the liberal Yarborough, but the senator was defeated in the Democratic primary by the more conservative Lloyd Bentsen. Despite help from President Nixon, Bush lost by nearly 160,000 votes.

Executive Career

Bush entered the second phase of his public career in December 1970, when Nixon appointed him ambassador to the United Nations, an appointment that drew criticism because of Bush's lack of experience in foreign affairs. As ambassador, Bush worked out an agreement to reduce the U.S. share of the organization's funding. He also defended the administration's policy of allowing "two Chinas" — Taiwan and the People's Republic — to be represented in the General Assembly.

Bush's next job was more controversial. In December 1972 Nixon picked Bush to head the Republican National Committee, replacing Kansas senator Robert Dole. That left Bush with the unenviable task of chairing the party during the Watergate investigation. Although he remained publicly loyal to the embattled president throughout the crisis, Bush later said he had privately urged Nixon to resign.

In August 1974, when Ford succeeded Nixon, Bush was mentioned as a possibility to fill the vacant vice presidency. Instead, Ford named Bush to be the U.S. envoy to Peking. Bush attracted little attention in that post. Slightly more than a year later, Ford fired William E. Colby as CIA director and named Bush to replace him.

Idaho Democrat Frank Church, chairman of the Senate Intelligence Committee, opposed the selection of Bush for the CIA because of his past political roles, particularly as Republican chairman. Church also was concerned that Bush might be chosen as Ford's 1976 running mate. After Ford promised not to pick Bush as his vice president, Bush was confirmed by the Senate.

Presidential Campaign

Bush's next public role was as a candidate for the 1980 Republican presidential nomination. His selection by Reagan as his vice presidential choice marked the first time in 20 years that a presidential nominee had named a pre-convention rival as his ticket partner.

The independently wealthy Bush had spent almost two years in his quest for the presidency. Following the script that won Jimmy Carter the 1976 Democratic nomination, he assiduously worked states with primaries scheduled for early in the election season in hopes of attracting attention to his candidacy.

The plan worked well in the fall of 1979, when Bush won several straw votes at state and local GOP meetings. The aim was to attract news media notice, and it worked. The plan also worked well in the important Iowa precinct caucuses in January 1980, when Bush defeated front-runner Reagan. Gaining on Reagan in the polls, Bush extolled his "Big Mo," or momentum.

The turning point in Bush's campaign came during a Feb. 23 debate with Reagan in Nashua, N.H. Bush, who wanted the debate to be limited to himself and Reagan, said nothing when the former California governor denounced banning other candidates from the debate. The incident deflated Bush's image. Although the Texan went on to win six primaries, he never could match Reagan's delegate totals. He withdrew from the race on May 26.

James S. Brady
(Press Secretary)

Presidential press secretary James S. Brady was seriously wounded in the March 30, 1981, assassination attempt on President Reagan. Larry Speakes, deputy press secretary, took over Brady's duties, but not his title, after the shooting.

Affable and witty, Brady had extensive Washington experience before being named presidential press secretary. Brady had been a communications consultant to the House of Representatives, an aide to James T. Lynn when Lynn headed the Office of Management and Budget and the Department of Housing and Urban Development, assistant to Defense Secretary Donald Rumsfeld and press assistant to Sen. William V. Roth Jr., R-Del.

A native of Illinois, Brady graduated from the University of Illinois in 1962; he majored in communications and political science. He later received a graduate degree in public administration from Southern Illinois University. He also had worked for Sen. Everett M. Dirksen, R-Ill. (1951-69), the Illinois State Medical Society and several Chicago business firms.

Patrick J. Buchanan
(Communications Director)

In appointing Patrick J. Buchanan as assistant to the president and director of communications in the White House, President Reagan brought to his team an experienced journalist and government servant. His new job placed him in charge of the White House media operation, including the president's speechwriting team.

For 10 years Buchanan had been writing a thrice-weekly column of political and social commentary, which was distributed to 125 newspapers across the United States. He also had been co-host for three years of a nightly interview program on the Cable News Network, "Crossfire," and a weekly panelist on "The McLaughlin Group," a public affairs show distributed nationally by PBS. From 1978 to 1984 he also was co-host of a daily radio show from Washington, D.C., and delivered daily commentary on the NBC radio network. In his nationally syndicated column and on a number of television and radio shows, he had sharply criticized liberalism and had been unflagging in his support for the conservative cause.

Born Nov. 2,. 1938, in Washington, D.C., Buchanan graduated with a bachelor of arts degree in English and philosophy from Georgetown University. Later, in 1962, he received a master's degree in journalism from Columbia University. From 1962 to 1966 he worked as a newspaper writer for the *St. Louis Globe-Democrat*. He first came to national attention in 1966 when he served as press aide, executive assistant and speechwriter to former vice president Richard Nixon, traveling with him during the 1966 and 1968 campaigns.

He was named special assistant to President Nixon in 1969 and served throughout his presidency, resigning from the Ford White House in November 1974. During his tenure at the White House, Buchanan had written speeches for both the president and vice president, helped develop political strategy, published the president's daily news summaries and prepared the foreign and domestic briefing books for presidential news conferences. In 1972 he was a member of the 15-person official delegation to the People's Republic of China, and he accompanied President Nixon to the summit in Moscow, Yalta and Minsk in 1974.

Buchanan never wavered in his support of Nixon throughout the Watergate affair, but he was one of the few top White House officials who remained untouched by the scandal.

In addition to his syndicated column, Buchanan had written two books, *The New Majority* and *Conservative Votes, Liberal Victories*. He also had contributed to *The Nation, Rolling Stone, National Review, Conservative Digest, Skeptic* and *The American Spectator*.

Max L. Friedersdorf
(Chief White House Lobbyist)

Having delivered an ambitious legislative program to an increasingly skeptical Congress in 1985, President Reagan persuaded his first chief White House lobbyist to return to map second-term strategy.

Max L. Friedersdorf, who began his new White House duties in February, was a veteran presidential lobbyist who served in the administrations of Richard Nixon and Gerald R. Ford. He headed the White House lobbying staff during Reagan's first year in office, overseeing the successful campaign for budget reductions and the three-year tax cut that passed in 1981. "I didn't want to sit around the rest of my life and say that I could've helped Reagan achieve his second-term aims," said Friedersdorf.

Friedersdorf, 55, left the White House at the end of 1981 and was named U.S. consul general to Bermuda. He left that post in September 1983 to become vice president for public affairs at Pepsico in Purchase, N.Y.

His return to the administration was part of a second-term shakeup that was changing the look of the senior White House staff. As the "legislative strategy coordinator," Friedersdorf would answer to Chief of Staff Donald T. Regan, the former secretary of the Treasury who swapped jobs with James A. Baker III.

Friedersdorf noted in a telephone interview with a reporter that as Reagan began his second term he enjoyed less support in the House for his positions than he had in 1981. He also said there had been some "ideological slippage" in the Senate even though Republicans remained in the majority. Still, Friedersdorf said Reagan's landslide victory in November 1984 over Walter F. Mondale should translate into legislative success on Capitol Hill.

Friedersdorf's return to his former position was expected to beef up the White House lobbying office in numbers and talent. Regan was thought by some to be less familiar with the ins and outs of legislative strategy than was Baker, thus requiring a skilled strategist to guide administration lobbying.

M. B. Oglesby Jr., the former chief White House lobbyist, had developed a reputation for being an effective lobbyist but not so good a planner of overall strategy. Oglesby remained at the White House, with responsibility for overseeing day-to-day lobbying on Capitol Hill.

A lobbyist with close ties to the White House said Friedersdorf's appointment would be "reassuring" to Congress because it signaled the administration's intent to place lobbying responsibility with someone who was "well regarded as a statesman, who knows the Hill and who knows the White House operation."

Friedersdorf said health problems that had hastened his departure from the White House in 1982 had dissipated. "I was pretty worn out when I left after '81. That was a pretty rough year. It's been three years since I left. . . . I feel great."

Friedersdorf had been a newspaper reporter, served as administrative assistant to Rep. Richard L. Roudebush, R-Ind. (1961-71), and worked on the congressional affairs staff at the Office of Economic Opportunity. President Jimmy Carter appointed him

to the Federal Election Commission in 1979, and he became chairman in 1980, before leaving to join the Reagan administration.

Robert C. McFarlane
(National Security Adviser)

On Oct. 17, 1983, President Reagan named Robert C. McFarlane, an experienced insider, as his national security adviser. McFarlane succeeded William P. Clark, who replaced James G. Watt as interior secretary.

McFarlane had been the deputy national security adviser since 1982 and the president's special Middle East envoy since July 1983. He was Reagan's third national security adviser. Clark, a Reagan friend and confidant, had replaced Richard V. Allen, who resigned in January 1982 as the result of charges that he had accepted an improper $1,000 honorarium from a Japanese magazine.

In the weeks prior to the Watt-Clark-McFarlane shuffle, there had been numerous reports of disagreements between Clark and Secretary of State George P. Shultz. The changes came at a time when issues affecting the Middle East, Central America and the spectrum of East-West relations seemed especially pressing.

Reagan's choice of McFarlane angered some conservatives, who had favored for the job Jeane J. Kirkpatrick, at the time the U.S. representative to the United Nations. The appointment of McFarlane was praised on Capitol Hill. He had won respect for his negotiations with congressional leaders on defense and foreign policy issues.

McFarlane said he would not be a high-profile adviser, as were his predecessors Henry A. Kissinger, who had served presidents Nixon and Ford, and Zbigniew Brzezinski, who had served Carter. "My role now is not to be an advocate, but to be a coordinator," he told reporters.

Despite his years of high-level government service, McFarlane's personal views on foreign and defense policies were not widely known. Some observed that he was less dogmatic than Clark in his approach to issues such as U.S.-Soviet relations.

In announcing the appointment, Reagan called McFarlane "someone of strong principle" who "shares my view about the need for . . . an effective, bipartisan foreign policy based on peace through strength."

Some administration officials reportedly had worried that McFarlane would not have the easy access to the president that Clark had enjoyed. But McFarlane said Reagan had assured him on that point: "The importance of that access is clearly understood."

McFarlane played a central role in negotiations in summer 1982 between the White House and members of Congress who had been urging the administration to moderate its stance in arms control talks with the Soviet Union. Sen. Larry Pressler, R-S.D., Rep. Albert Gore Jr., D-Tenn., and other members said that McFarlane, while standing behind the president's basic policies, apparently had pressed other White House officials for some accommodation with the congressional critics.

McFarlane, a retired Marine Corps lieutenant colonel, had more than 10 years of experience in national security affairs. During the Nixon and Ford years, he was military assistant to national security advisers Kissinger and Brent Scowcroft.

He returned to active military duty in 1977 but retired in 1979 and joined the Republican minority staff of the Senate Armed Services Committee. In 1981, then secretary of state Alexander M. Haig Jr. named McFarlane as the State Department counselor — where he served as troubleshooter. In July 1983 Reagan sent him to the Middle East, where he spent three months helping to negotiate a fragile cease-fire in Lebanon.

Donald T. Regan
(White House Chief of Staff)

The job switch between James A. Baker III, chief of staff during Reagan's first term, and Donald T. Regan was expected to have a stylistic, rather than a substantive, impact on White House relations with Capitol Hill. Regan, in his former role as Treasury secretary, had garnered a reputation for subordinating himself to the president, becoming one of his most ardent cheerleaders. Yet some maintained that he had lain low while others in the administration bore the brunt of criticism for the Reagan administration's budget cutting tactics.

It was also conjectured that Regan's presence in the White House could lessen the president's determination to make difficult deficit-cutting decisions. Regan had argued that large deficits were not so damaging to the economy as some purported, and he had supported the notion, also pushed by the president, that economic growth would resolve many of the deficit problems.

One top Republican Senate Budget Committee aide said the switch "adds another note of uncertainty in what is already a very fluid situation."

Wall Street Career

The 66-year-old Regan spent his entire career on Wall Street before joining the administration in 1981.

He went to work for Merrill Lynch in 1946 after receiving his undergraduate degree from Harvard University, his law degree from the University of Pennsylvania and serving as a Marine in World War II.

At Merrill Lynch he worked his way up the corporate ladder, becoming chairman of the financial conglomerate in 1971 through what had been described as a combination of hard work, shrewdness and toughness, which he attributed to his Marine training.

As head of the investment firm, Regan also became known as a maverick, developing Merrill Lynch into one of the largest and most innovative companies on Wall Street.

Although Regan was active in influential organizations such as the Business Roundtable, the Committee for Economic Development and the Council on Foreign Relations, he had not been active in politics.

He amassed a sizable fortune at Merrill Lynch; records showed he owned more than 244,000 shares of stock in the investment firm, worth nearly $9 million.

Regan's Influence on Reagan

Regan also moved up in the Reagan administration, where he became the president's chief economic adviser, in large part by remaining a consistent supporter of Reagan and his views on tax and budget policy. He had risen in stature above Reagan's other economic advisers, including David A. Stockman, director of OMB, and former Council of Economic Advisers chairman Martin Feldstein, both of whom had publicly challenged the president's fiscal views.

Regan's main weakness as chief of staff, noted some on Capitol Hill, would be his lack of knowledge of foreign affairs. But he was a close friend of Secretary of State George P. Shultz and the two were expected to work well together. It was questionable whether he would get along as well with Defense Secretary Caspar W. Weinberger, whose defense budget requests he had criticized as too large.

Regan's installation as the chief White House aide was expected to boost prospects for the Treasury Department's plan to overhaul the tax code, announced on Nov. 27, 1984. The president's initial reaction to the proposal —which would eliminate most special tax breaks and lower rates for businesses — was cautious, but aides said since then that he would push for similar revisions once Congress acted on the deficit.

"There was some question how enthusiastically Reagan would embrace the Treasury tax reform proposal," said Rep. Bill Gradison, R-Ohio, a member of the tax-writing House Ways and Means Committee. "To make the architect of the plan chief of staff, I think, is a great vote of confidence."

Larry Speakes
(Principal Deputy Press Secretary)

Larry Speakes handled most presidential news briefings after Press Secretary James S. Brady was seriously wounded in the March 30, 1981, assassination attempt on President Reagan.

Speakes had served as a press spokesman in Reagan's transition office in 1980. He returned to the White House as Brady's deputy after having been a member of the staff of the Nixon White House and assistant press secretary under President Ford. In 1977 he joined the public relations firm of Hill and Knowlton in Washington, D.C., and acted as a liaison between Ford and the Reagan-Bush committee in the 1980 presidential campaign.

Speakes was born and educated in Mississippi, where he was an editor and publisher of several small newspapers before coming to Washington in 1968 as press secretary to Sen. James O. Eastland, D-Miss. (1941, 1943-78).

Speakes generally was given high marks by the Washington press corps for his loyalty to the president, his punctuality and his self-effacing humor. A hard worker, Speakes was said to put in 14-hour days. Senior administration officials also reportedly had been pleased with Speakes' consistent improvement in the job. Reporters complained, however, that Speakes lacked credibility and that he was not plugged in to the White House decision-making apparatus.

Speakes bore the brunt of criticism

from the press for the news blackout of the October 1983 Grenada invasion and for his ignorance about the details of the operation. He was briefed on the invasion only after it had begun and was insufficientlty informed to be able to answer questions from the press.

Fred F. Fielding

President Reagan appointed Fred F. Fielding to be White House Counsel in 1981, and Fielding continued to serve in this capacity during Reagan's second term. As a member of the Reagan transition staff, Fielding acted as counsel on conflict-of-interest matters and headed the office of government ethics. During the Nixon administration, Fielding was deputy to White House Counsel John W. Dean III. Fielding practiced law with the firm of Morgan, Lewis and Bockius, where he eventually became a partner, between his stints at the White House. He received an undergraduate degree from Gettysburg College in 1961 and was graduated from the University of Virginia School of Law in 1964.

Beryl W. Sprinkel

Allaying fears that he would abolish the Council of Economic Advisers (CEA), President Reagan on Feb. 22, 1985, named Treasury Under Secretary Beryl W. Sprinkel as chairman. He replaced Martin S. Feldstein, who resigned after repeatedly incurring administration wrath with his negative assessments of budget deficits. The council was to provide the president with independent economic analyses.

Sprinkel had been serving as under secretary of the Treasury since March 1981. He previously worked for 28 years as executive vice president and economist at Harris Trust and Savings Bank in Chicago. He was director of "Harris Economics," an economic and financial forecasting service

published by the bank; a member of *Time* magazine's Board of Economists; chairman of the Economic Advisory Committee of the American Bankers Association; and a consultant to various government agencies and congressional committees.

Before joining Harris Trust and Savings, he taught economics and finance at the University of Chicago (1949-52) and at the University of Missouri School of Business and Public Administration (1948-49). He is the author of two books and co-author of a third on the effects of monetary policy on financial markets and the economy.

Born Nov. 20, 1923, on a farm near Richmond, Mo., Sprinkel received an undergraduate degree in public administration from the University of Missouri in 1947, a master's degree in business administration from the University of Chicago in 1948, and a Ph.D. in economics and finance from the University of Chicago in 1952.

Edward J. Rollins

Edward J. Rollins had been a longtime insider at the Reagan White House. Before his Feb. 5, 1985, appointment as assistant to the president for political and governmental affairs, Rollins had advised Reagan on political affairs in various other posts. He served as national director of the president's 1984 re-election campaign.

Born on March 19, 1943, Rollins graduated from the California state university system, where he completed graduate studies in political science. From 1969 to 1973 he was assistant vice chancellor for student affairs at Washington University in St. Louis, where he also taught political science and public administration. In 1968 he worked as assistant to the president of California State University, at Chico.

Long active in the Republican Party, Rollins managed numerous campaigns for the GOP in the West. He was principal assistant to the Republican leader and Speaker of the California Assembly. From 1973 to 1977 he worked at the U.S. Department of Transportation, where he oversaw the department's liaison with Congress and state and local governments. Immediately before accepting his first White House appointment in January 1981, Rollins was Republican chief of staff for the California Assembly.

John A. Svahn

On Sept. 12, 1983, John A. Svahn, under secretary of health and human services and commissioner of Social Security, was appointed as assistant to the president for policy development. Svahn had served on the Reagan transition team in 1980, heading the Task Force on the Health Care Financing Administration. Before joining the Reagan administration he was a consultant specializing in public policy management problems.

Beginning in 1968 Svahn held several positions in California government, first in the State Highway Department and later as chief deputy director and then director of Social Welfare. He was a principal member of California's Welfare Reform Task Force. From 1973 to 1976 he held major federal positions in the Social and Rehabilitation Service of the Department of Health, Education and Welfare, which would later become Health and Human Services. While there, he was credited with developing and implementing the Title XX Social Services program and the Child Support Enforcement Program.

Svahn was born in New London, Conn., on May 13, 1943. He received an undergraduate degree in political science from the University of Washington in 1966, after which he served for two years in the Air Force.

Robert H. Tuttle

Robert H. Tuttle was named director of presidential personnel on Feb. 7, 1985, to replace John S. Herrington, who left the White House to become Reagan's secretary of energy. Tuttle had served as special assistant to the president for presidential personnel since December 1982.

A West Coast business executive for 15 years before going to the White House, Tuttle had been president of three automobile dealerships in Los Angeles and Tucson. Tuttle was an active member of the Republican Party and in 1980 served as the co-chairman of the California Reagan for President Committee.

Tuttle, 41, received an undergraduate degree from Stanford University and a master's in business administration from the University of Southern California.

Appendix

President Reagan's 2nd Inaugural Address

Following is the text of President Reagan's second inaugural address as delivered Jan. 21, 1985:

Senator Mathias, Chief Justice Burger, Vice President Bush, Speaker O'Neill, Senator Dole, Reverend Clergy, members of my family and friends, and my fellow citizens:

This day has been made brighter with the presence here of one who, for a time, has been absent — Senator John Stennis.

God bless you and welcome back.

[Applause.]

There is, however, one who is not with us today: Representative Gillis Long of Louisiana left us last night. I wonder if we could all join in a moment of silent prayer.*

[Moment of silent prayer.]

Amen.

There are no words adequate to express my thanks for the great honor that you have bestowed on me. I will do my utmost to be deserving of your trust.

This is, as Senator Mathias told us, the 50th time that we the people have celebrated this historic occasion. When the first President, George Washington, placed his hand upon the Bible, he stood less than a single day's journey by horseback from raw, untamed wilderness.

There were 4 million Americans in a union of 13 States. Today we are 60 times as many in a union of 50 States. We have lighted the world with our inventions, gone to the aid of mankind wherever in the world there was a cry for help, journeyed to the Moon and safely returned.

So much has changed. And yet we stand together as we did two centuries ago.

When I took this oath 4 years ago, I did so in a time of economic stress. Voices were raised saying we had to look to our past for the greatness and glory. But we, the present-day Americans, are not given to looking backward. In this blessed land, there is always a better tomorrow.

Four years ago, I spoke to you of a new beginning and we have accomplished that. But in another sense, our new beginning is a continuation of that beginning created two centuries ago when, for the first time in history, government, the people said, was not our master, it is our servant; its only power that which we the people allow it to have.

That system has never failed us, but, for a time, we failed the system. We asked things of government that government was not equipped to give. We yielded authority to the National Government that properly belonged to States or to local governments or to the people themselves. We allowed taxes and inflation to rob us of our earnings and savings and watched the great industrial machine that had made us the most productive people on Earth slow down and the number of unemployed increase.

By 1980, we knew it was time to renew our faith, to strive with all our strength toward the ultimate in individual freedom consistent with an orderly society.

We believed then and now: There are no limits to growth and human progress when men and women are free to follow their dreams. And we were right.

[Applause.]

And we were right to believe that. Tax rates have been reduced, inflation cut dramatically, and more people are employed than ever before in our history.

We are creating a nation once again vibrant, robust, and alive. But there are many mountains yet to climb. We will not rest until every American enjoys the fullness of freedom, dignity, and opportunity as our birthright. It is our birthright as citizens of this great Republic.

And, if we meet this challenge, these will be years when Americans have restored their confidence and tradition of progress; when our values of faith, family, work, and neighborhood were restated for a modern age; when our economy was finally freed from government's grip; when we made sincere efforts at meaningful arms reduction, rebuilding our defenses, our economy, and developing new technologies, and helped preserve peace in a troubled world; when Americans courageously supported the struggle for liberty, self-government, and free enterprise throughout the world, and turned the tide of history away from totalitarian darkness and into the warm sunlight of human freedom.

[Applause.]

My fellow citizens, our Nation is poised for greatness. We must do what we know is right and do it with all our might. Let history say of us, these were golden years — when the American Revolution was reborn, when freedom gained new life, when America reached for her best.

Our two-party system has served us well over the years, but never better than in those times of great challenge when we came together not as Democrats or Republicans, but as Americans united in a common cause.

[Applause.]

Two of our Founding Fathers, a Boston lawyer named Adams and a Virginia planter named Jefferson, members of that remarkable group who met in Independence Hall and dared to think they could start the world over again, left us an important lesson. They had become political rivals in the Presidential election of 1800. Then years later, when both were retired, and age had softened their anger, they began to speak to each other again through letters. A bond was reestablished between those two who had helped create this Government of ours.

In 1826, the 50th anniversary of the Declaration of Independence, they both died. They died on the same day, within a few hours of each other, and that day was the Fourth of July.

In one of those letters exchanged in the sunset of their lives, Jefferson wrote:

> It carries me back to the times when, beset with difficulties and dangers, we were fellow laborers in the same cause, struggling for what is most valuable to man, his right to self-government. Laboring always at the same oar, with some wave ever ahead threatening to overwhelm us, and yet passing harmless . . . we rode through the storm with heart and hand.

Well, with heart and hand, let us stand as one today: One people under God determined that our future shall be worthy of our past. As we do, we must not repeat the well-intentioned errors of our past. We must

President Reagan takes the oath of office from Chief Justice Warren E. Burger at noon Jan. 21, 1985, in the Capitol Rotunda, as Nancy Reagan and Sen. Charles McC. Mathias Jr., R-Md., look on.

never again abuse the trust of working men and women, by sending their earnings on a futile chase after the spiraling demands of a bloated Federal establishment. You elected us in 1980 to end this prescription for disaster, and I don't believe you reelected us in 1984 to reverse course.

[Applause.]

At the heart of our efforts is one idea vindicated by 25 straight months of economic growth: Freedom and incentives unleash the drive and entrepreneurial genius that are the core of human progress. We have begun to increase the rewards for work, savings, and investment, reduce the increase in the cost and size of government and its interference in people's lives.

We must simplify our tax system,

make it more fair, and bring the rates down for all who work and earn. We must think anew and move with a new boldness, so every American who seeks work can find work; so the least among us shall have an equal chance to achieve the greatest things — to be heroes who heal our sick, feed the hungry, protect peace among nations, and leave this world a better place.

The time has come for a new American Emancipation — a great national drive to tear down economic barriers and liberate the spirit of enterprise in the most distressed areas of our country. My friends, together we can do this, and do it we must, so help me God.

From new freedom will spring new opportunities for growth, a more productive, fulfilled and united people, and a stronger America — an America that will lead the technological revolution, and also open its mind and heart and soul to the treasures of literature, music and poetry, and the values of faith, courage, and love.

A dynamic economy, with more citizens working and paying taxes, will be our strongest tool to bring down budget deficits. But an almost unbroken 50 years of deficit spending has finally brought us to a time of reckoning.

We have come to a turning point, a moment for hard decisions. I have asked the Cabinet and my staff a question, and now I put the same question to all of you: If not us, who? And if not now, when? It must be done by all of us going forward with a program aimed at reaching a balanced budget. We can then begin reducing the national debt.

I will shortly submit a budget to the Congress aimed at freezing Government program spending for the next year. Beyond that, we must take further steps to permanently control Government's power to tax and spend.

We must act now to protect future generations from Government's desire to spend its citizens' money and tax them into servitude when the bills come due. Let us make it unconstitutional for the Federal Government to spend more than the Federal Government takes in.

[Applause.]

We have already started returning to the people and to State and local governments responsibilities better handled by them. Now, there is a place for the Federal Government in matters of social compassion. But our fundamental goals must be to reduce dependency and upgrade the dignity of those who are infirm or disadvantaged. And here a growing economy and support from family and community offer our best chance for a society where compassion is a way of life, where the old and infirm are

cared for, the young and, yes, the unborn protected, and the unfortunate looked after and made self-sufficient.

[Applause.]

And there is another area where the Federal Government can play a part. As an older American, I remember a time when people of different race, creed, or ethnic origin in our land found hatred and prejudice installed in social custom and, yes, in law. There is no story more heartening in our history than the progress that we have made toward the "brotherhood of man" that God intended for us. Let us resolve there will be no turning back or hesitation on the road to an America rich in dignity and abundant with opportunity for all our citizens.

[Applause.]

Let us resolve that we the people will build an American opportunity society in which all of us — white and black, rich and poor, young and old — will go forward together arm in arm. Again, let us remember that though our heritage is one of blood lines from every corner of the Earth, we are all Americans pledged to carry on this last, best hope of man on Earth.

[Applause.]

National Security

I have spoken of our domestic goals and the limitations which we should put on our National Government. Now let me turn to a task which is the primary responsibility of National Government — the safety and security of our people.

Today we utter no prayer more fervently than the ancient prayer for peace on Earth. Yet history has shown that peace will not come nor will our freedom be preserved by good will alone. There are those in the world who scorn our vision of human dignity and freedom. One nation, the Soviet Union, has conducted the greatest military buildup in the history of man, building arsenals of awesome offensive weapons.

We have made progress in restoring our defense capability. But much remains to be done. There must be no wavering by us, nor any doubts by others, that America will meet her responsibilities to remain free, secure, and at peace.

[Applause.]

There is only one way safely and legitimately to reduce the cost of national security, and that is to reduce the need for it. And this we are trying to do in negotiations with the Soviet Union. We are not just discussing limits on a further increase of nuclear weapons. We seek, instead, to reduce their number. We seek the total elimination one day of nuclear weapons from the face of the Earth.

[Applause.]

Now, for decades, we and the Soviets have lived under the threat of mutual assured destruction; if either resorted to the use of nuclear weapons, the other could retaliate and destroy the one who had started it. Is there either logic or morality in believing that if one side threatens to kill tens of millions of our people, our only recourse is to threaten killing tens of millions of theirs?

I have approved a research program to find, if we can, a security shield that would destroy nuclear missiles before they reach their target. It wouldn't kill people, it would destroy weapons. It wouldn't militarize space, it would help demilitarize the arsenals of Earth. It would render nuclear weapons obsolete. We will meet with the Soviets, hoping that we can agree on a way to rid the world of the threat of nuclear destruction.

We strive for peace and security, heartened by the changes all around us. Since the turn of the century, the number of democracies in the world has grown fourfold. Human freedom is on the march, and nowhere more so than in our own hemisphere. Freedom is one of the deepest and noblest aspirations of the human spirit. People worldwide hunger for the right of self-determination, for those inalienable rights that make for human dignity and progress.

America must remain freedom's staunchest friend, for freedom is our best ally —

[Applause.]

And it is the world's only hope, to conquer poverty and preserve peace. Every blow we inflict against poverty will be a blow against its dark allies of oppression and war. Every victory for human freedom will be a victory for world peace.

So we go forward today, a Nation still mighty in its youth and powerful in its purpose. With our alliances strengthened, with our economy leading the world to a new age of economic expansion, we look forward to a world rich in possibilities. And all this because we have worked and acted together, not as members of political parties, but as Americans.

Echoes of the Past

My friends, we live in a world that is lit by lightning. So much is changing and will change, but so much endures, and transcends time.

History is a ribbon, always unfurling; history is a journey. And as we continue our journey, we think of those who traveled before us. We stand together again at the steps of this symbol of our democracy — or we would have been standing at the steps if it hadn't gotten so cold. Now we are standing inside this symbol of our democracy. Now we hear again the echoes of our past.

A General falls to his knees in the hard snow of Valley Forge; a lonely President paces the darkened halls, and ponders his struggle to preserve the Union; the men of the Alamo call out encouragement to each other; a settler pushes west and sings a song, and the song echoes out forever and fills the unknowing air.

It is the American sound. It is hopeful, big-hearted, idealistic, daring, decent, and fair. That's our heritage; that is our song.

We sing it still. For all our problems, our differences, we are together as of old, as we raise our voices to the God who is the Author of this most tender music. And may He continue to hold us close as we fill the world with our sound — sound in unity, affection, and love. One people under God, dedicated to the dream of freedom that He has placed in the human heart, called upon now to pass that dream on to a waiting and hopeful world.

God bless you and may God bless America.

* *The president referred to Sen. John C. Stennis, D-Miss., who had his leg amputated Nov. 30, 1984, because of cancer, and Rep. Gillis W. Long, D-La., who died Jan. 20.*

Reagan's Budget Message to Congress

To the Congress of the United States:

In the past 2 years we have experienced one of the strongest economic recoveries of the post-war period. The prospect of a substantially brighter future for America lies before us. As 1985 begins, the economy is growing robustly and shows considerable upward momentum. Favorable financial conditions presage a continuation of the expansion. Production, productivity, and employment gains have been impressive, and inflation remains well under control. I am proud of the state of our economy. Let me highlight a few points:

● The economy expanded at a 6.8% rate in 1984 and at a 6% annual rate over the 2 years since the recession trough at the end of 1982 — faster than any other upturn since 1951.

● Confidence in the economy has prompted business firms to expand their capital facilities. Real investment in new plant and equipment has grown 15.4% an-

nually since the end of 1982 — faster than in any other post-war recovery.

● The ratio of real investment to real GNP has reached its highest level in the post-war period.

● Industrial production is 23% above its level at the recession trough in November 1982 — a greater advance than in any other recovery since 1958.

● Corporate profits have risen nearly 90% since the recession trough in 1982 — the fastest 8-quarter increase in 37 years.

● Civilian employment has grown 7.2 million over the past 25 months and the number of unemployed has fallen by 3.7 million. In the last 4 months alone, more than 1.1 million Americans have found jobs.

● Inflation remains well under control. The December 1984 CPI was 4% higher than a year earlier, about a third of the rate of inflation this administration inherited. The GNP deflator, the broadest measure of inflation, increased only 3.5% last year and at only a 2.4% annual rate in the fourth quarter.

● The prime rate of interest is now only half of what it was when I took office.

Contrast our current circumstances with the situation we faced just 4 years ago. Inflation was raging at double-digit rates. Oil prices had soared. The prime rate of interest was over 20%. The economy was stagnating. Unemployment had risen sharply and was to rise further. America's standing in world opinion was at low ebb.

All that, mercifully, is behind us now. The tremendous turnaround in our fortunes did not just happen. In February 1981, I presented the four fundamentals of my economic program. They were:

● Reducing the growth of overall Federal spending by eliminating activities that are beyond the proper sphere of Federal Government responsibilities and by restraining the growth of spending for other activities.

● Limiting tax burdens to the minimum levels necessary to finance only essential government services, thereby strengthening incentives for saving, investment, work, productivity, and economic growth.

● Reducing the Federal regulatory burden where the Federal Government intrudes unnecessarily into our private lives, the efficient conduct of private business, or the operations of State and local governments.

● Supporting a sound and steady monetary policy, to encourage economic growth and bring inflation under control.

Four Years of Accomplishment

These policies were designed to restore economic growth and stability. They succeeded.

The past 4 years have also seen the beginning of a quiet but profound revolution in the conduct of our Federal Government. We have halted what seemed at the time an inexorable set of trends toward greater and greater Government intrusiveness, more and more regulation, higher and higher taxes, more and more spending, higher and higher inflation, and weaker and weaker defense. We have halted these trends in our first 4 years.

● The rate of Federal spending growth was out of control at 17.4% a year in 1980. Under my budget proposals the growth of programmatic spending — that is, total Federal spending except for debt service — will be zero next year — frozen at this year's levels.

● Further, spending will grow only 30% over the 4 years from 1982 to 1986, compared to its record pace of 66% between 1977 and 1981, and this despite legislated additions to my program and the needed rebuilding of our defense capabilities.

● The Federal tax system was changed for the better — marginal tax rates were reduced and depreciation reform introduced. These reforms were designed to increase incentives for work, training and education, saving, business growth, and capital expansion. Tax loopholes have been

closed, improving the equity of the system.

● Domestic spending, which previously grew faster than any other major part of the budget (nearly four-fold in real terms between 1960 and 1980), will have been virtually frozen from 1981 to 1985.

● Our defense capabilities are now getting back to a level where we can protect our citizens, honor our commitments to our allies, and participate in the long-awaited arms control talks from a position of respected strength.

● Federal credit programs, which had also grown out of control, have been cut back, and their management has been vastly improved.

● The rapid growth of regulations and red tape has also been halted. The number of Federal rules published by agencies has fallen by over 35% during the past 4 years, and many unnecessary old rules have been eliminated. For the first time, the *Federal Register* of new regulatory actions has grown shorter for 4 consecutive years; it is now 41% shorter than it was in 1980.

● Major management improvement initiatives are underway that will fundamentally change the way the Federal Government operates. The President's Private Sector Survey on Cost Control has completed its report, and many of its recommendations are included in this budget. The President's Council on Integrity and Efficiency has reported $46 billion in improved use of funds through reduction of waste and fraud.

● The Federal nondefense work force has been reduced by over 78,000.

The proposals contained in this budget will build on the accomplishments of the last 4 years and put into action a philosophy of government that is working and that has received the overwhelming endorsement of the American people.

If we took no action to curb the growth of spending, Federal outlays would rise to over a trillion dollars in 1986. This would result in deficits exceeding $200 billion in each of the next 5 years. This is unacceptable. The budget I propose, therefore, will reduce spending by $51 billion in 1986, $83 billion in 1987, and $105 billion in 1988. Enactment of these measures would reduce the deficit projected for 1988 to $144 billion — still a far cry from our goal of a balanced budget, but a significant step in the right direction and a 42% reduction from the current services level projected for that year.

Last year my administration worked with Congress to come up with a downpayment on reducing the deficit. This budget commits the Government to a second installment. With comparable commitments to further reductions in the next two budgets, and, I hope, other spending reduction ideas advanced by the Congress, we can achieve our goal in an orderly fashion.

The budget proposes a 1-year freeze in total spending other than debt service. This will be achieved through a combination of freezes, reforms, terminations, cutbacks, and management improvements in individual programs. For a number of reasons, a line-by-line budget freeze is not possible or desirable. Further, such an approach would assume that all programs are of equal importance. Taken together, the specific proposals in this budget hold total Federal spending excluding debt service constant in 1986 at its 1985 level.

The budget proposals provide for substantial cost savings in the medicare program, in Federal payroll costs, in agricultural and other subsidies to business and upper-income groups, in numerous programs providing grants to State and local governments, and in credit programs. A freeze is proposed in the level of some entitlement program benefits, other than social security, means-tested programs, and programs for the disabled, that have hitherto received automatic "cost-of-living ad-

justments" every year. The budget proposes further reductions in defense spending below previously reduced mid-year levels.

Despite the reforms of the past 4 years, our Federal tax system remains complex and inequitable. Tax rates are still so high that they distort economic decisions, and this reduces economic growth from what it otherwise could be. I will propose, after further consultation with the Congress, further tax simplification and reform. The proposals will not be a scheme to raise taxes — only to distribute their burden more fairly and to simplify the entire system. By broadening the base, we can lower rates.

There will be substantial political resistance to every deficit reduction measure proposed in this budget. Every dollar of current Federal spending benefits someone, and that person has a vested self-interest in seeing these benefits perpetuated and expanded. Prior to my administration, such interests had been dominant and their expectations and demands had been met, time and time again.

At some point, however, the question must be raised: "Where is the political logrolling going to stop?" At some point, the collective demands upon the public Treasury of all the special interests combined exceed the public's ability and willingness to pay. The single most difficult word for a politician to utter is a simple, flat "No." The patience of the American people has been stretched as far as it will go. They want action; they have demanded it.

We said "no" frequently in 1981, and real spending for discretionary domestic programs dropped sharply. But we did not accomplish enough. We now have no choice but to renew our efforts with redoubled vigor. The profusion of Federal domestic spending programs must be reduced to an acceptable, appropriate, and supportable size.

It will require political courage of a high order to carry this program forward in the halls of Congress, but I believe that with good faith and goodwill on all sides, we can succeed. If we fail to reduce excessive Federal benefits to special interest groups, we will be saddled either with larger budget deficits or with higher taxes — either of which would be of greater harm to the American economy and people.

1986 Efficiency Program

Not only must both the scope and scale of Federal spending be drastically cut back to reduce the deficit: we must also institute comprehensive management improvements and administrative reforms to make sure that we use available funds as efficiently as possible.

Tough but necessary steps are being taken throughout the Federal Government to reduce the costs of management and administration. Substantial savings in overhead costs have been achieved under provisions of the Deficit Reduction Act of 1984. A 5% Federal civilian employee salary cut has been proposed; a 10% reduction in administrative overhead has been ordered; termination of programs that have outlived their usefulness is proposed; outmoded, inefficient agency field structures that have evolved over the past half-century are being consolidated and streamlined to take advantage of efficiencies made possible by modern transportation, communication, and information technology.

Administration of Federal agencies is being made more efficient through the adoption of staffing standards, automation of manual processes, consolidation of similar functions, and reduction of administrative overhead costs. A program to increase productivity by 20% by 1992 in all appropriate Government functions is being instituted, as are improved cash and credit management systems and error rate reduction programs.

This management improvement program will result in a leaner and more effi-cient Federal structure and will be described in a management report that I am submitting to the Congress for the first time shortly after my annual budget submission.

We have also made a great deal of progress in reducing the costs imposed on businesses and State and local governments by Federal regulations. These savings are estimated to total $150 billion over a 10-year period. We have reduced the number of new regulations in every year of my first term and have eliminated or reduced paperwork requirements by over 300 million hours each year. In addition, the regulations are more carefully crafted to achieve the greatest protection for the least cost, and wherever possible to use market forces instead of working against them.

A recent Executive Order will strengthen the executive branch coordination that has made these accomplishments possible. For the first time, we will publish an annual program of the most significant regulatory activities, including those that precede the publication of a proposed rule. This will give Congress and the public an earlier opportunity to understand the administration's regulatory policies and priorities.

Conclusion

The key elements of the program I set out 4 years ago are in place and working well. Our national security is being restored; so, I am happy to report, is our economy. Growth and investment are healthy; and inflation, interest rates, tax rates, and unemployment are down and can be reduced further. The proliferation of unnecessary regulations that stifled both economic growth and our individual freedoms has been halted. Progress has been made toward the reduction of unwarranted and excessive growth in domestic spending programs.

But we cannot rest on these accomplishments. If we are to attain a new era of sustained peace, prosperity, growth, and freedom, Federal domestic spending must be brought firmly under control. This budget presents the steps that I believe must be taken. I do not exclude other economies that Congress may devise, so long as they do not imperil my fundamental constitutional responsibilities to look after the national defense and the general welfare of the American people.

Let us get on with the job. The time for action is now.

Ronald Reagan
February 4, 1985

Reagan's Economic Report to Congress

To the Congress of the United States:

In 1981, when I first assumed the duties of the Presidency, our Nation was suffering from declining productivity and the highest inflation in the postwar period — the legacy of years of government overspending, overtaxing, and overregulation.

We bent all of our efforts to correct these problems, not by unsustainable short-run measures, but by measures that would increase long-term growth without renewed inflation. We removed unnecessary regulations, cut taxes, and slowed the growth of Federal spending, freeing the private sector to develop markets, create jobs, and increase productivity. With conviction in our principles, with patience and hard work, we restored the economy to a condition of healthy growth without substantial inflation.

Although employment is now rising, business opportunities are expanding, and interest rates and inflation are under control, we cannot relax our economic vigilance. A return to the policies of excessive government spending and control that led to the economic "malaise" of the late seventies would quickly draw us back into that same disastrous pattern of inflation and recession. Now is the time to recommit ourselves to the policies that broke that awful pattern: policies of reduced Federal spending, lower tax rates, and less regulation to free the creative energy of our people and lead us to an even better economic future through strong and sustained economic growth.

Economic Developments, 1981-1984

The Program for Economic Recovery that we initiated in February 1981 had four key elements:

● Budget reform to cut the rate of growth in Federal spending,

● Reductions in personal and business taxes,

● A far-reaching program of regulatory relief, and

● Restoration of a stable currency and a healthy financial market through sound monetary policy.

The success of this program is now obvious — the U.S. economy is experiencing the strongest recovery in 30 years:

● Real business fixed investment in plant and equipment is higher, relative to real gross national product, than at any time in the postwar period.

● Productivity growth in the business sector has averaged 2.2 percent since the fourth quarter of 1980, compared with a rate of less than 0.3 percent over the prior 4 years.

● The inflation rate is now about one-third the rate in 1980, and short-term interest rates are less than one-half their peak 1981 levels.

But the quantitative record alone does not tell the full story. Four years ago, there was a widespread and growing anxiety about the economy. Many thought that the Nation had entered a condition of permanent economic decline, and that we would have to live with permanent double-digit inflation unless we were willing to suffer massive long-term unemployment.

We did not share this pessimism. It was clear to us that the Nation's economic problems were not the product of the economic system, but of the onerous influence of government on that system. The creative potential of the American people, choosing their own economic futures, was more constrained than helped by the increasingly heavy hand of government. Nor did we share the negative views that a reduction of inflation would increase long-term unemployment; that economic growth, by itself, would increase inflation; and that the government had to protect a "fragile" market system by regulating oil prices and interest rates.

The primary economic responsibility of the Federal Government is not to make choices for people, but to provide an environment in which people can make their own choices. The performance of the economy in the past 2 years under our Program for Economic Recovery fully justifies our faith in the Nation's basic economic health. In 1983 and 1984 the economy generated about 300,000 new jobs per month without an increase in inflation. Real gross national product increased 5.6 percent during 1984, and the unemployment rate declined from 8.1 percent to 7.1 percent. Inflation was steady at its lowest level in more than a decade, and most interest rates are now lower than a year ago. Yet while the U.S. economy grew rapidly in 1984, it maintains the potential for continued strong growth. The inventory/sales ratio is low by historical standards, and capacity utilization rates in most industries are well below prior peak rates.

Economic conditions in 1984 were more favorable than during the second year of a typical recovery, and we see none of the warning signs that usually precede the end of an expansion. The temporary slowing of economic growth starting in July — reflecting the combination of a minor adjustment of consumer spending and inventories and little growth of the basic money supply — seems to have ended in November. These conditions, plus an expectation that the Federal Reserve System will maintain sufficient money growth, support our forecast that the present recovery will continue. *The thriving venture capital market is financing a new American revolution of entrepreneurship and technological change. The American economy is once again the envy of the world.*

Economic Outlook

For the years 1985 through 1988, we assume real gross national product growth of 4 percent per year, slowing slightly in 1989-90. We know that economic recoveries have not been stable in either duration or magnitude, in part because monetary and fiscal policies have often been erratic. We may not be able to eliminate recessions entirely, but a sustained commitment to policies that promote long-term growth and stability can reduce their frequency and severity. Our forecast that the unemployment rate, the inflation rate, and interest rates will decline gradually in the years ahead reflects this commitment to sound, sustainable, and predictable policies.

The Task Ahead

Our 1981 Program for Economic Recovery was designed for the long run with priority attention to the major problems we faced at that time. Our second-term Program for Growth and Opportunity represents a continuation and expansion of the earlier program, with priority attention to the major problems we face in 1985 and beyond. Our objectives — economic growth, stability of the general price level, and increased individual economic opportunity — have not changed. Federal economic policy will continue to be guided by the four key elements of the earlier program. Our progress in solving the most important economic problems we inherited in 1981, however, has allowed us to refocus our attention on the remaining problems and to shift our priorities and resources toward their solution.

Several significant problems remain to be addressed. The rate of growth of Federal spending has been substantially reduced from the rate projected in the budget we inherited in fiscal 1981, but spending growth continues to outpace the economy. Spending too much has left us with a large budget deficit that must and will be reduced. In our efforts to reduce the deficit, we must not forget that the cause of the deficit is increased spending and insufficient growth, not decreased taxes. Federal tax receipts are now almost the same share of gross national product as in the late 1970s, even after the substantial reduction in tax rates that we initiated in 1981.

Another economic problem demanding resolution is unemployment and its effects on the Nation's workers and families. Despite significant progress, much remains to be done. More than 6 million more Americans are now employed than in January 1981, but the unemployment rate is still too high. We will not be satisfied until every American who wants a job is employed at a wage that reflects the market value of his or her skills. Another aspect of this problem is that the poverty rate remains stubbornly high, despite a strong recovery and a continued increase in government assistance. Also, although the inflation rate has been reduced substantially, it is still higher than during most of our peacetime history prior to 1965. We will not be satisfied until we have totally and permanently wrung inflation out of our economy.

Work also remains to be done in the areas of regulatory and monetary policy. Many Federal regulations still impose a substantial cost to the economy. In addition, we need to strengthen the commitment to a sound monetary policy that never again retards economic growth, or reaccelerates inflation.

Our trade deficit, another area of concern, has been caused in large part by a stronger dollar. Investors around the world have bid up the dollars as they have become increasingly confident in our economy. That confidence is an asset and not a liability. However, the conditions that have led to the trade deficit have increased the obstacles faced by some important industries. Agriculture, one of our most productive export sectors, has been harmed by a combination of rigid and outdated Federal agricultural policies and subsidized foreign competition and the strong dollar. In one respect the trade deficit is like the budget deficit; both are too large to be sustained, but there are both beneficial and detrimental ways to reduce them. Our goal is a system of free and fair trade in goods, services, and capital. We will work toward this goal through both bilateral and multilateral agreements.

Economic conditions during the past 4 years are best characterized as transitional — from a period of low productivity growth to a period of high productivity growth; from a period of high inflation and interest rates to a period of much lower inflation and interest rates; from a period of economic "malaise" to a period of economic opportunity. Our task is to consolidate and extend these gains.

Federal Spending, the Deficit

The rate of growth of Federal spending has been reduced from 14.8 percent in fiscal 1981 to an average rate of 9.1 percent in fiscal years 1982 through 1985. During this period, however, current dollar gross national product has increased at an average rate of 7.6 percent. The continued growth of the Federal spending share of gross national product and lost revenues from the recession are the main reasons we are now faced with such large Federal deficits.

The projected Federal deficits are much too large, and they must be reduced. As explained in the accompanying report, however, the economic consequences of reducing these deficits depend critically on how they are reduced. A sustained reduction of the growth of Federal spending will contribute to economic growth, while an increase in tax rates would constrain economic growth. Federal spending on many programs is far larger than necessary, and far larger than desired by most Americans.

My fiscal 1986 budget proposal will protect the social safety net and essential programs, such as defense, for which the Federal Government has a clear constitutional responsibility, and will reform or eliminate many programs that have proven ineffective or nonessential. With no resort to a tax increase, this budget will reduce the deficit to about 4 percent of gross national product in fiscal 1986 and to a steadily lower percentage in future years. Additional spending reductions will probably be necessary in future years to achieve a balanced budget by the end of the decade.

The problems of excessive spending and deficits are not new. In the absence of fundamental reform, they may recur again and again in the future. I therefore support two important measures — one to authorize the President to veto individual line items in comprehensive spending bills, and another to constrain the federal authority to borrow or to increase spending in the absence of broad congressional support. These structural changes are *not* substitutes for the hard fiscal choices that will be necessary in 1985 and beyond, nor for the need to simplify our tax system to stimulate greater growth; but they are important to provide the mechanisms and discipline for longer term fiscal health.

The case for a line-item veto should by now be obvious. The Governors of 43 States have used this authority effectively, and such authority has only once been withdrawn, only later to be reinstated. For over a century, Presidents of both parties have requested such authority.

The proposed constitutional amendment providing for a balanced budget and a tax limitation would constrain the long-run growth of Federal spending and the national debt. In 1982 a proposed amendment to constrain Federal authority to spend and borrow was approved by more than two-thirds of the Senate and by more than a majority of the House of Representatives; a balanced budget amendment has also been endorsed by the legislatures of 32 States. Approval of the proposed balanced budget/tax limitation amendment would ensure that fiscal decisions by future Presidents and Members of Congress are more responsive to the broad interests of the American population.

Federal Taxation

The Economic Recovery Tax Act of 1981 was one of the most important accomplishments of my first term. Individual income tax rates were reduced nearly 25 percent, effective tax rates on the income from new investment were substantially reduced, and beginning this year tax brackets are adjusted for inflation.

But more needs to be done. Personal tax rates should be reduced further to encourage stronger economic growth which, in itself, is our best tool for putting deficits on a steady downward path. Our tax system needs basic reform. It is extraordinarily complicated; it leads to substantial economic inefficiency; and it is widely perceived to be unfair.

At my request, the Treasury Department has developed a comprehensive proposal to simplify and reform the Federal tax system, one that for expected economic conditions would yield about the same revenues as the present system. This proposal, by substantially broadening the tax base, would permit a significant further reduction of marginal tax rates. Shortly, I will be submitting my own proposal for tax simplification, and will urge the Congress to give serious sustained attention to tax simplification — in order to enact a program that will increase fairness and stimulate future savings, investment, and growth.

Federal Regulation

We have made major efforts in the past 4 years to reduce and eliminate Federal regulation of economic activity. Executive Office review of new regulations was streamlined. Oil prices were deregulated by Executive authority early in 1981. New legislation was approved to reduce regulation of banking and to largely eliminate regulation of interstate bus travel.

Regulatory reform, however, has been painfully slow. The Congress failed to approve our proposals to further deregulate banking and natural gas prices, and to reform the regulation of private pensions. In addition, the reauthorization of several major environmental laws has been delayed for several years.

I urge the Congress to consider further deregulation efforts in several areas. The experience with deregulation of oil prices makes clear that continued regulation of natural gas prices is not appropriate. Reform of nuclear licensing requirements also deserves attention. Further deregulation of the banking system should be paired with a major reform of the deposit insurance systems.

Some changes in the single-employer pension law and an increased premium are necessary to preserve the pension insurance system. We should also seriously consider eliminating the remaining Federal regulation of trucking and railroads. Finally, I remain hopeful that the Administration and the Congress can work together to reauthorize the major environmental laws in a way that serves our common environmental and economic goals.

Monetary Policy

The Constitution authorizes the Congress "To coin Money (and) regulate the Value thereof," and Congress has delegated this authority to the Federal Reserve System. The role of the executive branch is restricted to advising the Congress and the Federal Reserve about the conduct of monetary policy, and to nominating members of the Board of Governors as positions become vacant.

During my first term, the Federal Reserve reduced the rate of money growth relative to the high rates of the late 1970s. This change in policy, assisted by the related strong increase in the exchange value of the dollar, helped produce a substantial reduction of inflation and market interest rates. On occasion, however, the rate of money growth has been quite volatile, contributing to instability in interest rates and a decline in economic activity. The sharp reduction in money growth through mid-1982, for example, undoubtedly added to the length and severity of the 1981-1982 recession. And a similar reduction in money growth in the second half of 1984 contributed to the temporary slowing of economic growth late in the year.

We reaffirm our support for a sound monetary policy that contributes to strong, steady economic growth and price stability. Moreover, we expect to cooperate closely with the Federal Reserve in defining and carrying out a prudent and predictable monetary policy.

Conclusion

The Federal Government has only a few important economic responsibilities. Given a proper conduct of these important roles, additional Federal intervention is more often a part of the problem than a part of the solution. We should continue to reduce the many less-important economic activities of the Federal Government so that individuals, private institutions, and State and local governments will have more resources and more freedom to pursue their own interests. Good stewardship of our constitutional responsibilities and the creative energies of the American people will ensure a future of continued economic growth and opportunity.

Ronald Reagan
February 5, 1985

Reagan's State of the Union Address

Following is the **Congressional Record** *text of President Reagan's State of the Union address to a joint session of Congress Feb. 6, 1985:*

Mr. Speaker, Mr. President, distinguished Members of the Congress, honored guests, and fellow citizens. I come before you to report on the state of our Union. And I am pleased to report that, after 4 years of united effort, the American people have brought forth a Nation renewed — stronger, freer and more secure than before.

Four years ago, we began to change — forever, I hope — our assumptions about Government and its place in our lives. Out of that change has come great and robust growth — in our confidence, our economy, and our role in the world.

Tonight, America is stronger because of the values that we hold dear. We believe that faith and freedom must be our guiding stars, for they show us truth, they make us brave, give us hope, and leave us wiser than we were. Our progress began not in Washington, D.C., but in the hearts of our families, communities, workplaces, and voluntary groups which, together, are unleashing the invincible spirit of one great Nation under God.

Four years ago, we said we would invigorate our economy by giving people greater freedom and incentives to take risks, and letting them keep more of what they earned.

We did what we promised, and a great industrial giant is reborn. Tonight we can take pride in 25 straight months of economic growth, the strongest in 34 years; a three-year inflation average of 3.9 percent, the lowest in 17 years; and 7.3 million new jobs in two years, with more of our citizens working than ever before.

New freedom in our lives has planted the rich seeds for future success:

For an America of wisdom that honors the family, knowing that as the family goes, so goes our civilization;

For an America of vision that sees tomorrow's dreams in the learning and hard work we do today;

For an America of courage whose servicemen and women, even as we meet, proudly stand watch on the frontiers of freedom;

For an America of compassion that opens its heart to those who cry out for help.

We have begun well. But it's only a beginning. We are not here to congratulate ourselves on what we have done, but to challenge ourselves to finish what has not yet been done.

We are here to speak for millions in our inner cities who long for real jobs, safe neighborhoods, and schools that truly teach. We are here to speak for the American farmer, the entrepreneur, and every worker in industries fighting to modernize and compete. And, yes, we are here to stand, and proudly so, for all who struggle to break free from totalitarianism; for all who know in their hearts that freedom is the one true path to peace and human happiness.

Proverbs tells us, without a vision the people perish. When asked what great principle holds our Union together, Abraham Lincoln said, "Something in (the) Declara-

Sitting with First Lady Nancy Reagan for the State of the Union address were two "American heroes" hailed by the president in his speech: West Point cadet Jean Nguyen (left) and Clara "Mother" Hale (center) of Harlem.

tion giving liberty, not alone to the people of this country, but hope to the world for all future time."

We honor the giants of our history, not by going back, but forward to the dreams their vision foresaw. My fellow citizens, this Nation is poised for greatness. The time has come to proceed toward a great new challenge — a Second American Revolution of hope and opportunity; a revolution carrying us to new heights of progress by pushing back frontiers of knowledge and space; a revolution of spirit that taps the soul of America, enabling us to summon greater strength than we have ever known; and, a

revolution that carries beyond our shores the golden promise of human freedom in a world at peace.

Let us begin by challenging our conventional wisdom: There are no constraints on the human mind, no walls around the human spirit, no barriers to our progress except those we ourselves erect. Already, pushing down tax rates has freed our economy to vault forward to record growth.

In Europe, they are calling it "the American Miracle." Day by day, we are shattering accepted notions of what is possible. When I was growing up, we failed to see how a new thing called radio would transform our marketplace. Well, today many have not yet seen how advances in technology are transforming our lives.

In the late 1950s, workers at the AT&T semiconductor plant in Pennsylvania produced five transistors a day for $7.50 apiece. They now produce over a million for less than a penny apiece.

New laser techniques could revolutionize heart bypass surgery, cut diagnosis time for viruses linked to cancer from weeks to minutes, reduce hospital costs dramatically, and hold out new promise for saving human lives.

Our automobile industry has overhauled assembly lines, increased worker productivity, and is competitive once again.

We stand on the threshold of a great ability to produce more, do more, be more. Our economy is not getting older and weaker, it is getting younger and stronger. It doesn't need rest and supervision, it needs new challenge and greater freedom. And that word, freedom, is the key to the Second American Revolution that we mean to bring about.

Tax Simplification

Let us move together with a historic reform of tax simplification for fairness and growth. Last year I asked then Treasury Secretary Regan to develop a plan to simplify the tax code, so all taxpayers would be treated more fairly, and personal tax rates could come further down.

We have cut tax rates by almost 25 percent, yet the tax system remains unfair and limits our potential for growth. Exclusions and exemptions cause similar incomes to be taxed at different levels. Low-income families face steep tax barriers that make hard lives even harder. The Treasury Department has produced an excellent reform plan whose principles will guide the final proposal that we will ask you to enact.

One thing that tax reform will not be is a tax increase in disguise. We will not jeopardize the mortgage interest deduction that families need. We will reduce personal tax rates as low as possible by removing many tax preferences. We will propose a top rate of not more than 35 percent, and possibly lower. And we will propose reducing corporate rates while maintaining incentives for capital formation.

To encourage opportunity and jobs rather than dependency and welfare, we will propose that individuals living at or near the poverty line be totally exempt from Federal income tax. To restore fairness to families, we will propose increasing significantly the personal exemption.

And tonight, I am instructing Treasury Secretary James Baker — I have to get used to saying that — to begin working with congressional authors and committees for bipartisan legislation conforming to these principles. We will call upon the American people for support and upon every man and woman in this chamber. Together we can pass, this year, a tax bill for fairness, simplicity and growth, making this economy the engine of our dreams, and America the investment capital of the world. So let us begin.

Enterprise, Not Dependency

Tax simplification will be a giant step toward unleashing the tremendous pent-up power of our economy. But a Second American Revolution must carry the promise of opportunity for all. It is time to liberate the spirit of enterprise in the most distressed areas of our country.

This Government will meet its responsibility to help those in need. But policies that increase dependency, break up families and destroy self-respect are not progressive, they are reactionary. Despite our strides in civil rights, blacks, Hispanics, and all minorities will not have full and equal power until they have full economic power.

We have repeatedly sought passage of enterprise zones to help those in the aban-

doned corners of our land find jobs, learn skills, and build better lives. This legislation is supported by a majority of you. Mr. Speaker, I know we agree that there must be no forgotten Americans. Let us place new dreams in a million hearts and create a new generation of entrepreneurs by passing enterprise zones this year.

And "Tip," you could make that a birthday present.

Nor must we lose the chance to pass our Youth Employment Opportunity Wage proposal. We can help teenagers who have the highest unemployment rate find summer jobs, so they can know the pride of work, and have confidence in their futures.

We will continue to support the Job Training Partnership Act, which has a nearly two-thirds job placement rate. Credits and education and health care vouchers will help working families shop for services they need.

Our Administration is already encouraging certain low-income public housing residents to own and manage their own dwellings. It is time that all public housing residents have that opportunity of ownership.

The Federal Government can help create a new atmosphere of freedom. But States and localities, many of which enjoy surpluses from the recovery, must not permit their tax and regulatory policies to stand as barriers to growth.

Let us resolve that we will stop spreading dependency and start spreading opportunity; that we will stop spreading bondage and start spreading freedom.

Cutting Government Spending

There are some who say that growth initiatives must await final action on deficit reductions. Well, the best way to reduce deficits is through economic growth. More businesses will be started, more investments made, more jobs created, and more people will be on payrolls paying taxes. The best way to reduce Government spending is to reduce the need for spending by increasing prosperity. Each added percentage point per year of real GNP growth will lead to a cumulative reduction in deficits of nearly $200 billion over five years.

To move steadily toward a balanced budget we must also lighten Government's claim on our total economy. We will not do this by raising taxes. We must make sure that our economy grows faster than the growth in spending by the Federal Government. In our Fiscal Year 1986 budget, overall Government program spending will be frozen at the current level; it must not be one dime higher than Fiscal Year 1985. And three points are key:

First, the social safety net for the elderly, the needy, the disabled, and unemployed will be left intact. Growth of our major health care programs, Medicare and Medicaid, will be slowed, but protections for the elderly and needy will be preserved.

Second, we must not relax our efforts

to restore military strength just as we near our goal of a fully equipped, trained, and ready professional corps. National security is Government's first responsibility, so, in past years, defense spending took about half the Federal budget. Today it takes less than a third.

We have already reduced our planned defense expenditures by nearly $100 billion over the past 4 years, and reduced projected spending again this year. You know, we only have a military industrial complex until a time of danger. Then it becomes the arsenal of democracy. Spending for defense is investing in things that are priceless: peace and freedom.

Third, we must reduce or eliminate costly Government subsidies. For example, deregulation of the airline industry has led to cheaper airfares, but on Amtrak taxpayers pay about $35 per passenger every time an Amtrak train leaves the station. It's time we ended this huge Federal subsidy.

Our farm program costs have quadrupled in recent years. Yet I know from visiting farmers, many in great financial distress, that we need an orderly transition to a market-oriented farm economy. We can help farmers best, not by expanding Federal payments, but by making fundamental reforms, keeping interest rates heading down, and knocking down foreign trade barriers to American farm exports.

We are moving ahead with Grace Commission reforms to eliminate waste, and improve Government's management practices. In the long run, we must protect the taxpayers from Government. And I ask again that you pass, as 32 States have now called for, an amendment mandating the Federal Government spend no more than it takes in. And I ask for the authority used responsibly by 43 Governors to veto individual items in appropriations bills. Senator Mattingly has introduced a bill permitting a 2-year trial run of the line-item veto. I hope you will pass and send that legislation to my desk.

Nearly 50 years of Government living beyond its means has brought us to a time of reckoning. Ours is but a moment in history. But one moment of courage, idealism, and bipartisan unity can change American history forever.

Sound monetary policy is key to long-running economic strength and stability. We will continue to cooperate with the Federal Reserve Board, seeking a steady policy that ensures price stability, without keeping interest rates artificially high or needlessly holding down growth.

Reducing unneeded red tape and regulations, and deregulating the energy, transportation, and financial industries, have unleashed new competition, giving consumers more choices, better services, and lower prices. In just one set of grant programs we have reduced 905 pages of regulations to 31.

We seek to fully deregulate natural gas to bring on new supplies and bring us closer to energy independence. Consistent with safety standards, we will continue removing restraints on the bus and railroad industries; we will soon send up legislation to return Conrail to the private sector, where it belongs; and we will support further deregulation of the trucking industry.

Every dollar the Federal Government does not take from us, every decision it does not make for us, will make our economy stronger, our lives more abundant, our future more free.

The New Frontier: Space

Our Second American Revolution will push on to new possibilities not only on Earth, but in the next frontier of space. Despite budget restraints, we will seek record funding for research and development.

We have seen the success of the space shuttle. Now we are going to develop a permanently manned Space Station, and new opportunities for free enterprise because in the next decade Americans and our friends around the world will be living and working together in space.

In the zero gravity of space we could manufacture in 30 days lifesaving medicines it would take 30 years to make on Earth. We can make crystals of exceptional purity to produce super computers, creating jobs, technologies, and medical breakthroughs beyond anything we ever dreamed possible.

As we do all this, we will continue to protect our natural resources. We will seek reauthorization and expanded funding for the Superfund program, to continue cleaning up hazardous waste sites which threaten human health and the environment.

Rediscovery of Values

Now, there is another great heritage to speak of this evening. Of all the changes that have swept America the past four years, none brings greater promise than our rediscovery of the values of faith, freedom, family, work, and neighborhood.

We see signs of renewal in increased attendance in places of worship; renewed optimism and faith in our future; love of country rediscovered by our young who are leading the way. We have rediscovered that work is good in and of itself; that it ennobles us to create and contribute no matter how seemingly humble our jobs. We have seen a powerful new current from an old and honorable tradition — American generosity.

From thousands answering Peace Corps appeals to help boost food production in Africa, to millions volunteering time, corporations adopting schools, and communities pulling together to help the neediest among us at home, we have refound our values. Private sector initiatives are crucial to our future.

I thank the Congress for passing equal access legislation giving religious groups the same right to use classrooms after school that other groups enjoy. But no citizen should tremble, nor the world shudder, if a child stands in a classroom and breathes a prayer. We ask you again — give children back a right they had for a century and a half or more in this country.

The question of abortion grips our Nation. Abortion is either the taking of a human life or it isn't; and if it is — and medical technology is increasingly showing it is — it must be stopped.

It is a terrible irony that while some turn to abortion, so many others who cannot become parents cry out for children to adopt. We have room for these children; we can fill the cradles of those who want a child to love. Tonight I ask you in the Congress to move this year on legislation to protect the unborn.

In the area of education, we are returning to excellence and again the heroes are our people, not government. We are stressing basics of discipline, rigorous testing, and homework, while helping children become computer smart as well. For 20 years Scholastic Aptitude Test scores of our high school students went down. But now they have gone up two of the last three years.

We must go forward in our commitment to the new basics, giving parents greater authority and making sure good teachers are rewarded for hard work and achievement through merit pay.

Violence and Crime

Of all the changes in the past 20 years, none has more threatened our sense of national well-being than the explosion of violent crime. One does not have to be attacked to be a victim. The woman who must run to her car after shopping at night is a victim; the couple draping their door with locks and chains are victims; as is the tired, decent cleaning woman who can't ride a subway home without being afraid.

We do not seek to violate the rights of defendants. But shouldn't we feel more compassion for the victims of crime than for those who commit crime? For the first time in 20 years the crime index has fallen two years in a row; we have convicted over 7,400 drug offenders, and put them, as well as leaders of organized crime, behind bars in record numbers.

But we must do more. I urge the House to follow the Senate and enact proposals permitting use of all reliable evidence that police officers acquire in good faith. These proposals would also reform the habeus corpus laws and allow, in keeping with the will of the overwhelming majority of Americans, the use of the death penalty where necessary.

There can be no economic revival in ghettos when the most violent among us are allowed to roam free. It is time we restored domestic tranquility. And we mean to do just that.

Working for Peace

Just as we are positioned as never before to secure justice in our economy, we are poised as never before to create a safer, freer, more peaceful world.

Our alliances are stronger than ever. Our economy is stronger than ever. We have resumed our historic role as a leader of the free world — and all of these together are a great force for peace.

Since 1981 we have been committed to seeking fair and verifiable arms agreements that would lower the risk of war and reduce the size of nuclear arsenals. Now our determination to maintain a strong defense has influenced the Soviet Union to return to the bargaining table. Our negotiators must be able to go to that table with the united support of the American people. All of us have no greater dream than to see the day when nuclear weapons are banned from this Earth forever.

Each Member of the Congress has a role to play in modernizing our defenses, thus supporting our chances for a meaningful arms agreement. Your vote this spring on the Peacekeeper missile will be a critical test of our resolve to maintain the strength we need and move toward mutual and verifiable arms reductions.

For the past 20 years we have believed that no war will be launched as long as each side knows it can retaliate with a deadly counterstrike. Well, I believe there is a better way of eliminating the threat of nuclear war.

It is a Strategic Defense Initiative aimed ultimately at finding a non-nuclear defense against ballistic missiles. It is the most hopeful possibility of the nuclear age. But it is not well understood.

Some say it will bring war to the heavens — but its purpose is to deter war, in the heavens and on Earth. Some say the research would be expensive. Perhaps, but it could save millions of lives, indeed humanity itself. Some say if we build such a system the Soviets will build a defense system of their own. Well, they already have strategic defenses that surpass ours; a civil defense system, where we have almost none; and a research program covering roughly the same areas of technology we are exploring. And finally, some say the research will take a long time. The answer to that is: "Let's get started."

Aid and Trade

Harry Truman once said that ultimately our security and the world's hopes for peace and human progress, "lie not in measures of defense or in the control of weapons, but in the growth and expansion of freedom and self-government."

Tonight we declare anew to our fellow citizens of the world: Freedom is not the sole prerogative of a chosen few; it is the universal right of all God's children. Look to where peace and prosperity flourish today. It is in homes that freedom built. Victories against poverty are greatest and peace most secure where people live by laws that ensure free press, free speech, and freedom to worship, vote, and create wealth.

Our mission is to nourish and defend freedom and democracy and to communicate these ideals everywhere we can.

America's economic success is freedom's success; it can be repeated a hundred times in a hundred different nations. Many countries in East Asia and the Pacific have few resources other than the enterprise of their own people. But through low tax rates and free markets they have soared ahead of centralized economies. And now China is opening up its economy to meet its needs.

We need a stronger and simpler approach to the process of making and implementing trade policy and will be studying potential changes in that process in the next few weeks.

We have seen the benefits of free trade and lived through the disasters of protectionism. Tonight I ask all our trading partners, developed and developing alike, to join us in a new round of trade negotiations to expand trade and competition, and strengthen the global economy — and to begin it in this next year.

There are more than 3 billion human beings living in Third World Countries with an average per capita income of $650 a year. Many are victims of dictatorships that impoverish them with taxation and corruption. Let us ask our allies to join us in a practical program of trade and assistance that fosters economic development through personal incentives to help these people climb from poverty on their own. We cannot play innocents abroad in a world that is not innocent. Nor can we be passive when freedom is under siege. Without resources, diplomacy cannot succeed. Our security assistance programs help friendly governments defend themselves, and give them confidence to work for peace. And I hope that you in the Congress will understand that dollar for dollar security assistance contributes as much to global security as our own defense budget.

We must stand by all our democratic allies. And we must not break faith with those who are risking their lives on every continent, from Afghanistan to Nicaragua, to defy Soviet-supported aggression and secure rights which have been ours from birth.

The Sandinista dictatorship of Nicaragua, with full Cuban Soviet-bloc support, not only persecutes its people, the church, and denies a free press, but arms and provides bases for communist terrorists attacking neighboring states. Support for freedom fighters is self-defense, and totally consistent with the OAS [Organization of American States] and U.N. Charters. It is essential that the Congress continue all facets of our assistance to Central America. I want to work with you to support the democratic forces whose struggle is tied to our own security.

Two American Heroes

Tonight I have spoken of great plans and great dreams. They are dreams we can make come true. Two hundred years of American history should have taught us that nothing is impossible.

Ten years ago a young girl left Vietnam with her family, part of the exodus that followed the fall of Saigon. They came to the United States with no possessions and not knowing a word of English, 10 years ago. The young girl studied hard, learned English, and finished high school in the top of her class. And this May, May 22 to be exact, is a big date on her calendar. Just 10 years from the time she left Vietnam she will graduate from the United States Military Academy at West Point.

I though you might like to meet an American hero named Jean Nguyen.

Now, there is someone else here tonight — born 79 years ago. She lives in the inner city where she cares for infants born of mothers who are heroin addicts. The children born in withdrawal are sometimes even dropped at her doorstep. She helps them with love.

Go to her house some night and maybe you will see her silhouette against the window as she walks the floor, talking softly, soothing a child in her arms. Mother Hale of Harlem, and she, too, is an American hero.

Jean, Mother Hale, your lives tell us that the oldest American saying is new again — anything is possible in America if we have the faith, the will, and the heart.

History is asking us once again to be a force for good in the world. Let us begin — in unity, with justice and love.

Thank you and God bless you.

[Applause, the Members rising.]

Index